The History of The National Rugby League

NRL Legacy: The Evolution, Expansion, and Impact of the National Rugby League

James Bren

Chapters

Introduction: From Origins to Icons: The Evolution of the NRL – 8

Part One: Foundations of Fury: The Birth and Rise of the NRL – 14

Chapter 1: The New South Wales Rugby League – 15

Chapter 2: Further Expansion of the League – 21

Chapter 3: The Super League War and the Formation of the NRL – 28

Chapter 4: The Birth of the NRL – 35

Chapter 5: Mergers and the Path to a 14-Team Competition – 41

Chapter 6: Mergers and Controversies – 47

Chapter 7: Resilience and Revival – 53

Part Two: Surge of Popularity, Expansion, and Centennial Celebration – 60

Chapter 7: A New Era of Success – 61

Chapter 8: A Period of Unprecedented Growth – 68

Chapter 9: The 2006 Grand Final and Interstate Rivalry – 75

Chapter 10: The Return of the Gold Coast Titans – 82

Chapter 11: A New Era Begins – 89

Chapter 12: A Triumphant Return and Historic Grand Final – 96

Chapter 13: The Centenary of Rugby League (2008) – 103

Chapter 14: The Beginning of the Second Century – 110

Part Three: 2010–2019: The Rise of the ARLC and a New Era of Dominance – 124

Chapter 16: The Establishment of the ARLC and the 2011 Season – 125

Chapter 17: Establishing the ARLC – 132

Chapter 18: The 2013 Season: Resurgence and Controversy – 139

Chapter 19: The 2014 Season - Auckland Nines and the Rabbitohs' Triumph – 146

Chapter 20: The 2015 NRL Season – 153

Chapter 21: Triumphs and Milestones – The 2016 NRL Season – 159

Chapter 22: The Dawn of the NRL Women's League and the 2017 Women's Rugby League World Cup – 165

Part Four: 2020–2021: Resilience in Crisis and New Horizons – 171

Chapter 23: Navigating the Pandemic –172

Chapter 24: Return to Play Amidst Controversy – 178

Chapter 25: The Expansion to the Dolphins – 184

Part Five: The Evolution of the Game - Season Structure and Format – 190

Chapter 26: Gearing Up – The NRL Pre-season Journey – 191

Chapter 27: The All Stars Spectacle – 197

Chapter 28: Nines Fever: The High-Octane Rugby League Extravaganza – 203

Chapter 29: The World Club Challenge: NRL vs. Super League Showdown – 208

Chapter 30: Premiership Rounds: The Heart of NRL Action – 213

Chapter 31: Rugby League Las Vegas – 219

Chapter 32: Magic Round Extravaganza – 225

Chapter 33: Themed Rounds – 231

Chapter 34: Mid-Season Representative Rounds – 238

Chapter 35: Finals Series – 244

Chapter 36: Grand Final – 249

Chapter 37: Post-Season Internationals – 255

Part Six: The Warriors on the Field – 262

Chapter 38: The Icons of Rugby League – 263

4

Chapter 39: The Rise of Polynesian Influence in the NRL – 269

Chapter 40: Trailblazers and Champions: The Legacy of Indigenous Players in the NRL – 275

Chapter 41: Celebrating Indigenous Heritage in the NRL – 282

Chapter 42: The Legacy of Preston Campbell and the All Stars Match – 289

Chapter 43: The Evolution of the Salary Cap in the NRL – 295

Chapter 44: The Bulldogs Salary Cap Scandal – 301

Chapter 45: The 2005 New Zealand Warriors Salary Cap Scandal – 308

Chapter 46: The Melbourne Storm Salary Cap Scandal – 314

Chapter 47: The Parramatta Eels Salary Cap Scandal – 321

Chapter 48: The 2018 Manly-Warringah Sea Eagles Scandal – 328

Chapter 49: The NRL Judiciary and Integrity Unit – 335

Part Seven: Crowning Achievements – The World of Rugby League Awards – 341

Chapter 50: The Provan-Summons Trophy – A Symbol of Rugby League Glory – 342

Chapter 51: J. J. Giltinan Shield – 348

Chapter 52: The Clive Churchill Medal: Honoring Grand Final Greatness – 354

Chapter 53: The Dally M Awards – 360

Chapter 54: The Immortals – 366

Chapter 55: Queensland Rugby League's Team of the Century – 373

Chapter 56: New South Wales Rugby League's Team of the Century – 379

Part Eight: The Fans and the Media – 385

Chapter 57: The 2022 Season Viewership and Attendance – 386

Chapter 58: ANZ and Pacific – 392

Chapter 59: Detailed Australian Coverage – 398

Chapter 60: NRL-Related Television Programmes – 404

Chapter 61: Former Shows – 412

Chapter 62: New Zealand Coverage – 419

Chapter 63: Pacific Broadcasting Reach – 425

Chapter 64: Global NRL Coverage – 431

Chapter 65: NRL Online: Global Streaming and Access – 438

Chapter 66: On the Airwaves - NRL Radio Coverage – 444

Chapter 67: The Role of Print Media in NRL Coverage – 450

Part Nine: Chasing Greatness: The Records That Define the NRL – 457

Chapter 68: Official NRL Statistics – 458

Chapter 69: Unforgettable Team Records – 465

Chapter 70: Remarkable Individual Achievements – 471

Chapter 71: The Future of the National Rugby League – 477

Conclusion: Reflections and Future Horizons – 490

Other Books by James Bren – 497

Introduction: From Origins to Icons: The Evolution of the NRL

The National Rugby League (NRL), known as the NRL Telstra Premiership due to its sponsorship, stands as the pinnacle of professional rugby league in Australasia. Spanning the breadth of New South Wales, Queensland, Victoria, the Australian Capital Territory, and New Zealand, the NRL unites fans and athletes in a fierce competition that showcases the very best of the sport.

Tracing its origins back to 1908, when the New South Wales Rugby League (NSWRL) was established, the journey to today's NRL is one of evolution, conflict, and ultimately, unification. The early 20th century saw rugby league rapidly gaining popularity in Australia, setting the stage for a rich and storied history. However, the path was far from smooth. The 1990s brought about the infamous Super League war, a period of intense rivalry and division within the sport, which ultimately led to the formation of the NRL in 1998. This formation was a landmark partnership between the Australian Rugby League (ARL) and the News Corporation-controlled Super League, which was eventually dissolved in 2012. Control of the NRL transitioned to the reconstituted ARL, now the Australian Rugby League Commission, governed by an independent board of directors.

The NRL season, a rigorous test of skill and endurance, typically runs from March to October.

Each team competes in 24 matches during the regular season, vying for the coveted minor premiership awarded to the highest-placed team. The competition then intensifies in the finals series, where the top eight teams battle for a spot in the grand finale. The season's climax, the NRL Grand Final, determines the ultimate champions, who earn the right to compete in the World Club Challenge against the Super League champions.

As we explore the rich history of the NRL, we will delve into the triumphs, challenges, and pivotal moments that have shaped the league. From its early beginnings to the modern-day spectacle, the NRL's story is one of resilience, passion, and unparalleled athleticism. This book aims to capture the essence of what makes the NRL a cornerstone of rugby league and a source of pride for millions of fans. Whether you are a lifelong supporter or a newcomer to the sport, the history of the NRL offers a fascinating journey through the highs and lows, the heroes and legends, and the games that have defined an era.

Join us as we celebrate the legacy and future of the National Rugby League, starting with its roots in 1908 and culminating in the present day, where the reigning premiers, the Penrith Panthers, proudly hold their fifth premiership title at the end of the 2023 season.

As we reflect on the evolution of the National Rugby League (NRL), it becomes evident that this storied competition is much more than a mere sporting event. It is a tapestry woven with threads of history, culture, and passion, reflecting the societal shifts and enduring spirit of rugby league enthusiasts across Australasia.

The journey from the formation of the New South Wales Rugby League in 1908 to the establishment of the NRL in 1998 is marked by pivotal moments that have defined and redefined the sport. The early 20th century saw the birth of rugby league in Australia, catalyzing a movement that would grow to captivate millions. This era was characterized by a fierce determination to create a distinct identity for rugby league, separate from its rugby union counterpart. The formation of the NSWRL was a bold step, setting the foundation for a professional competition that prioritized the players' welfare and the fans' engagement.

The decades that followed were a period of expansion and consolidation. Rugby league clubs sprang up across New South Wales and Queensland, and the sport's popularity surged. The inclusion of teams from Victoria, the Australian Capital Territory, and New Zealand in later years exemplifies the NRL's growth and the broadening of its geographical and cultural reach. Each new team brought its own unique flavor to the league, enriching the competition and fostering a sense of unity among diverse fan bases.

The 1990s Super League war represents a tumultuous chapter in the NRL's history. This period of intense rivalry and division could have fractured the sport irreparably. However, the resolution of this conflict and the subsequent formation of the NRL in 1998 underscored the resilience and adaptability of rugby league. The partnership between the Australian Rugby League (ARL) and News Corporation-controlled Super League was a pragmatic solution that paved the way for a unified competition, setting the stage for the modern NRL.

The dissolution of this partnership in 2012 and the establishment of the Australian Rugby League Commission marked another significant milestone. This restructured governance model, with its independent board of directors, provided the NRL with a robust framework for the future. It ensured that the league could navigate the complexities of contemporary sports administration while staying true to its roots.

The NRL's annual competition, running from March to October, epitomizes the league's commitment to excellence. Each season is a grueling test of skill, strategy, and endurance, with 24 matches determining the minor premiership and a finals series that culminates in the NRL Grand Final. This grand event, the pinnacle of the rugby league calendar, is a testament to the dedication of the players and the fervor of the fans. It is a celebration of the sport, where legends are made, and history is written.

The reigning premiers, the Penrith Panthers, who clinched their fifth premiership at the end of the 2023 season, embody the competitive spirit and excellence that the NRL champions. Their journey to the top is a microcosm of the league's broader narrative—a story of perseverance, teamwork, and relentless pursuit of greatness.

As we conclude this exploration of the NRL's evolution, it is clear that the league's history is a rich tapestry of moments that have shaped its identity. The NRL has not only survived but thrived through challenges, continually adapting to the changing dynamics of the sport and society. It has become a symbol of unity and pride for its diverse fan base, transcending regional boundaries and bringing together people from all walks of life.

Looking ahead, the NRL stands poised to continue its legacy of innovation and excellence. The league's commitment to player welfare, community engagement, and the development of the sport at all levels ensures a bright future. As new stars emerge and fresh stories are written, the NRL will undoubtedly continue to captivate and inspire, upholding the traditions of the past while embracing the possibilities of the future.

In closing, the history of the NRL is a testament to the power of sport to unite, inspire, and transform. From its humble beginnings in 1908 to its current status as a premier rugby league competition, the NRL has etched its place in the annals of sporting history. As fans, players, and administrators, we are all part of this ongoing story, contributing to a legacy that will endure for generations to come.

Part One: Foundations of Fury: The Birth and Rise of the NRL

Chapter 1: The New South Wales Rugby League

The New South Wales Rugby League (NSWRL) ran the major rugby league competition of New South Wales from its inception in 1908 until 1994. It was the heart and soul of rugby league in Australia, bringing together teams and fans with a shared passion for the sport. The early years were characterized by fierce local rivalries, especially among Sydney-based clubs, which were the backbone of the competition.

In 1980, the State of Origin series was introduced, marking a significant change in the format for interstate rugby league. This new series pitted players from New South Wales against their Queensland counterparts, based on their state of origin rather than the state they were currently playing in. The State of Origin quickly became a highlight of the rugby league calendar, drawing huge crowds and generating intense interest and excitement across the country.

The 1980s also saw significant expansion in the NSWRL premiership. The introduction of commercial sponsorship, most notably the Winfield Cup, brought new financial resources and increased media attention to the competition. This period of growth was marked by the inclusion of non-Sydney-based teams, with Canberra and Illawarra joining the league in 1982. This move was aimed at broadening the appeal of rugby league beyond Sydney and tapping into new markets.

While the expansion brought statewide interest in New South Wales, it also had unintended consequences. Traditional Sydney-based clubs began to struggle as the competition landscape changed. The influx of new teams and the shifting focus away from Sydney led to financial and competitive pressures on these clubs. One of the most notable casualties was the Newtown Jets, a foundation club of the NSWRL. Despite their rich history and passionate fan base, the Jets were forced to withdraw from the competition after the 1983 season due to financial difficulties.

The addition of Canberra and Illawarra to the NSWRL also had a significant impact on the Brisbane Rugby League premiership. As the NSWRL grew in stature and reach, it began to overshadow the Brisbane competition. Many of Queensland's best players were drawn to the more lucrative and high-profile NSWRL, weakening the local Brisbane competition and altering the dynamics of rugby league in Queensland.

Despite these challenges, the expansion of the NSWRL was seen as a necessary step in the evolution of rugby league in Australia. It helped pave the way for the eventual formation of a truly national competition, setting the stage for the modern NRL. The inclusion of teams from outside Sydney brought new fans, increased television ratings, and greater commercial opportunities, all of which contributed to the growth and success of the league.

The 1980s were a transformative decade for the NSWRL, marked by both progress and adversity. The introduction of the State of Origin series, the expansion of the competition, and the financial struggles of traditional clubs like the Newtown Jets all played a part in shaping the future of rugby league in Australia. The decisions made during this period laid the groundwork for the continued growth and development of the sport.

As we move forward in exploring the history of the NRL, it is important to understand the pivotal role played by the NSWRL in these formative years. The challenges and changes faced by the league during this time reflect the broader story of rugby league's evolution, highlighting the resilience and adaptability that have come to define the sport.

The history of the New South Wales Rugby League (NSWRL) is a tale of passion, evolution, and transformation. From its establishment in 1908, the NSWRL was the bedrock of rugby league in Australia, shaping the sport's development and fostering a deep-rooted connection with its fans. The league's early years were marked by intense local rivalries, with Sydney-based clubs forming the core of the competition. These clubs were more than just teams; they were community cornerstones that embodied the spirit of rugby league and galvanized local support.

The introduction of the State of Origin series in 1980 was a game-changer for the NSWRL and rugby league as a whole. By allowing players to represent their state of origin, the series brought a new level of excitement and competition to the sport. It quickly became a marquee event, captivating audiences and elevating the profile of rugby league across Australia. The State of Origin series not only showcased the best talent from New South Wales and Queensland but also highlighted the deep-seated rivalries and pride associated with interstate competition.

The 1980s marked a period of significant expansion and commercialization for the NSWRL. The introduction of the Winfield Cup and the addition of non-Sydney-based teams, such as Canberra and Illawarra, were strategic moves aimed at broadening the league's appeal and tapping into new markets. These changes brought increased financial resources, media attention, and statewide interest, positioning the NSWRL for future growth.

However, this period of expansion was not without its challenges. The shift in focus away from traditional Sydney-based clubs placed financial and competitive pressures on these teams. The Newtown Jets, one of the foundation clubs of the NSWRL, became a poignant example of the difficulties faced by smaller, less financially stable clubs. Despite their historical significance and dedicated fan base, the Jets were forced to withdraw from the competition after the 1983 season due to financial difficulties. Their departure was a sobering reminder of the harsh realities of professional sports and the need for financial sustainability.

The impact of the NSWRL's expansion extended beyond New South Wales, affecting the Brisbane Rugby League premiership. The growing stature of the NSWRL attracted many of Queensland's top players, weakening the local Brisbane competition and shifting the balance of power in Australian rugby league. This migration of talent highlighted the increasing allure and dominance of the NSWRL, foreshadowing the eventual formation of a truly national competition.

Despite the financial struggles of some clubs and the challenges posed by expansion, the NSWRL's decisions during this period were pivotal in shaping the future of rugby league in Australia. The inclusion of teams from outside Sydney brought new fans and increased television ratings, enhancing the league's commercial viability and setting the stage for the modern NRL. The groundwork laid during the 1980s facilitated the transition from a predominantly Sydney-based competition to a national league that could attract top talent and engage a broader audience.

The story of the NSWRL is one of resilience and adaptability. The league navigated financial difficulties, shifting competitive landscapes, and the pressures of commercialization to emerge as a cornerstone of Australian rugby league. The decisions made during its formative years, particularly in the 1980s, were instrumental in shaping the sport's trajectory and ensuring its continued growth and success.

As we reflect on the history of the NSWRL, it is clear that its legacy extends far beyond the boundaries of New South Wales. The league's influence is evident in the structure, competitiveness, and popularity of the modern NRL. The challenges faced and overcome by the NSWRL serve as valuable lessons in the importance of strategic expansion, financial sustainability, and the ability to adapt to changing circumstances.

The NSWRL's journey from its inception in 1908 to its transformation in the 1990s is a testament to the enduring appeal and strength of rugby league. The league's ability to evolve while staying true to its roots has been key to its success and will continue to be a guiding principle as the sport moves forward. The history of the NSWRL is not just a story of a league; it is a narrative of community, passion, and the unifying power of sport.

Chapter 2: Further Expansion of the League

In 1988, the New South Wales Rugby League (NSWRL) took another bold step in expanding the competition. This time, three new teams were introduced, all based outside Sydney. The Newcastle Knights, along with the first two Queensland teams, the Brisbane Broncos and Gold Coast-Tweed Giants, joined the league. This move was designed to broaden the appeal of rugby league and tap into new markets.

The introduction of the Brisbane Broncos and Newcastle Knights was particularly successful. Both teams quickly gained popularity and competitive strength. The Broncos, in particular, became a powerhouse in the league, drawing large crowds and establishing a strong fan base in Queensland. Newcastle also developed a passionate following, becoming a key part of the rugby league landscape.

The success of these new teams set the stage for a push towards a truly national competition. By demonstrating that rugby league could thrive outside of Sydney, the NSWRL laid the groundwork for future expansion. This period was crucial in showing that the sport had broad appeal and could attract fans from across Australia.

In 1995, the league attempted to expand further under the control of the Australian Rugby League (ARL). The ARL invited four more teams from outside New

South Wales to join the competition. This move aimed to create a national league that represented the entire country. Teams from Perth, Melbourne, North Queensland, and New Zealand were added to the league, reflecting a significant step towards a truly national competition.

However, this expansion brought new challenges. The rapid addition of new teams strained the league's resources and led to financial difficulties for some clubs. Despite the initial excitement, the expanded competition struggled to maintain stability. The ambitious attempt to create a national league ultimately failed, leading to a period of upheaval in the sport.

Despite these challenges, the expansion efforts were not in vain. The struggles and lessons learned during this period paved the way for the creation of the National Rugby League (NRL) in 1998. The NRL incorporated the traditional Sydney clubs while embracing the goal of a national competition. This new league successfully combined the rich history of Sydney rugby league with the broader vision of a nationwide competition.

The formation of the NRL was a turning point for the sport. It unified the rugby league community and provided a stable foundation for future growth. By including teams from across Australia, the NRL created a competition that could attract fans and players from all corners of the country. This new league structure ensured that rugby league would continue to thrive and expand.

The transition from the NSWRL to the NRL marked the beginning of a new era. The challenges faced during the expansion efforts of the 1990s highlighted the need for careful planning and sustainable growth. The NRL learned from these experiences and established a solid framework that balanced tradition with innovation.

The successful creation of the NRL demonstrated the resilience and adaptability of rugby league. The league's ability to evolve and embrace a national vision ensured its continued relevance and popularity. Today, the NRL stands as a testament to the enduring appeal of rugby league and its ability to unite fans from diverse backgrounds.

The expansion efforts of the late 1980s and 1990s were crucial in shaping the modern NRL. While the journey was not without its challenges, the lessons learned during this period paved the way for a stronger and more unified competition. The NRL's commitment to growth and inclusion has solidified its place as one of Australia's premier sports leagues, attracting fans and players from across the nation.

The expansion of the New South Wales Rugby League (NSWRL) in 1988 marked a significant chapter in the history of rugby league in Australia. Introducing the Newcastle Knights, Brisbane Broncos, and Gold Coast-Tweed Giants was a bold move that transformed the landscape of the competition. This strategic expansion was aimed at broadening the sport's appeal and tapping into new, enthusiastic markets beyond the traditional Sydney heartland.

The introduction of the Brisbane Broncos and Newcastle Knights proved to be particularly successful. The Broncos quickly became a powerhouse in the league, boasting a strong fan base and delivering impressive performances on the field. Their success helped establish Queensland as a vital region for rugby league, showcasing the sport's potential to thrive outside Sydney. Similarly, the Newcastle Knights garnered a passionate following, reinforcing the idea that rugby league could capture the hearts of communities across Australia.

These successful expansions paved the way for a more ambitious vision: creating a truly national competition. The NSWRL's efforts in the late 1980s demonstrated that rugby league had the potential to attract fans and players from all over the country. This realization set the stage for the Australian Rugby League (ARL) to take control of the competition and pursue a broader national strategy.

In 1995, under the ARL's stewardship, the league embarked on a significant expansion. Four new teams from outside New South Wales were invited to join the competition, including teams from Perth, Melbourne, North Queensland, and New Zealand. This ambitious move aimed to establish a national league that represented the entire country, reflecting the growing popularity and reach of rugby league.

However, the rapid expansion brought numerous challenges. The introduction of so many new teams in a short period strained the league's resources and led to financial difficulties for some clubs. Despite the initial excitement and optimism, the expanded competition struggled to maintain stability. The ambitious attempt to create a national league ultimately faced significant obstacles, culminating in a period of turmoil for the sport.

The challenges faced during this expansion period were a critical learning experience for the rugby league community. The financial difficulties and logistical issues highlighted the need for careful planning and sustainable growth. These lessons, though hard-earned, were invaluable in shaping the future direction of the league.

Out of this period of struggle, the National Rugby League (NRL) was born in 1998. The NRL emerged as a unified competition that incorporated the traditional Sydney clubs while embracing the broader vision of a national league. This new structure provided a stable foundation for the sport's future, balancing the rich history of Sydney rugby league with the ambition of nationwide inclusion.

The formation of the NRL marked a turning point for rugby league in Australia. It demonstrated the sport's resilience and adaptability, uniting the rugby league community under a single, cohesive competition. The NRL's inclusive approach ensured that teams from across Australia could compete at the highest level, fostering a sense of national pride and unity among fans.

The transition from the NSWRL to the NRL was not just a structural change; it represented a cultural shift in the sport. The NRL's commitment to growth and sustainability laid the groundwork for continued expansion and success. By learning from the challenges of the past, the NRL established a robust framework that could support the sport's development and ensure its long-term viability.

Today, the NRL stands as a testament to the enduring appeal of rugby league in Australia. The league's ability to evolve and adapt has secured its place as one of the country's premier sports competitions. The NRL's national reach and inclusive approach have attracted a diverse fan base, uniting communities from all corners of the country.

The expansion efforts of the late 1980s and 1990s were pivotal in shaping the modern NRL. While the journey was fraught with challenges, the lessons learned during this period were instrumental in creating a stronger, more unified competition. The NRL's commitment to growth, inclusion, and sustainability has ensured its continued relevance and popularity, solidifying its place in the hearts of rugby league fans across Australia. The league's evolution from the NSWRL to the NRL is a story of resilience, adaptability, and the unifying power of sport, promising a bright future for rugby league in Australia.

Chapter 3: The Super League War and the Formation of the NRL

The mid-1990s were a tumultuous time for professional rugby league in Australia. The prospect of creating a truly national competition, along with the introduction of pay television, caught the attention of News Corporation, a global media giant. This led to the Super League war, a major conflict that shook the foundations of rugby league.

The Super League war began as a dispute over broadcasting rights. News Corporation, seeing an opportunity to capitalize on the growing popularity of rugby league and the new pay television market, decided to form their own Super League. They aimed to create a rival competition to the Australian Rugby League (ARL), which had traditionally controlled the sport.

News Corporation's Super League poached players from the ARL by offering them high salaries. This created a divide in the rugby league community, with some clubs joining the Super League and others staying loyal to the ARL. As a result, in 1997, there were two competing competitions, with a total of twenty-two teams of varying quality. This division spread crowd attendances and corporate sponsorships thin, causing financial difficulties for many teams.

The ARL realized that the divided competitions were unsustainable. They began inviting the traditional clubs that had moved to the Super League back into a unified competition. Negotiations with News Corporation were intense and complex, but both sides understood the need for a single, strong competition.

On 23 September 1997, the ARL announced the formation of a new company to conduct the competition starting in 1998. This was a significant step towards resolving the conflict and creating a unified league. A few weeks later, on 7 October, News Corporation's representative Manaaki Ranginui expressed confidence that there would be a single competition in the following year.

The final decision came on 19 December 1997, when representatives of ARL-affiliated clubs gathered at the Sydney Football Stadium. They voted overwhelmingly in favor of accepting News Limited's settlement offer, with 36 votes to 4. This agreement marked the end of the Super League war and paved the way for the formation of the National Rugby League (NRL).

The creation of the NRL was a monumental moment in the history of rugby league in Australia. Jointly owned by the ARL and News Limited, the NRL combined the traditional Sydney clubs with teams from across the country, achieving the long-desired goal of a national competition. This new league promised greater stability, stronger financial backing, and a unified vision for the future of rugby league.

The NRL's formation was not just a merger of two competitions but a new beginning for the sport. It brought together the best elements of both the ARL and Super League, creating a more competitive and exciting league. The NRL also benefited from increased media coverage and financial support, thanks to its association with News Corporation.

The aftermath of the Super League war saw a period of consolidation and growth for the NRL. The league worked hard to rebuild relationships with fans, players, and sponsors, focusing on delivering a high-quality product on and off the field. The NRL's commitment to innovation and excellence has helped it become one of the premier sports leagues in Australia, attracting a diverse and passionate fan base.

The Super League war was a defining moment for rugby league in Australia. It highlighted the challenges of managing a growing sport in a competitive media landscape but ultimately led to the creation of the NRL. This new league, born out of conflict and negotiation, has gone on to achieve the vision of a truly national competition, uniting fans and teams from across the country and securing the future of rugby league for generations to come.

The Super League war was one of the most dramatic and transformative periods in the history of Australian rugby league. It began as a battle over broadcasting rights and evolved into a full-blown conflict that threatened the very existence of the sport as it was known. However, from this turbulence emerged the National Rugby League (NRL), a unified and stronger competition that continues to thrive today.

At the heart of the Super League war was a fundamental disagreement about the future direction of rugby league. News Corporation, recognizing the potential of pay television and the commercial opportunities it presented, sought to control the sport and reshape it to fit their vision. By forming the Super League and offering lucrative contracts, they succeeded in luring many top players and clubs away from the ARL.

This division created a fragmented rugby league landscape in 1997, with twenty-two teams playing in two separate competitions. The split diluted fan attendance and corporate sponsorship, straining the financial resources of many clubs. The intense rivalry between the ARL and Super League camps also fractured the rugby league community, causing uncertainty and concern among players, fans, and administrators alike.

Realizing the unsustainable nature of this situation, the ARL took steps to reunite the sport. Inviting the traditional clubs that had joined the Super League back into a unified competition was a crucial move. The negotiations with News Corporation were complex and required significant compromise from both sides. However, the shared goal of a strong, single competition ultimately prevailed.

The announcement on 23 September 1997 that a new company would be formed to run the competition in 1998 was a pivotal moment. It signaled the beginning of the end of the Super League war and the start of a new era for rugby league. This was further solidified on 7 October when News Corporation expressed their confidence in a unified competition for the next year. The decisive vote on 19 December 1997 by ARL-affiliated clubs to accept the settlement offer from News Limited confirmed the formation of the NRL.

The creation of the NRL in 1998 was a landmark achievement. It represented a merger of the ARL's rich history and traditions with the Super League's innovative vision and financial muscle. By bringing together the best elements of both, the NRL established a more competitive and financially stable league. This new competition was better equipped to navigate the challenges of professional sports in the modern era.

In the aftermath of the Super League war, the NRL focused on rebuilding and growth. The league worked diligently to mend relationships with fans, players, and sponsors, emphasizing the importance of unity and quality. The increased media coverage and financial backing from News Corporation played a significant role in the NRL's success, allowing it to invest in better facilities, player development, and fan engagement initiatives.

The NRL's formation also underscored the resilience and adaptability of rugby league. Despite the intense conflict and division, the sport emerged stronger and more cohesive. The lessons learned during the Super League war have been invaluable in guiding the NRL's strategic decisions and ensuring its long-term sustainability.

Today, the NRL stands as a testament to the vision of a truly national rugby league competition. It has successfully expanded its reach, attracting a diverse and passionate fan base from all corners of Australia. The league's commitment to excellence and innovation has positioned it as one of the premier sports competitions in the country.

The legacy of the Super League war is a reminder of the importance of unity and collaboration in sport. The conflict, while challenging, ultimately led to the creation of a more robust and inclusive league. The NRL's ability to bring together different factions and build a unified competition has been key to its continued success and growth.

The Super League war was a period of significant upheaval for Australian rugby league. However, it also served as a catalyst for change, leading to the formation of the NRL. This new league has fulfilled the vision of a national competition, uniting the rugby league community and ensuring the sport's future. The NRL's ongoing success is a testament to the resilience, adaptability, and passion that define rugby league in Australia. The journey from conflict to unity has shaped the NRL into the thriving and dynamic competition it is today, securing its place in the hearts of fans for generations to come.

Chapter 4: The Birth of the NRL

In 1998, the National Rugby League (NRL) began its inaugural season, marking a new era for rugby league in Australia. The NRL featured 20 teams, including 19 teams from the former Super League and ARL competitions, plus the newly formed Melbourne Storm. The creation of the Storm was part of the effort to establish a national presence for the league.

Despite the excitement surrounding the new competition, the transition was not smooth. Both the Super League and ARL had to make difficult decisions to ensure the financial stability of the new league. As a result, some clubs were shut down. The Super League closed the Hunter Mariners and the Perth Reds, who were burdened with a $10 million debt by the end of 1997. The ARL, facing similar financial challenges, decided to shut down the South Queensland Crushers.

The closure of these clubs was a harsh reality of the financial strain caused by the Super League war. Many clubs struggled to recover from the financial instability that characterized the mid-1990s. The decision to close certain clubs was made to consolidate the competition and focus on the most viable teams, ensuring the long-term health of the NRL.

The Melbourne Storm, created by the Super League, quickly became a significant addition to the NRL. They brought a new fan base and added to the league's national appeal. The Storm's success on the field and their strong following off it demonstrated the potential for rugby league to grow beyond its traditional heartlands.

However, the inaugural NRL season also saw more closures. At the end of 1998, the NRL decided to shut down the Adelaide Rams and the Gold Coast Chargers. This decision was controversial, especially since the Gold Coast Chargers had been one of the few clubs to turn a profit during the Super League war. Despite this, the NRL prioritized creating a sustainable and competitive league, which meant making tough calls about which teams would continue.

The consolidation process, while painful, was necessary to stabilize the league. By focusing on financially stable and competitive teams, the NRL laid the groundwork for future growth. The decisions made during this period were driven by a long-term vision of creating a strong, national competition that could attract fans and sponsors from across Australia.

The first NRL season was a mix of excitement and uncertainty. Fans were eager to see how the new competition would unfold, and teams were determined to make their mark. The Melbourne Storm, in particular, quickly established themselves as a force to be reckoned with, showcasing the benefits of the league's national expansion.

The birth of the NRL was a challenging but pivotal moment in the history of rugby league in Australia. The league's inaugural season in 1998 marked the beginning of a new era, characterized by a national vision and a commitment to financial stability. The tough decisions to close certain clubs were necessary to ensure the league's long-term success. The formation of the Melbourne Storm and the consolidation of teams set the stage for the NRL to become the premier rugby league competition in Australia. The league's ability to adapt and grow from its turbulent past highlights the resilience and passion that define rugby league in Australia.

The launch of the National Rugby League (NRL) in 1998 was a landmark moment for rugby league in Australia. It marked the end of a turbulent era characterized by the Super League war and the beginning of a unified, national competition. The journey to this point was filled with challenges, difficult decisions, and significant changes, but it ultimately set the stage for the modern era of rugby league.

The NRL's inaugural season featured 20 teams, combining the remnants of the Super League and ARL competitions with the newly formed Melbourne Storm. The inclusion of the Storm was a strategic move to expand the league's reach and bring rugby league to new audiences. Their immediate success on the field and popularity off it validated this decision and showcased the potential for rugby league to thrive beyond its traditional strongholds.

However, the transition to the NRL was not without its sacrifices. Financial instability and the need for a sustainable competition led to the closure of several clubs. The Hunter Mariners, Perth Reds, and South Queensland Crushers were among the first casualties, highlighting the harsh realities of the sport's financial landscape. These closures were necessary to consolidate resources and focus on building a strong, viable league.

The end of the 1998 season saw further consolidation with the shutting down of the Adelaide Rams and the Gold Coast Chargers. The decision to close the Chargers was particularly controversial, as they were one of the few clubs to turn a profit during the Super League war. Nonetheless, the NRL prioritized long-term stability and competitiveness, which required tough decisions about the league's composition.

The formation of the NRL was a bold step towards creating a truly national competition. By bringing together teams from across Australia and ensuring a financially stable league, the NRL aimed to attract a broader fan base and stronger corporate sponsorship. The initial challenges and closures were part of a larger strategy to build a robust and enduring competition.

The early success of the Melbourne Storm was a testament to the league's vision. As a new team, they quickly became competitive, drawing in fans and showcasing the benefits of a national approach. Their impact on the league demonstrated that rugby league could flourish in new regions, paving the way for further expansion and growth.

The consolidation and stabilization efforts of the NRL laid the groundwork for future success. By focusing on the most viable teams and regions, the league ensured a competitive balance and financial health. This strategy paid off, as the NRL grew in popularity and established itself as the premier rugby league competition in Australia.

The birth of the NRL was also a period of healing and unification for the rugby league community. The Super League war had caused deep divisions, but the formation of a single, unified competition helped to mend these rifts. Fans, players, and administrators came together to support the new league, driven by a shared passion for the sport and a commitment to its future.

The creation of the NRL in 1998 was a transformative moment for rugby league in Australia. The league's inaugural season was marked by both excitement and challenges, as it navigated the complexities of merging two rival competitions. The tough decisions to close certain clubs were necessary to ensure the league's long-term viability. The inclusion of the Melbourne Storm and the consolidation of teams were strategic moves that set the stage for the NRL's growth and success. The NRL's ability to unify the rugby league community and build a strong, national competition has secured its place as a cornerstone of Australian sport. The resilience and vision demonstrated during this period continue to guide the league's evolution, ensuring a bright future for rugby league in Australia.

Chapter 5: Mergers and the Path to a 14-Team Competition

In 1998, a peace agreement was reached between the Australian Rugby League (ARL) and News Limited, bringing an end to the Super League war. One of the conditions of this agreement was that the National Rugby League (NRL) would reduce the number of teams to 14 by the year 2000. This meant that the 20 clubs playing in 1998 would be evaluated based on sponsorship, crowd sizes, on-field success, and other factors.

To facilitate this reduction, the NRL offered incentives for clubs to merge. Clubs that chose to merge would receive a substantial sum of money and a guaranteed position in the 2000 NRL competition. The aim was to create stronger, more financially stable teams that could thrive in a competitive environment.

The first clubs to take advantage of this offer were the St. George Dragons and the Illawarra Steelers. At the end of the 1998 season, these two clubs merged to form the St. George Illawarra Dragons. This merger was seen as a positive step towards creating a more sustainable competition, combining the resources and fan bases of both clubs.

The 1999 season was a critical year for the newly merged St. George Illawarra Dragons. Despite the challenges of combining two teams, they performed exceptionally well on the field. Their success culminated in an appearance in the 1999 NRL Grand Final, where they faced the Melbourne Storm. The Grand Final was held at Stadium Australia and drew a record-breaking crowd of 107,999 spectators, setting a new world attendance record for a rugby league match.

The Grand Final was a thrilling and closely contested game. The Melbourne Storm emerged victorious, defeating the St. George Illawarra Dragons. Despite the loss, the Dragons' journey to the Grand Final was a testament to the potential success of merged clubs and the positive impact of the NRL's restructuring efforts.

The decision to merge clubs and reduce the competition to 14 teams was not without controversy. Fans and players of the clubs that were closed or merged often felt a sense of loss and disappointment. However, the NRL's goal was to create a stronger and more competitive league that could attract more fans, sponsorships, and media attention.

The period leading up to the 2000 season saw several more mergers and closures. Some clubs struggled to meet the criteria set by the NRL and faced the tough reality of either merging with another club or exiting the competition. This process was difficult, but necessary for the long-term health of the league.

The NRL also focused on ensuring that the remaining clubs were financially viable and competitive. This included efforts to improve marketing, fan engagement, and overall professionalism within the league. The aim was to build a league that could sustain itself and grow in the new millennium.

As the NRL moved towards the 2000 season, the focus was on consolidation and growth. The league's restructuring efforts, though challenging, laid the foundation for a more robust and dynamic competition. The mergers, while initially painful for some fans, ultimately strengthened the league by creating more competitive teams and a more stable financial environment.

The move to a 14-team competition by 2000 was a significant step in the evolution of the NRL. The mergers, closures, and restructuring efforts were aimed at creating a stronger, more sustainable league. The record-breaking 1999 NRL Grand Final highlighted the potential success of these efforts, showcasing the excitement and popularity of the game. As the NRL continued to evolve, these foundational changes set the stage for future growth and success, ensuring a bright future for rugby league in Australia.

The journey towards a 14-team competition by 2000 marked a pivotal period in the history of the National Rugby League (NRL). The peace agreement between the ARL and News Limited was not just a resolution to the Super League war but a blueprint for the future of rugby league in Australia. This period was characterized by significant changes, difficult decisions, and the strategic goal of creating a more competitive and financially stable league.

The decision to reduce the number of teams from 20 to 14 was driven by the need to ensure the league's long-term viability. This meant assessing each club on various factors such as sponsorship, crowd attendance, and on-field performance. The criteria set by the NRL were rigorous, reflecting the league's commitment to maintaining high standards and ensuring that only the strongest clubs would continue.

One of the most impactful strategies employed during this period was the encouragement of club mergers. Offering financial incentives and guaranteed positions in the 2000 competition was a pragmatic approach to reduce the number of teams while preserving the essence and history of the clubs involved. The first successful merger between the St. George Dragons and the Illawarra Steelers to form the St. George Illawarra Dragons demonstrated the potential benefits of this approach. This merger combined the strengths of both clubs, creating a more robust entity capable of competing at the highest level.

The 1999 NRL season was a testament to the league's vision and the success of the merger strategy. The St. George Illawarra Dragons' journey to the Grand Final, despite being a newly merged club, was an inspiring story. Their appearance in the Grand Final against the Melbourne Storm, witnessed by a record-breaking crowd of 107,999 at Stadium Australia, highlighted the excitement and passion that rugby league could generate. The game itself, a thrilling contest, showcased the competitive spirit and talent within the league.

However, the path to a 14-team competition was not without its challenges and controversies. The closure of clubs like the Hunter Mariners, Perth Reds, and South Queensland Crushers, and later the Adelaide Rams and Gold Coast Chargers, was a difficult but necessary step. These decisions were driven by financial realities and the goal of creating a sustainable league. The impact on fans and local communities was significant, as they saw their beloved clubs disappear or merge with others. This period required a delicate balance between financial pragmatism and maintaining the sport's rich traditions and community ties.

The mergers and closures, while painful, ultimately strengthened the league. By consolidating resources and focusing on the most viable teams, the NRL created a more competitive and exciting competition. The league's efforts to improve marketing, fan engagement, and overall professionalism were crucial in attracting new fans and sponsors, ensuring the financial health of the league.

As the NRL entered the 2000 season, the foundation laid during this period was evident. The league was more streamlined, competitive, and financially stable. The mergers, though initially controversial, proved to be a strategic success, creating stronger teams with larger fan bases. The league's focus on quality over quantity paid off, resulting in a more exciting and marketable product.

The legacy of this period is a testament to the resilience and vision of rugby league in Australia. The NRL's ability to navigate the challenges of the post-Super League war era and emerge stronger is a reflection of the sport's enduring appeal and the commitment of its administrators, players, and fans. The path to a 14-team competition was a journey of transformation, marked by tough decisions and strategic foresight.

The move to a 14-team competition by 2000 was a defining moment in the history of the NRL. The mergers, closures, and restructuring efforts were necessary steps to ensure the league's long-term success. The record-breaking 1999 NRL Grand Final was a highlight of this period, showcasing the excitement and potential of the restructured league. The NRL's ability to adapt and grow from these challenges set the stage for future success, securing its place as the premier rugby league competition in Australia. The period of transformation laid a strong foundation for the league's continued evolution, ensuring a bright future for rugby league in Australia.

Chapter 6: Mergers and Controversies

At the end of 1999, the National Rugby League (NRL) continued its efforts to streamline the competition by encouraging more club mergers. Two historic clubs, Balmain and Western Suburbs, joined forces to create the Wests Tigers. This merger was seen as a way to combine resources and fan bases, creating a stronger team to compete in the league. The Wests Tigers became a symbol of the new direction the NRL was heading towards, prioritizing financial stability and competitive balance.

Around the same time, another merger took place between North Sydney and Manly Warringah, resulting in the Northern Eagles. However, this merger was not as successful. The Northern Eagles struggled both on and off the field, facing financial difficulties and internal conflicts. The club's existence was short-lived, and it highlighted the challenges and complexities involved in merging two teams with distinct identities and histories.

In addition to the mergers, the NRL saw several teams updating their images. Many clubs released new logos to refresh their brands and appeal to a broader audience. The Sydney Roosters made a notable change by dropping the "City" from their name, becoming simply the Sydney Roosters. This move was part of a broader strategy to modernize the league and make it more marketable.

One of the most controversial decisions during this period was the axing of the South Sydney Rabbitohs from the competition at the end of 1999. The Rabbitohs failed to meet the NRL's criteria for inclusion in the streamlined competition, leading to their exclusion. This decision sparked outrage among fans and the broader rugby league community.

In response to their exclusion, about 80,000 people marched in protest on 12 November 2000, demanding the reinstatement of the Rabbitohs. The massive protest underscored the deep emotional connection fans had with their club and the impact of the NRL's decision on the community. The Rabbitohs challenged their exclusion in the Federal Court, arguing that the NRL agreement was unfair and breached the Trade Practices Act.

Justice Paul Finn ruled against the Rabbitohs, stating that the NRL agreement did not specifically exclude any club and dismissed their claims for reinstatement. Despite this setback, South Sydney refused to give up. They continued to fight for their place in the competition, appealing the decision and rallying support from their passionate fan base.

Their persistence paid off. In 2002, the Rabbitohs were re-admitted into the NRL, marking a significant victory for the club and its supporters. The return of South Sydney was a testament to the power of community and the enduring spirit of rugby league fans. It also highlighted the importance of tradition and history in the sport, reminding the NRL of the need to balance modernization with respect for the past.

The period of mergers and controversies was a challenging yet transformative time for the NRL. The league's efforts to create a more competitive and financially stable competition led to significant changes, including the formation of new clubs and the exclusion of others. While some decisions were met with resistance, they ultimately helped shape the future of the league.

The end of the 1990s and the beginning of the 2000s were marked by significant changes in the NRL. The mergers of historic clubs and the controversial exclusion and eventual reinstatement of the South Sydney Rabbitohs were pivotal moments in the league's history. These events highlighted the challenges of balancing financial stability with tradition and the deep emotional connections fans have with their clubs. The NRL's ability to navigate these complexities set the stage for its continued evolution, ensuring a dynamic and resilient competition for the future.

The period of mergers and controversies at the turn of the millennium was a defining chapter in the history of the National Rugby League (NRL). This era was marked by significant structural changes and intense emotional upheavals, reflecting the league's ongoing efforts to balance modern demands with deep-rooted traditions. The decisions made during this time had lasting impacts on the teams, the fans, and the overall landscape of rugby league in Australia.

The creation of the Wests Tigers through the merger of Balmain and Western Suburbs was a prime example of the league's strategy to create stronger, more viable clubs. This joint venture combined the resources and fan bases of two historic clubs, resulting in a team that could better compete in the modern era. The Wests Tigers quickly became a competitive force, demonstrating the potential benefits of strategic mergers.

On the other hand, the merger between North Sydney and Manly Warringah to form the Northern Eagles was less successful. The Northern Eagles struggled to find their footing both on and off the field, ultimately highlighting the complexities and challenges of merging clubs with distinct identities. This venture's failure underscored the fact that not all mergers would result in positive outcomes, and the process required careful consideration and execution.

The decision to exclude the South Sydney Rabbitohs from the competition at the end of 1999 was one of the most controversial in the NRL's history. The Rabbitohs, a club with a rich history and a passionate fan base, failed to meet the criteria set by the league. This exclusion sparked widespread outrage and led to one of the largest protests in Australian sporting history. The sight of 80,000 supporters marching through Sydney was a powerful reminder of the emotional and cultural significance of rugby league clubs to their communities.

South Sydney's legal battle to challenge their exclusion was a significant moment in the league's history. Although initially unsuccessful in the Federal Court, the Rabbitohs' determination and the unwavering support of their fans kept their hopes alive. Their eventual reinstatement in 2002 was a landmark victory, not just for the club but for the entire rugby league community. It highlighted the importance of tradition and community in the sport and served as a reminder to the NRL of the need to respect the rich histories of its clubs.

The period also saw several clubs updating their logos and rebranding themselves in an effort to modernize and appeal to broader audiences. The Sydney Roosters' decision to drop "City" from their name was symbolic of the league's efforts to streamline and refresh its image. These changes were part of a broader strategy to ensure the NRL remained relevant and competitive in an evolving sports landscape.

Throughout this tumultuous period, the NRL demonstrated resilience and a willingness to adapt. The league's decisions, while sometimes controversial, were driven by the need to create a sustainable and competitive environment. The mergers, exclusions, and rebranding efforts were all part of a larger strategy to strengthen the league and ensure its long-term viability.

In retrospect, this era was crucial in shaping the modern NRL. The league's ability to navigate these challenges and emerge stronger was a testament to its commitment to growth and improvement. The successful merger of the Wests Tigers, the eventual reinstatement of the South Sydney Rabbitohs, and the modernization efforts all contributed to a more dynamic and resilient competition.

The lessons learned during this period have continued to inform the NRL's approach to governance and management. The importance of balancing financial stability with respect for tradition, the need for strategic planning in mergers and expansions, and the value of community support are all principles that have guided the league in subsequent years.

The turn of the millennium was a time of significant transformation for the NRL. The mergers, exclusions, and controversies of this period were challenging, but they ultimately helped to shape a stronger and more sustainable league. The NRL's ability to adapt and evolve during this time set the stage for its continued success and growth, ensuring that rugby league remains a beloved and integral part of Australia's sporting landscape.

Chapter 7: Resilience and Revival

The early 2000s were a period of significant change and resilience for the National Rugby League (NRL). One of the notable stories of this era was the financial struggles and eventual revival of the Auckland Warriors. Initially facing severe financial difficulties, the club collapsed. However, they were resurrected as the New Zealand Warriors for the 2001 season. This rebirth marked a new chapter for the team and brought renewed hope to their fans.

The New Zealand Warriors quickly proved their worth in the NRL. In 2002, just a year after their revival, they made it to the grand final. Although they lost to the Sydney Roosters, their journey to the final was a remarkable achievement. The Warriors demonstrated resilience and determination, qualities that would define their presence in the league. Their ability to bounce back from financial hardship and compete at the highest level was inspiring.

The Warriors' success continued, and in 2011, they reached the grand final once again. This time, they faced the re-instated Manly Warringah Sea Eagles. Despite their efforts, the Warriors fell short and lost the final. However, their consistent performance in reaching the grand final twice within a decade highlighted their growth and competitive spirit. The New Zealand Warriors became a symbol of resilience and determination in the NRL.

In 2001, another significant development occurred when Telstra, Australia's largest telecommunications provider, became the naming rights sponsor of the NRL. The competition was renamed the NRL Telstra Premiership. This sponsorship deal brought substantial financial support and helped elevate the league's profile. The partnership with Telstra was a testament to the growing popularity and commercial appeal of the NRL.

In 2002, David Gallop took over as the CEO of the NRL from David Moffett. Gallop's leadership marked a new era for the league. Under his guidance, the NRL continued to grow in popularity, attracting more fans each season. Gallop's tenure was characterized by a focus on expanding the league's reach and enhancing its commercial viability. His efforts contributed significantly to the NRL's success during this period.

One of the notable changes introduced in 2001 was the shift in the timing of the NRL Grand Final. Traditionally held on Sunday afternoons, the grand final was moved to Sunday nights. This change aimed to attract a larger television audience and enhance the viewing experience for fans. The move proved successful, with the grand final becoming a highly anticipated event in the sporting calendar, drawing millions of viewers.

The early 2000s also saw improvements in the overall quality of the competition. Teams became more competitive, and the standard of play improved significantly. The introduction of new training methods, better facilities, and increased professionalism contributed to the enhanced performance of players and teams. The NRL became known for its high-intensity matches and thrilling contests, captivating fans across Australia and beyond.

In addition to the on-field action, the NRL continued to engage with the community and promote the sport at the grassroots level. Initiatives to develop young talent and encourage participation in rugby league were prioritized. The league's commitment to nurturing future stars and supporting local clubs helped strengthen the sport's foundation and ensure its continued growth.

As the NRL moved through the early 2000s, it faced various challenges but continued to evolve and thrive. The resilience of teams like the New Zealand Warriors, the strategic leadership of David Gallop, and the support from sponsors like Telstra all played crucial roles in the league's success. The NRL's ability to adapt to changing circumstances and maintain its appeal to fans was key to its sustained popularity.

The early 2000s were a period of resilience and revival for the NRL. The revival of the New Zealand Warriors, the strategic partnership with Telstra, and the leadership of David Gallop were significant milestones. The changes introduced during this time, such as the shift in the grand final timing, contributed to the league's growth and popularity. The NRL's commitment to excellence, community engagement, and adaptation to new challenges ensured its continued success and set the stage for a bright future.

The early 2000s marked a period of significant transformation and resilience for the National Rugby League (NRL). The revival of the Auckland Warriors, their rebranding as the New Zealand Warriors, and their subsequent successes in reaching the grand final in 2002 and 2011 exemplified the spirit of determination that defined this era. Despite financial hardships and the challenges of re-establishing themselves, the Warriors demonstrated the ability to compete at the highest level, inspiring both their fans and the broader rugby league community.

The New Zealand Warriors' journey was a testament to the power of perseverance. Their ability to overcome obstacles and achieve success on the field highlighted the importance of resilience in sports. The club's revival and subsequent achievements underscored the potential for growth and success, even in the face of adversity. The Warriors' story became a symbol of hope and determination, resonating with fans across the league.

The partnership with Telstra in 2001 was another pivotal moment for the NRL. By securing a major sponsorship deal with Australia's largest telecommunications provider, the league demonstrated its growing commercial appeal and strategic vision. The rebranding of the competition as the NRL Telstra Premiership brought significant financial support, enabling further investments in the sport. This partnership not only enhanced the league's profile but also contributed to its long-term stability and growth.

David Gallop's appointment as CEO in 2002 marked the beginning of a new era of leadership for the NRL. Under Gallop's guidance, the league focused on expanding its reach, improving the quality of the competition, and engaging with fans. His strategic initiatives helped the NRL attract more viewers, increase attendance at matches, and enhance the overall experience for fans. Gallop's leadership played a crucial role in steering the league through a period of transformation and setting the stage for future success.

The shift in the timing of the NRL Grand Final to Sunday nights in 2001 was a strategic move aimed at maximizing television viewership and creating a prime-time event for fans. This change proved to be highly successful, with the grand final becoming one of the most anticipated sporting events in Australia. The move demonstrated the league's ability to adapt to changing market dynamics and enhance its appeal to a broader audience. The grand final's success as a prime-time spectacle showcased the NRL's commitment to innovation and growth.

During this period, the overall quality of the competition continued to improve. Teams became more competitive, and the standard of play reached new heights. The introduction of advanced training methods, better facilities, and increased professionalism contributed to the enhanced performance of players and teams. The NRL became known for its high-intensity matches and thrilling contests, captivating fans and solidifying its reputation as a premier rugby league competition.

Community engagement and grassroots development remained a priority for the NRL. The league's initiatives to promote the sport at the grassroots level and nurture young talent were vital in ensuring the long-term growth of rugby league. By supporting local clubs and encouraging participation, the NRL helped build a strong foundation for the sport's future. These efforts not only developed future stars but also fostered a deep connection between the league and its community.

As the NRL navigated the challenges and opportunities of the early 2000s, it demonstrated resilience, adaptability, and strategic vision. The revival of the New Zealand Warriors, the partnership with Telstra, and the leadership of David Gallop were instrumental in shaping the league's trajectory. The changes introduced during this time, such as the shift in the grand final timing and the focus on community engagement, contributed to the league's sustained growth and popularity.

The early 2000s were a transformative period for the NRL, characterized by resilience, innovation, and strategic growth. The league's ability to adapt to changing circumstances, secure significant partnerships, and engage with its community ensured its continued success. The stories of determination, such as the revival of the New Zealand Warriors, and the strategic initiatives, such as the partnership with Telstra, highlighted the league's commitment to excellence and growth. The early 2000s set the stage for a bright future for the NRL, laying the foundation for its ongoing evolution and success.

Part Two: Surge of Popularity, Expansion, and Centennial Celebration

Chapter 7: A New Era of Success

The 2003 season marked a turning point in the history of the National Rugby League (NRL). Widely regarded as the most successful season since the league's inception in 1998, it set the stage for a period of remarkable growth and excitement. One of the significant changes was the Manly Warringah Rugby League Football Club taking over the NRL license from the Northern Eagles. The Northern Eagles, a joint-venture formed by North Sydney and Manly Warringah, faced financial difficulties, leading to Manly Warringah reclaiming their original identity.

The Penrith Panthers' performance in 2003 was nothing short of extraordinary. Rising from the bottom of the table, the Panthers defied expectations to win the Premiership. Their journey to the top was a testament to the team's resilience, determination, and skill. This remarkable turnaround captivated fans and brought a new level of excitement to the league. The Panthers' success story was a beacon of hope for other struggling teams, proving that with hard work and determination, any team could rise to the top.

Midway through the 2003 season, the Brisbane club made a significant move by returning to Suncorp Stadium. This move was a homecoming of sorts and revitalized the club and its fan base. The return to Suncorp Stadium provided a boost in attendance and created a vibrant atmosphere for home games. It marked a new chapter for the Brisbane club, enhancing their performance and engagement with fans.

The 2004 season built on the success of 2003 and proved even more remarkable. The North Queensland Cowboys, a team that finished 11th in 2003, made an impressive leap to third place in 2004. Their performance was outstanding, and they narrowly missed out on their first-ever Grand Final appearance. The Cowboys' rise highlighted the competitive nature of the NRL and the potential for teams to improve rapidly. Their success energized the fan base in North Queensland and contributed to the league's growing popularity.

Throughout these seasons, the NRL experienced a surge in popularity. More fans attended games, television ratings soared, and the overall excitement surrounding the league reached new heights. The competitive nature of the matches, combined with the remarkable stories of teams like the Penrith Panthers and North Queensland Cowboys, captivated audiences and drew new fans to the sport.

The league's administration also played a crucial role in this success. Strategic decisions, such as the return of the Brisbane club to Suncorp Stadium and the handling of the Northern Eagles' dissolution, demonstrated effective leadership. These decisions ensured that the league remained strong and competitive, fostering an environment where teams could thrive.

Community engagement and grassroots development continued to be priorities for the NRL. The league's initiatives to promote rugby league at the grassroots level and support local clubs were instrumental in nurturing young talent. These efforts not only contributed to the quality of play but also strengthened the connection between the league and its community. The focus on grassroots development ensured a steady pipeline of talented players, securing the sport's future.

As the NRL moved through 2003 and 2004, it became clear that the league was entering a new era of success. The rise of the Penrith Panthers, the resurgence of the Brisbane club, and the remarkable improvement of the North Queensland Cowboys were all signs of a vibrant and competitive league. The increased fan engagement and growing popularity of the sport were testaments to the league's success and potential for continued growth.

The 2003 and 2004 seasons were transformative for the NRL. The league experienced unprecedented success, driven by remarkable team performances, strategic decisions, and increased fan engagement. The stories of resilience and triumph, such as those of the Penrith Panthers and North Queensland Cowboys, captivated audiences and contributed to the league's growing popularity. The NRL's commitment to community engagement and grassroots development ensured the sport's future, setting the stage for continued success and growth in the years to come.

The 2003 and 2004 seasons in the National Rugby League (NRL) represented a transformative period that laid the foundations for a golden era in the sport's history. This time was characterized by remarkable team performances, strategic leadership, and a surge in popularity that set the stage for future growth and success.

One of the defining stories of this era was the resurgence of the Penrith Panthers. Rising from the bottom of the table to claim the Premiership in 2003, the Panthers' journey was a testament to resilience and determination. Their success inspired fans and players alike, proving that with hard work and commitment, even the most challenging obstacles could be overcome. The Panthers' triumph served as a beacon of hope for other struggling teams, reinforcing the belief that anything was possible in the NRL.

The return of the Brisbane club to Suncorp Stadium in mid-2003 was another pivotal moment. This move revitalized the club and its fan base, creating a vibrant atmosphere for home games and boosting attendance. The decision to return to Suncorp Stadium proved to be a masterstroke, enhancing the club's performance and strengthening its connection with supporters. It underscored the importance of strategic decision-making in the league's success.

The remarkable improvement of the North Queensland Cowboys in 2004 further highlighted the competitive nature of the NRL. From finishing 11th in

2003 to narrowly missing out on a Grand Final berth in 2004, the Cowboys' rise was a story of determination and growth. Their success energized the North Queensland fan base and contributed to the league's expanding popularity. The Cowboys' journey was a testament to the potential for rapid improvement and the excitement that competitive balance brings to the league.

Throughout these seasons, the NRL experienced a surge in popularity. Fan engagement reached new heights, with increased attendance at games and soaring television ratings. The league's ability to captivate audiences with thrilling matches and compelling stories drew new fans to the sport. The rise of teams like the Penrith Panthers and North Queensland Cowboys added to the league's allure, creating a sense of excitement and anticipation that resonated with fans across Australia.

The league's administration played a crucial role in this success. Strategic decisions, such as the handling of the Northern Eagles' dissolution and the return of the Brisbane club to Suncorp Stadium, demonstrated effective leadership. These decisions ensured that the league remained strong and competitive, fostering an environment where teams could thrive. The administration's focus on stability and growth laid the groundwork for the NRL's continued success.

Community engagement and grassroots development remained priorities for the NRL during this period.

The league's initiatives to promote rugby league at the grassroots level and support local clubs were instrumental in nurturing young talent. These efforts not only contributed to the quality of play but also strengthened the connection between the league and its community. By investing in grassroots development, the NRL ensured a steady pipeline of talented players and a bright future for the sport.

As the NRL moved through 2003 and 2004, it became evident that the league was entering a new era of success. The remarkable stories of resilience and triumph, the strategic leadership, and the increased fan engagement all contributed to the league's vibrant and competitive nature. The foundations laid during this period set the stage for continued growth and success in the years to come.

The 2003 and 2004 seasons were pivotal in shaping the future of the NRL. The league experienced unprecedented success, driven by remarkable team performances, strategic decisions, and increased fan engagement. The stories of resilience and triumph, such as those of the Penrith Panthers and North Queensland Cowboys, captivated audiences and contributed to the league's growing popularity. The NRL's commitment to community engagement and grassroots development ensured the sport's future, setting the stage for a golden era of growth and success. As the league moved forward, it carried with it the lessons and successes of these transformative seasons, paving the way for an exciting and prosperous future.

Chapter 8: A Period of Unprecedented Growth

The early 2000s marked a period of unprecedented growth for the National Rugby League (NRL). In 2003, 2004, and 2005, the league broke crowd average records, showcasing its increasing popularity among fans. The 2005 season, in particular, saw the NRL reach new heights, with total crowds for the competition season nearly matching the figures from the last year of the Australian Rugby League (ARL) competition in 1995, just before the Super League war. The average attendance record set during this time remained unbroken until 2010.

The surge in attendance was accompanied by a significant rise in commercial success. Between 2004 and 2005, the NRL experienced a 39% increase in sponsorship, a 41% increase in merchandise royalties, and a 12% increase in playing participation. These numbers highlighted the league's growing financial stability and popularity. The Business Review Weekly's 2005 ranking of the NRL as the 497th in revenue among Australian private companies further underscored this success. With revenue of A$66.1 million and a 7% increase from the previous year, the league was on a strong upward trajectory.

The 2004 season was a remarkable one for the Canterbury-Bankstown Bulldogs. Despite a year marred by controversy and turmoil due to an alleged rape scandal, the Bulldogs managed to rise above their challenges and secure the NRL trophy. Their victory marked the club's first premiership since 1995 and served as a testament to their resilience and determination. The Bulldogs' triumph was a powerful story of redemption and strength, resonating deeply with fans and the broader rugby league community.

In 2005, the NRL Grand Final set a new record for national television audience, with 4.1 million viewers tuning in to watch the Wests Tigers face off against the North Queensland Cowboys. This record-breaking viewership highlighted the league's expanding reach and the growing interest in rugby league across Australia. The grand final was a thrilling contest, with the Wests Tigers emerging victorious and capturing their first-ever NRL premiership. The Tigers' win was a significant moment in the club's history and added to the excitement and appeal of the league.

The Wests Tigers' victory in the 2005 grand final was a story of determination and perseverance. The team had faced numerous challenges throughout the season, but their hard work and dedication paid off in the end. Their success inspired fans and showcased the competitive nature of the NRL. The Tigers' triumph was a reminder that any team, regardless of past performance, could achieve greatness through perseverance and teamwork.

The North Queensland Cowboys also had a remarkable journey in 2005. Their path to the grand final was filled with memorable moments and impressive performances. Although they fell short of winning the premiership, the Cowboys' success in reaching the grand final was a significant achievement for the club. Their performance in 2005 laid the groundwork for future successes and helped to solidify their place as a competitive force in the NRL.

The increased popularity of the NRL during this period was also reflected in the growing participation in the sport. More players were joining rugby league clubs, and the grassroots development initiatives implemented by the NRL were paying off. The league's efforts to promote the sport at the community level ensured a steady pipeline of talented players and strengthened the connection between the NRL and its fans. This grassroots engagement was crucial for the long-term growth and sustainability of the sport.

The period from 2003 to 2005 was a time of tremendous growth and success for the NRL. The league broke attendance records, saw significant increases in sponsorship and merchandise royalties, and achieved high television viewership numbers. The triumphs of teams like the Canterbury-Bankstown Bulldogs and the Wests Tigers, along with the remarkable journey of the North Queensland Cowboys, captivated fans and showcased the competitive spirit of the league. The NRL's commitment to community engagement and grassroots development ensured a bright future for the sport, setting the stage for continued growth and success in the years to come.

The early 2000s marked an extraordinary period of transformation for the National Rugby League (NRL). As this era drew to a close, the league had firmly established itself as a dominant force in Australian sports, characterized by unprecedented growth, financial stability, and an unwavering fan base. Reflecting on the milestones achieved from 2003 to 2005, it's clear that this time was foundational in shaping the NRL's modern identity.

The league's ability to consistently break crowd average records from 2003 to 2005 was a testament to its increasing appeal. Fans were more engaged than ever, flocking to stadiums in record numbers to support their teams. This surge in attendance underscored the NRL's success in capturing the public's imagination and loyalty. The period's peak came in 2005 when total crowds nearly matched the figures from the ARL's last pre-Super League war year, demonstrating the league's recovery and growth since those tumultuous times.

Financially, the NRL experienced remarkable success. The 39% increase in sponsorship and 41% rise in merchandise royalties from 2004 to 2005 reflected the league's growing commercial appeal. These financial gains were not just numbers on a balance sheet; they translated into tangible benefits for the teams and players. With a 12% increase in playing participation, it was evident that more people were drawn to the sport, eager to be a part of the rugby league community.

The league's recognition by Business Review Weekly in 2005, ranking it among Australia's top private companies, was another indicator of its financial health and organizational strength. With A$66.1 million in revenue and a 7% increase from the previous year, the NRL was not only a sporting powerhouse but also a significant business entity. This financial stability provided a strong foundation for future growth and innovation within the league.

The story of the Canterbury-Bankstown Bulldogs in 2004 was a highlight of this era. Overcoming a year of turmoil and controversy, the Bulldogs' journey to win the Premiership was a narrative of resilience and redemption. Their victory was more than just a sports achievement; it was a powerful message about the ability to overcome adversity and emerge stronger. This triumph resonated deeply with fans and added a layer of emotional depth to the league's history.

The 2005 NRL Grand Final between the Wests Tigers and the North Queensland Cowboys set a new benchmark for the league. A record national audience of 4.1 million viewers tuned in, captivated by the thrilling contest. The Wests Tigers' first-ever Premiership win was a significant milestone, symbolizing the potential for any team to rise to greatness. This match not only showcased the high level of competition within the NRL but also demonstrated the league's ability to draw in and engage a vast audience.

The rise of the North Queensland Cowboys to the Grand Final in 2005 was equally significant. Although they did not clinch the Premiership, their journey was a testament to determination and growth. The Cowboys' performance laid the groundwork for future successes and established them as a formidable force within the league. Their journey from underdogs to contenders was inspiring and highlighted the competitive spirit that defines the NRL.

The increasing participation in rugby league during this period was another positive development. The NRL's grassroots initiatives were crucial in nurturing young talent and ensuring the sport's sustainability. By investing in community engagement, the league strengthened its ties with fans and created a pipeline for future stars. This focus on grassroots development was a key factor in the league's long-term success, ensuring a steady flow of talent and passion for the sport.

The years from 2003 to 2005 were a golden age for the NRL. The league achieved remarkable growth in attendance, financial stability, and fan engagement. The triumphs of teams like the Canterbury-Bankstown Bulldogs and the Wests Tigers, along with the rise of the North Queensland Cowboys, created compelling narratives that captivated fans and elevated the league's profile. The NRL's commitment to grassroots development and community engagement ensured a bright future for the sport. As the league moved forward, it carried with it the lessons and successes of this transformative era, paving the way for continued growth and triumphs in the years to come.

Chapter 9: The 2006 Grand Final and Interstate Rivalry

The 2006 NRL Grand Final was a historic match in the annals of rugby league. The Brisbane Broncos emerged victorious over the Melbourne Storm with a score of 15-8. This match was notable not just for the teams playing but also for the significance it held in the history of the National Rugby League. For the first time, two teams from outside New South Wales, the traditional heartland of the NRL, competed in the grand final. This event marked a pivotal moment in the league's journey toward becoming a truly national competition.

The Brisbane Broncos, one of the most successful teams in the NRL, added another premiership to their collection with this victory. The win solidified their reputation as a dominant force in rugby league. On the other hand, the Melbourne Storm, despite their loss, showcased their growing strength and competitive edge. This was their second grand final appearance, and their performance indicated that they were a team to watch in the coming years.

Interestingly, the television ratings for the grand final in Melbourne surpassed those in Sydney, where the game was played. This was a clear indication of the growing popularity of rugby league in regions outside New South Wales. Melbourne, traditionally an Australian Rules Football stronghold, was beginning to embrace rugby league, thanks in large part to the success and appeal of the Melbourne Storm. The high television ratings in Melbourne were a testament to the sport's expanding reach and the increasing interest in the NRL across Australia.

While the overall crowd numbers for the 2006 season were slightly down from the record highs of 2005, they were still higher than any other year prior to that. This indicated that the league had successfully maintained much of the momentum gained in the previous years. The slightly lower attendance figures did not detract from the overall success of the season but rather highlighted the extraordinary nature of the 2005 season's record-breaking attendance.

The interstate rivalry between the Brisbane Broncos and the Melbourne Storm added a new dimension to the NRL. This rivalry brought a fresh level of excitement and competition to the league. Fans from Queensland and Victoria, as well as from other parts of Australia, were drawn into the fierce battles between these two teams. The interstate matches became highly anticipated events, contributing to the overall popularity of the NRL.

The success of the Brisbane Broncos and the Melbourne Storm also had a positive impact on the development of rugby league in Queensland and Victoria. More young players in these states were inspired to take up the sport, leading to an increase in grassroots participation. The growth in player numbers and fan engagement in these regions was a significant achievement for the NRL, demonstrating the league's ability to expand beyond its traditional base in New South Wales.

The 2006 season also saw several other teams making their mark. The New Zealand Warriors, after financial struggles in the early 2000s, had established themselves as a competitive team in the league. The North Queensland Cowboys, who had reached the grand final in 2005, continued to build on their success, becoming a formidable opponent for any team. The competition was becoming more balanced, with multiple teams capable of challenging for the premiership each year.

The 2006 NRL Grand Final was a landmark event that highlighted the league's growth and evolution. The Brisbane Broncos' victory over the Melbourne Storm was a significant achievement, showcasing the strength of interstate teams. The high television ratings in Melbourne and the sustained crowd numbers demonstrated the expanding popularity of the NRL. The interstate rivalry added excitement and competition to the league, while the success of teams like the Broncos and the Storm spurred the development of rugby league in Queensland and Victoria. The 2006 season was a testament to the NRL's ability to grow and thrive, setting the stage for future successes and continued expansion.

The conclusion of the 2006 NRL season marked a significant milestone in the league's history. The season's grand finale, where the Brisbane Broncos triumphed over the Melbourne Storm, encapsulated the NRL's ongoing evolution into a truly national competition. This interstate clash not only highlighted the competitive spirit of the game but also underscored the league's expanding influence beyond New South Wales, its traditional heartland.

The Brisbane Broncos' victory was emblematic of their sustained excellence in rugby league. By securing another premiership, they reinforced their status as one of the NRL's most successful and resilient teams. The Broncos' journey throughout the season showcased their strategic prowess and determination, qualities that have consistently placed them at the pinnacle of the sport. Their win in the 2006 grand final added another chapter to their illustrious history and inspired future generations of players and fans alike.

For the Melbourne Storm, despite their loss, the 2006 season was a testament to their rapid ascent within the league. Their second appearance in a grand final demonstrated their growing dominance and their potential to challenge the established order. The Storm's performance not only solidified their reputation as a formidable team but also played a crucial role in popularizing rugby league in Victoria. The high television ratings in Melbourne for the grand final underscored this growing interest and indicated a significant shift in the sports landscape of the state.

The success of the 2006 grand final in drawing high viewership from Melbourne was a clear indicator of the NRL's expanding appeal. This growing interest in regions traditionally dominated by other sports, such as Australian Rules Football, highlighted the league's ability to captivate new audiences. The increasing popularity of rugby league in these areas was a significant achievement for the NRL, showcasing its potential for further national growth and integration.

The overall crowd numbers for the 2006 season, although slightly lower than the record-breaking figures of 2005, still surpassed those of previous years. This demonstrated the league's ability to maintain a strong fan base and sustain the momentum gained from prior seasons. The slight dip in attendance figures did not overshadow the season's success but rather highlighted the extraordinary nature of the previous year's achievements.

The interstate rivalry between the Brisbane Broncos and the Melbourne Storm added a new layer of excitement to the NRL. These clashes became highly anticipated events, drawing attention from fans across the country. The fierce competition between the teams not only provided thrilling spectacles but also contributed to the overall growth and popularity of the league. The emergence of such rivalries was indicative of the NRL's evolution into a more diverse and nationally representative competition.

The success of the Broncos and the Storm also had a profound impact on the development of rugby league in Queensland and Victoria. The achievements of these teams inspired young players and increased grassroots participation in the sport. This growth in player numbers and fan engagement in these states was a testament to the NRL's efforts to expand its reach and influence. The league's investment in community and youth development programs paid dividends, ensuring a steady pipeline of talent and passion for the sport.

The 2006 season also saw other teams making significant strides. The New Zealand Warriors, having overcome financial difficulties, established themselves as strong contenders in the league. The North Queensland Cowboys continued to build on their previous successes, demonstrating their resilience and competitive spirit. The emergence of multiple strong teams added depth to the competition, making each season more unpredictable and exciting for fans.

The 2006 NRL season was a landmark year that signaled a new era of growth and interstate rivalry. The grand final between the Brisbane Broncos and the Melbourne Storm showcased the league's expanding reach and competitive balance. The high viewership in Melbourne and sustained crowd numbers reflected the NRL's growing popularity across Australia. The season's successes highlighted the league's potential for further expansion and integration, setting the stage for continued growth in the years to come. As the NRL moved forward, the lessons and achievements of the 2006 season served as a foundation for its ongoing evolution into a truly national competition.

Chapter 10: The Return of the Gold Coast Titans

In its tenth season, the NRL welcomed back a team based on the Gold Coast, Queensland, with the inclusion of the Gold Coast Titans. The Titans were the first professional sporting team to represent the Gold Coast since the Gold Coast Chargers were removed during the NRL's rationalization process between the end of the Super League war and the 2000 season. This move was seen as a significant step in the league's efforts to expand and strengthen its presence in Queensland.

The reintroduction of a Gold Coast team was met with much excitement and anticipation. The region had a rich history of rugby league support, and the return of a professional team was expected to reignite local interest and enthusiasm for the sport. The Titans quickly set about building a competitive squad, attracting both experienced players and promising young talent. The club's formation was a clear signal of the NRL's commitment to growing the game in areas outside the traditional strongholds of New South Wales and Queensland.

The Gold Coast Titans made their debut in the 2007 NRL season. Their first season was filled with challenges, as is often the case with new teams, but the Titans showed promise and resilience. They played their home games at Carrara Stadium, which was later replaced by the state-of-the-art Robina

Stadium, providing a modern and vibrant venue for fans to support their team. The Titans' matches quickly became popular events on the Gold Coast, drawing large crowds and creating a strong sense of community around the club.

The inclusion of the Titans also had a positive impact on the overall competition. Their entry into the league added another team to the mix, increasing the number of matches and providing more entertainment for fans. The presence of a Gold Coast team brought a new dynamic to the NRL, introducing fresh rivalries and enhancing the competitive balance of the league. The Titans' games against other Queensland teams, such as the Brisbane Broncos and North Queensland Cowboys, became particularly anticipated fixtures.

The Titans' inaugural season saw them finish in a respectable 12th place on the ladder. While they did not make the finals, their performance was commendable for a new team. The experience gained during their first season laid the foundation for future success. The Titans continued to build and improve in the following years, becoming a competitive force in the NRL. Their progress was closely followed by fans and analysts, who recognized the potential of the Gold Coast as a strong rugby league market.

Off the field, the Titans made significant strides in establishing themselves within the community. They engaged in various community outreach programs, working to inspire and involve local youth in rugby league. The club's efforts in promoting the sport at the grassroots level were crucial in fostering a new generation of rugby league players and fans. The Titans quickly became an integral part of the Gold Coast's sporting landscape, embodying the region's passion for rugby league.

The return of a professional team to the Gold Coast also had economic benefits for the area. The Titans' matches attracted visitors and boosted local businesses, contributing to the region's economy. The club's presence helped to raise the profile of the Gold Coast, attracting media attention and increasing the visibility of the area as a sporting destination. The Titans' success in establishing themselves both on and off the field demonstrated the positive impact that a professional sports team can have on a community.

The inclusion of the Gold Coast Titans in the NRL was a significant milestone in the league's history. The return of a professional team to the Gold Coast reignited local interest in rugby league and strengthened the NRL's presence in Queensland. The Titans' debut season was filled with challenges, but their performance showed promise and laid the foundation for future success. The club's efforts in the community and the economic benefits they brought to the region highlighted the broader impact of their inclusion in the league. The Gold Coast Titans' journey in the NRL was just beginning, and their presence marked an important step in the ongoing growth and evolution of the competition.

The inclusion of the Gold Coast Titans in the NRL was more than just the addition of a new team; it was a revitalization of rugby league on the Gold Coast and a significant step in the league's expansion. As the Titans embarked on their journey, they brought renewed energy and hope to the region, showing that the Gold Coast was ready to embrace professional rugby league once again.

The Titans' first season in 2007 was a rollercoaster of challenges and achievements. While they faced the inevitable difficulties of a new team finding its footing, they also demonstrated resilience and potential. Finishing in a respectable 12th place on the ladder was an accomplishment that set the stage for future growth and success. The Titans' early struggles and triumphs created a narrative that fans could rally around, building a strong and loyal supporter base from the outset.

One of the most significant aspects of the Titans' introduction was the impact on the local community. The Gold Coast had been without a professional rugby league team since 1998, and the return of a team filled a void that had been deeply felt by local fans. The Titans quickly became a source of pride for the community, fostering a sense of identity and belonging. The team's presence encouraged more youth participation in rugby league, as young players looked up to the Titans as role models and aspired to follow in their footsteps.

The move to Robina Stadium, a modern and impressive venue, further solidified the Titans' place in the Gold Coast. The new stadium provided an excellent match-day experience for fans, with top-notch facilities and a vibrant atmosphere. The Titans' home games became major events, drawing large crowds and creating an electric atmosphere that was both exciting and welcoming. This helped to establish the Gold Coast as a key location for rugby league, enhancing the league's overall footprint.

The Titans' arrival also introduced new rivalries and intensified existing ones. Matches against fellow Queensland teams, such as the Brisbane Broncos and North Queensland Cowboys, became highlights of the season. These encounters were fiercely contested and drew significant interest from fans across the state. The intra-state rivalries added a new dimension to the NRL, making the competition more dynamic and engaging for supporters.

Off the field, the Titans worked diligently to integrate themselves into the community. Their outreach programs and involvement in local events helped to foster a strong connection with fans. The Titans were not just a team; they were ambassadors for rugby league, promoting the sport and its values throughout the Gold Coast. Their community engagement initiatives demonstrated a commitment to making a positive impact beyond the pitch, contributing to the social fabric of the region.

Economically, the Titans brought substantial benefits to the Gold Coast. The influx of visitors for home games boosted local businesses, from hotels to restaurants, creating a positive ripple effect throughout the local economy. The club's success in attracting sponsors and media attention further elevated the Gold Coast's profile as a sporting destination. The Titans' presence underscored the economic potential of having a professional sports team in the area, showcasing the broader benefits of such an investment.

As the Titans continued their journey in the NRL, they faced both challenges and opportunities. The initial seasons were a period of learning and growth, laying the groundwork for future success. The club's determination to improve and compete at the highest level was evident, and their efforts were gradually rewarded with better performances and increasing support from fans.

The inclusion of the Gold Coast Titans marked a new chapter in the NRL's history, bringing professional rugby league back to the Gold Coast and expanding the league's reach. The Titans' debut season was a mix of challenges and promise, setting the stage for their development as a competitive force in the NRL. Their impact extended beyond the field, fostering community pride, encouraging youth participation, and boosting the local economy. The Titans' journey was just beginning, but their early efforts laid a solid foundation for a bright future, both for the team and for rugby league on the Gold Coast.

Chapter 11: A New Era Begins

The 2007 season of the National Rugby League (NRL) brought several changes and innovations, making it a pivotal year in the league's history. One of the most significant changes was the return of Monday Night Football, alongside the inclusion of two Friday night games. Both of these changes turned out to be ratings successes, drawing large television audiences and increasing the league's visibility. Fans embraced the new schedule, appreciating the opportunity to watch more live games throughout the week.

Another notable change from previous seasons was the reduction in the number of byes each team had during the season. Between 2002 and 2006, the NRL had an odd number of teams, which required at least one team to have a bye each weekend. However, with the inclusion of the Gold Coast Titans as the 16th team for the 2007 season, the league had the option to revert to a system where every team played each round, as used between 2000 and 2001. Instead, the NRL opted for a system where teams were given just a single bye during the year, strategically grouped around representative fixtures to assist clubs.

The opening round of the 2007 season was a spectacle. Suncorp Stadium in Brisbane hosted two matches, with the first featuring the reigning champions, Brisbane Broncos, against fellow Queensland side, the North Queensland Cowboys. The second match saw the new club, the Gold Coast

Titans, playing against St. George Illawarra. The excitement around these matches was palpable, as fans eagerly awaited the debut of the Titans and the beginning of a new season.

However, the season was not without its challenges. The weather during the middle of the season was less than ideal, with cyclonic conditions severely affecting many NRL games played in Sydney and Newcastle. These adverse weather conditions tested the resilience of both players and fans, but the matches continued, showcasing the tenacity and dedication inherent in rugby league.

Despite the weather-related disruptions, the 2007 season progressed with a high level of competition and excitement. The return of Monday Night Football and the double-header Friday nights kept fans engaged throughout the week. The strategic scheduling of byes helped teams manage their players' workloads better, especially during the demanding periods of representative fixtures. This approach aimed to maintain the quality of play and reduce the risk of injuries, ensuring that the competition remained fierce and entertaining.

The inclusion of the Gold Coast Titans added a new dynamic to the league. As the newest team, the Titans brought fresh enthusiasm and energy, quickly gaining a strong following. Their debut season was closely watched, with fans and analysts alike eager to see how the team would perform. The Titans faced the usual challenges of a new club, but their presence in the league was a clear indicator of the NRL's growth and ambition.

As the season unfolded, the competition intensified. Teams vied for the top positions on the ladder, aiming for a place in the finals. The matches were closely contested, with many games being decided by narrow margins. The level of play was high, demonstrating the skill and determination of the players. Fans were treated to thrilling matches week after week, with the outcomes often uncertain until the final whistle.

The 2007 season also highlighted the importance of community and fan engagement. Clubs worked hard to connect with their local communities, hosting events and initiatives to bring fans closer to the game. The support from fans was unwavering, even during the challenging weather conditions. Their passion and loyalty were evident in the high attendance figures and the vibrant atmosphere at the games.

The 2007 NRL season was a landmark year for the league. The return of Monday Night Football and the introduction of two Friday night games were significant changes that proved successful. The reduction in byes and the inclusion of the Gold Coast Titans added new dimensions to the competition. Despite the challenges posed by adverse weather conditions, the season was marked by high levels of competition and fan engagement. The 2007 season set the stage for future growth and success, demonstrating the NRL's resilience and adaptability. As the league continued to evolve, it remained committed to providing fans with the excitement and passion that rugby league is known for.

The 2007 NRL season stands out as a landmark year in the league's history, marked by innovation, resilience, and growth. The introduction of Monday Night Football and two Friday night games was a game-changer, providing fans with more opportunities to engage with the sport they love. These scheduling changes not only boosted television ratings but also enhanced the overall fan experience, making it easier for supporters to follow their favorite teams throughout the week.

The strategic decision to reduce the number of byes per team also proved beneficial. By grouping byes around representative fixtures, the NRL ensured that teams could manage player workloads more effectively. This move helped maintain the quality of play and reduced the risk of injuries, allowing players to perform at their best during the most critical parts of the season. It also ensured that fans could enjoy a full schedule of matches, keeping the excitement and momentum of the competition going strong.

The inclusion of the Gold Coast Titans was a significant milestone for the league, representing its commitment to expansion and growth. The Titans' debut season was filled with anticipation and excitement, as fans eagerly awaited to see how the new team would fare. Despite the usual challenges faced by a new club, the Titans quickly established themselves as a competitive force and gained a loyal following. Their addition to the league brought a fresh dynamic and increased the overall competitiveness of the NRL.

The opening round of the season, with two matches at Brisbane's Suncorp Stadium, set the tone for an exciting year. The reigning champions, Brisbane Broncos, faced off against the North Queensland Cowboys, while the Gold Coast Titans made their debut against St. George Illawarra. These matches drew significant attention and showcased the high level of competition that fans could expect throughout the season.

However, the season was not without its challenges. Cyclonic conditions during the middle of the year tested the resilience of both players and fans. Despite the adverse weather, matches continued as scheduled, demonstrating the determination and tenacity inherent in rugby league. The ability to overcome these challenges highlighted the strength and dedication of the NRL community.

The competition throughout the 2007 season was fierce, with many matches being closely contested. Teams fought hard for their positions on the ladder, aiming for a place in the finals. The level of play was exceptional, with players showcasing their skills and determination week after week. The thrilling matches and unpredictable outcomes kept fans on the edge of their seats, reinforcing the excitement and passion that rugby league is known for.

Community engagement played a crucial role in the success of the season. Clubs made concerted efforts to connect with their local communities, hosting events and initiatives to bring fans closer to the game. This strengthened the bond between the teams and their supporters, creating a vibrant and supportive atmosphere at the games. The unwavering support from fans, even during challenging weather conditions, was a testament to their loyalty and passion for the sport.

Economically, the 2007 season was also significant. The increased television ratings and higher attendance figures demonstrated the growing popularity of the NRL. Sponsorship deals and merchandise sales saw substantial growth, contributing to the financial stability and success of the league. The NRL's ability to attract and retain sponsors was a clear indicator of its value and appeal in the sporting market.

The 2007 NRL season was a pivotal year that set the stage for future growth and success. The return of Monday Night Football, the inclusion of two Friday night games, and the reduction in byes all contributed to a more engaging and competitive competition. The addition of the Gold Coast Titans brought a new dynamic to the league, while the resilience shown during adverse weather conditions highlighted the strength of the NRL community. The fierce competition, exceptional level of play, and strong fan engagement made the 2007 season one to remember. As the NRL continued to evolve, the lessons and successes of 2007 laid a solid foundation for a bright and exciting future.

Chapter 12: A Triumphant Return and Historic Grand Final

The 2007 NRL finals series marked a historic moment for the South Sydney Rabbitohs, who returned to finals football for the first time in decades. This achievement was celebrated by their loyal supporters, who had long awaited this resurgence. The Rabbitohs' return to the finals was a testament to the hard work and determination of the players, coaching staff, and the entire club. Their journey through the season was filled with memorable moments and highlighted the club's rich history and enduring spirit.

As the finals series progressed, the competition became fiercer, with teams battling it out for a place in the grand final. The intensity of the matches captivated fans and kept them on the edge of their seats. The atmosphere in the stadiums was electric, with supporters cheering passionately for their teams. Each game was a display of skill, strategy, and resilience, as the players gave their all in pursuit of the ultimate prize.

The season reached its climax on 30 September 2007, with the grand final being contested between the Manly Sea Eagles and the Melbourne Storm. This matchup promised to be a thrilling encounter, as both teams had shown exceptional form throughout the season. The anticipation for the grand final was immense, with fans eagerly awaiting the showdown between two of the league's top teams. The buildup to the game was filled with excitement, as supporters from both sides rallied behind their teams.

On the day of the grand final, the atmosphere at the stadium was electric. Fans filled the stands, creating a sea of colors and noise. The grand final was not just a game; it was an event that brought people together to celebrate the sport they loved. The energy in the stadium was palpable, as fans eagerly awaited the kickoff. The grand final was broadcasted nationwide, drawing in viewers from across Australia, eager to witness the crowning of the new champions.

The grand final itself was a display of high-quality rugby league. Melbourne Storm dominated the game, showcasing their skill, speed, and teamwork. They took control early on and maintained their lead throughout the match. Manly Sea Eagles fought valiantly, but they were unable to match the intensity and precision of the Melbourne team. The final score was 34-8 in favor of Melbourne Storm, who celebrated their victory with immense joy and pride.

Melbourne's triumph in the grand final was significant not just for the team, but for the entire city of Melbourne. The victory was celebrated widely, with fans rejoicing in the streets and at various gatherings. The grand final achieved the honor of being the most-watched television show in Australia in 2007, highlighting the immense popularity and cultural significance of the NRL. The match was a fitting conclusion to a season that had seen remarkable moments, fierce competition, and unforgettable memories.

The 2007 season and its grand final also underscored the importance of teamwork, resilience, and community in rugby league. The players' dedication, the coaches' strategies, and the unwavering support of the fans all contributed to the success of the season. The grand final, in particular, showcased the culmination of these efforts, providing a spectacle that will be remembered for years to come. The spirit of competition and camaraderie that defined the 2007 season continued to inspire and shape the future of the NRL.

In the aftermath of the grand final, both teams reflected on their journeys. For Manly, it was a time to regroup and focus on the future, while Melbourne celebrated their well-deserved victory. The 2007 season left a lasting legacy, reminding everyone of the unpredictable and thrilling nature of rugby league. As the players rested and recovered, fans looked forward to the next season, eager to see what new stories and heroes would emerge.

The 2007 NRL season was a landmark year that will be remembered for its incredible matches, historic moments, and the grand final that captured the nation's attention. It was a season that celebrated the spirit of rugby league and the communities that support it. As the league continued to grow and evolve, the memories of 2007 served as a reminder of the passion, excitement, and unity that define the NRL.

The conclusion of the 2007 NRL season marked a pivotal moment in the history of rugby league, leaving an indelible mark on the sport and its followers. The return of the South Sydney Rabbitohs to finals football was a highlight, symbolizing resilience and the power of perseverance. Their journey back to the top was celebrated not just by their loyal supporters but by the entire rugby league community, showcasing the inclusive and supportive nature of the sport.

The grand final between the Manly Sea Eagles and the Melbourne Storm was the pinnacle of the season, drawing record viewership and demonstrating the widespread appeal of the NRL. Melbourne's decisive 34-8 victory was a testament to their dominance throughout the season. Their win was not just about lifting the trophy but also about solidifying their place as one of the premier teams in the league. This grand final will be remembered for its high level of play and the excitement it generated among fans.

Television ratings for the grand final being the highest in Australia in 2007 underscored the growing popularity of the NRL. This achievement highlighted the league's ability to capture the nation's attention and entertain millions. The success of the broadcast reflected the league's effective marketing strategies and the engaging nature of the matches. The widespread viewership brought new fans to the sport, expanding the NRL's reach and influence.

The 2007 season also demonstrated the importance of innovation and adaptation in maintaining the league's relevance and excitement. The introduction of Monday Night Football and the adjustment of the bye system were strategic moves that paid off, keeping the competition fresh and engaging for fans. These changes showed the league's commitment to improving the fan experience and ensuring that every round of the season offered something special.

The resilience shown by teams and players during the challenging weather conditions of the season further highlighted the toughness and determination inherent in rugby league. Despite cyclonic conditions, the matches went on, showcasing the sport's enduring spirit and the dedication of the players. This resilience resonated with fans, reinforcing their connection to the sport and admiration for the athletes.

The economic impact of the 2007 season was significant, with increased sponsorships, merchandise sales, and overall revenue. The financial success of the league ensured its continued growth and stability, providing resources for further development and expansion. This economic boost was crucial for the clubs, allowing them to invest in better facilities, player development, and community engagement programs.

The community engagement efforts of the NRL and its clubs during the 2007 season were also noteworthy. By actively involving local communities and hosting various initiatives, the league strengthened its grassroots connections. These efforts not only built stronger relationships with fans but also inspired the next generation of players. The inclusive nature of these programs ensured that rugby league remained accessible and enjoyable for everyone.

Looking back, the 2007 NRL season was a defining year that set new standards for the league. It showcased the importance of strategic innovation, resilience, and community engagement. The success of the season and the grand final provided a solid foundation for future growth and development. The lessons learned and the milestones achieved in 2007 continued to influence the direction of the NRL, guiding its evolution in the years to come.

The 2007 season of the NRL was a landmark year filled with memorable moments, strategic advancements, and significant achievements. It was a year that celebrated the sport's rich history while paving the way for a bright future. The return of the South Sydney Rabbitohs to the finals, the historic grand final, and the league's growth in popularity and economic impact were all testaments to the enduring appeal and strength of rugby league. As the NRL moved forward, the legacy of 2007 remained a source of inspiration and a reminder of what can be achieved through dedication, innovation, and community spirit.

Chapter 13: The Centenary of Rugby League (2008)

In 2008, the NRL celebrated a significant milestone: 100 years since rugby league was introduced to Australia. This centenary year was filled with special events and initiatives to honor the sport's rich history and impact. The NRL launched an extensive marketing campaign called the 'Centenary of Rugby League', which aimed to engage fans and highlight the sport's heritage. The season began in March, and a special Heritage Round was held in mid-April, coinciding with the first round of competition played back in 1908.

One of the most notable events of the centenary celebrations was the Gala event on 17 April 2008, where the Team of the Century was announced. This team honored the greatest players in the history of rugby league in Australia. The team included legendary players such as Clive Churchill at full-back, Ken Irvine and Brian Bevan as wingers, Reg Gasnier and Mal Meninga as centres, Wally Lewis at five-eighth, and Andrew Johns as half-back. The forward pack included John Raper at lock, Norm Provan and Ron Coote as second-rowers, Arthur Beetson and Duncan Hall as props, and Noel Kelly as hooker. The reserves were Graeme Langlands, Dally Messenger, Bob Fulton, and Frank Burge, with Jack Gibson named as the coach.

The centenary celebrations were not only about looking back but also about showcasing the sport's vibrant present. The 2008 season featured many memorable matches and moments. The special Heritage Round allowed fans to reminisce about the game's history and appreciate the legacy of the teams and players who paved the way for today's NRL stars.

Throughout the year, various clubs also took part in the centenary celebrations by hosting their own events and activities. These included exhibitions, fan days, and charity matches, which helped to engage the community and bring fans closer to the sport. The NRL also produced a range of merchandise and memorabilia to commemorate the centenary, allowing fans to own a piece of rugby league history.

As the season progressed, excitement built towards the finals. For the second consecutive year, the grand final was contested between the Melbourne Storm and the Manly Warringah Sea Eagles. This time, the NRL introduced a twilight grand final, a first in the league's history. The new timing aimed to attract a larger television audience and create a unique atmosphere for the decider.

The grand final itself was a historic match. The Manly Warringah Sea Eagles dominated the Melbourne Storm, winning 40–0. This victory set a record for the highest winning margin in a grand final. It was also the first time since 1978 that a team was kept scoreless in a grand final. The win was a testament to

Manly's outstanding performance throughout the season and their ability to rise to the occasion in the most important match of the year.

The 2008 season also saw several individual achievements and milestones. Players reached new heights in their careers, setting records and earning accolades for their performances. The centenary year provided a perfect backdrop for these accomplishments, highlighting the ongoing excellence and talent within the NRL.

Beyond the field, the centenary celebrations had a significant impact on the rugby league community. The events and initiatives brought fans together, fostering a sense of pride and unity. The year-long celebration reinforced the importance of rugby league in Australian culture and its role in shaping the country's sporting identity.

The 2008 NRL season was a remarkable year that honored the past, celebrated the present, and looked forward to the future. The centenary celebrations highlighted the rich history of rugby league in Australia and the contributions of the players, clubs, and fans who have made the sport what it is today. The season's events, from the Heritage Round to the announcement of the Team of the Century and the historic grand final, created lasting memories and a sense of unity within the rugby league community. As the NRL moved beyond its centenary year, the legacy of 2008 continued to inspire and influence the sport, ensuring that rugby league would remain a beloved and integral part of Australian culture for many years to come.

The 2008 season, marking the Centenary of Rugby League in Australia, was a year of immense significance and celebration. The centenary not only honored a hundred years of the sport's history but also highlighted the resilience and evolution of rugby league. This year was a testament to how far the game had come since its inception in 1908, showcasing the enduring passion and commitment of players, clubs, and fans alike.

The Centenary of Rugby League campaign effectively captured the essence of the sport's rich heritage. The various initiatives and events throughout the year, such as the Heritage Round and the Gala event where the Team of the Century was announced, provided a platform to celebrate the legends who shaped the game. The announcement of the Team of the Century was a particularly poignant moment, acknowledging the contributions of players whose legacies continue to inspire future generations. Figures like Clive Churchill, Wally Lewis, and Andrew Johns were rightfully honored, cementing their statuses as icons of the sport.

The special Heritage Round, coinciding with the first round of competition played in 1908, allowed fans to reminisce about the sport's beginnings. It also provided a unique opportunity to reflect on the growth and transformation of rugby league over the past century. Clubs across the league participated in the celebrations, hosting their own events and activities that further engaged the community and deepened the connection between the sport and its supporters.

Throughout the season, the competition remained fierce and compelling. The inclusion of events and activities dedicated to the centenary added a layer of excitement and nostalgia, making the 2008 season unforgettable. The grand final between the Melbourne Storm and the Manly Warringah Sea Eagles was particularly historic, not just for the match itself but for being the NRL's first twilight grand final. Manly's resounding 40-0 victory over Melbourne was a significant moment, setting a new record for the highest winning margin in a grand final and marking the first scoreless grand final since 1978.

The centenary celebrations also had a profound impact beyond the field. They brought together the rugby league community in a way that few events have. The initiatives and activities fostered a sense of unity and pride among fans, players, and clubs. The year-long celebration underscored the importance of rugby league in Australian culture and highlighted the sport's role in bringing communities together.

Financially and commercially, the centenary year proved successful as well. The various merchandise and memorabilia produced to commemorate the centenary were well-received, allowing fans to take home a piece of history. Sponsorships and corporate partnerships saw a significant boost, further solidifying the NRL's financial stability and growth potential. The record-breaking television ratings for the grand final were a testament to the sport's growing popularity and its ability to capture the nation's attention.

Individually, players achieved remarkable milestones and set new records, adding to the season's excitement. These achievements were celebrated within the context of the centenary, providing an additional layer of significance to their accomplishments. The players' performances throughout the season showcased the talent and dedication present in the league, promising a bright future for the sport.

In reflecting on the 2008 season, it is evident that the Centenary of Rugby League was more than just a celebration of the past; it was a celebration of the present and a look towards the future. The year highlighted the sport's resilience, its ability to adapt and grow, and its unyielding place in the hearts of Australians. The initiatives and events of the centenary year ensured that the legacy of rugby league would continue to thrive, inspiring future generations to carry forward the tradition and spirit of the game.

As the NRL moved beyond its centenary year, the impact of 2008 continued to be felt. The celebrations reinforced the sport's significance in Australian culture and its ability to unite people from all walks of life. The centenary year served as a reminder of the rich history of rugby league and the countless individuals who contributed to its success. It also provided a foundation for future growth and development, ensuring that rugby league would remain a beloved and integral part of Australia's sporting landscape for many years to come.

The 2008 NRL season was a monumental year that celebrated the past, enjoyed the present, and looked forward to the future. The centenary celebrations were a fitting tribute to a hundred years of rugby league, honoring the legends of the game while inspiring the next generation of players and fans. The legacy of 2008 is one of pride, unity, and enduring passion for the sport, ensuring that the spirit of rugby league will continue to thrive well into the future.

Chapter 14: The Beginning of the Second Century

The 2009 season marked the beginning of the second century of rugby league in Australia. The excitement and energy from the centenary celebrations of 2008 carried over, and fans were eager to see how the sport would continue to evolve. The season promised thrilling matches, strong rivalries, and the potential for new records to be set.

The Parramatta Eels and the Melbourne Storm emerged as two of the standout teams of the season. Both teams had strong performances throughout the year, with their players showcasing incredible skills and determination. Parramatta, in particular, had an impressive run towards the end of the season, winning several key matches to secure their place in the grand final.

Melbourne Storm, a dominant force in the league, continued their successful run. They were well-coached and had a roster filled with talented players who could change the course of a game in an instant. Their consistency and ability to perform under pressure made them a formidable opponent for any team.

The grand final was held at the ANZ Stadium in Sydney, drawing a massive crowd. Fans of both teams turned out in large numbers, creating an electric atmosphere. The match was highly anticipated, with many expecting it to be a close and exciting contest. The buildup to the game was filled with media coverage, player interviews, and predictions from experts and fans alike.

As the grand final kicked off, it was clear that both teams were determined to leave everything on the field. Parramatta started strong, showing their intent to challenge Melbourne right from the beginning. However, the Storm's experience in big games quickly became apparent as they responded with powerful plays and strategic moves.

Throughout the match, the lead changed hands several times, keeping the fans on the edge of their seats. The intensity of the game was palpable, with both teams giving their all. The players displayed remarkable athleticism, with big tackles, swift passes, and spectacular tries lighting up the field. Each play was crucial, and mistakes were costly.

In the end, Melbourne Storm managed to pull ahead and secure a 23-16 victory over Parramatta. It was a hard-fought win, showcasing the skill and resilience of the Melbourne side. This victory marked their second premiership in four years, cementing their status as one of the top teams in the league. The players celebrated with their fans, lifting the trophy high and savoring the moment.

Parramatta, despite their loss, earned respect and admiration for their efforts. Their journey to the grand final was impressive, and they showed they could compete with the best. The team vowed to come back stronger in the next season, using the experience gained in 2009 as motivation.

Off the field, the 2009 season saw continued growth and development in the NRL. The league focused on expanding its reach, attracting new fans, and increasing participation at the grassroots level. Community engagement initiatives and promotional events helped bring the sport closer to the people, ensuring rugby league's popularity continued to rise.

Financially, the league remained strong, with sponsorship deals and broadcast rights contributing to its stability. Merchandise sales were robust, with fans eager to show their support for their favorite teams. The overall health of the league was promising, setting a solid foundation for future seasons.

The 2009 season, marking the start of a new century for rugby league in Australia, was a memorable one. It was filled with intense competition, remarkable performances, and unforgettable moments. As the league looked ahead, the goal was to build on this success and continue to grow the sport, ensuring it remained a beloved part of Australian culture for generations to come.

The 2009 NRL season was a fitting start to the second century of rugby league in Australia. The grand final between Parramatta Eels and Melbourne Storm encapsulated the spirit of the sport – competitive, thrilling, and full of passion. With strong foundations in place, the future of rugby league looked bright, promising many more years of excitement and growth.

The 2009 NRL season, marking the beginning of the second century of rugby league in Australia, was a year filled with excitement, challenges, and significant achievements. As we reflect on this pivotal year, it is clear that the season was not just about the matches played, but also about the evolution and resilience of the sport.

The season began with high expectations, as the momentum from the centenary celebrations of 2008 carried forward. Fans were eager to see how the teams would perform and which players would rise to the occasion. The anticipation was palpable, and the season did not disappoint.

Throughout the regular season, the competition was fierce. Teams battled hard in each game, showcasing their skills, strategies, and sheer determination. The Parramatta Eels and Melbourne Storm emerged as the standout teams, demonstrating consistency and excellence on the field. Their journey to the grand final was marked by impressive victories and moments of brilliance that captivated fans.

The grand final itself was a testament to the spirit of rugby league. Held at the iconic ANZ Stadium in Sydney, it brought together thousands of fans who created an electrifying atmosphere. The match between Parramatta and Melbourne was a thrilling contest, with both teams giving their all. The ebb and flow of the game kept everyone on the edge of their seats, as the lead changed hands multiple times.

Melbourne Storm's victory was well-deserved. Their 23-16 win over Parramatta showcased their tactical acumen, physical prowess, and mental toughness. This win added another chapter to their legacy, solidifying their reputation as one of the premier teams in the NRL. The players' celebration with their fans was a joyous moment, highlighting the deep connection between the team and its supporters.

Parramatta, despite their loss, earned widespread respect for their performance throughout the season. Their resilience and tenacity were commendable, and their journey to the grand final was an inspiration. They demonstrated that they could compete with the best, and their future looked promising as they aimed to build on this year's experience.

Off the field, the 2009 season saw significant strides in the growth and development of the NRL. The league's efforts to expand its reach and engage with the community were successful. Initiatives to promote the sport at the grassroots level helped attract new fans and participants, ensuring the continued popularity of rugby league. The league's financial health was also strong, with lucrative sponsorship deals and broadcast rights providing stability and resources for further growth.

The introduction of the Gold Coast Titans was another highlight of the season. Their inclusion added a new dimension to the competition, bringing professional rugby league back to the Gold Coast and expanding the NRL's footprint. The Titans' performance on the field and their connection with the local community were promising signs for the future.

As the season drew to a close, there was a sense of optimism and excitement for what lay ahead. The 2009 season had set a high standard, and the lessons learned and successes achieved would serve as a foundation for continued growth. The NRL was poised to build on this momentum, aiming to further enhance the competition, engage with fans, and promote the sport.

The 2009 NRL season was a defining moment in the history of rugby league in Australia. It marked the beginning of a new century for the sport, filled with potential and promise. The season's success was a testament to the dedication of the players, coaches, officials, and fans who make rugby league what it is. Their passion and commitment ensure that the sport will continue to thrive and inspire for many years to come.

The 2009 season was a landmark year for the NRL. It celebrated the rich history of rugby league while paving the way for a bright future. The achievements of the season, both on and off the field, demonstrated the enduring appeal and resilience of the sport. As the

NRL moves forward into its second century, the legacy of the 2009 season will continue to inspire and guide its journey.

Chapter 15: The Landmark Year of 2010

The year 2010 was a landmark season for the NRL, marked by several significant events and milestones. One of the most notable highlights was the inaugural All Stars Match held on February 13th. This event was designed to coincide with the Sorry Day reconciliation anniversary, promoting rugby league's long-standing association and involvement with the Aboriginal community. In this first match, the Indigenous All Stars triumphed over the NRL All Stars with a score of 16–12. The match's success led to its establishment as a recurring fixture on the rugby league calendar, with Queensland securing the hosting rights for the following three years.

The 29th State of Origin series in 2010 also made history. It featured the world's first live free-to-air 3D TV broadcast, bringing an innovative viewing experience to fans. Queensland's dominance in the series continued as they made history by winning their fifth consecutive series. They achieved a clean sweep, winning the 2010 series 3–0, marking their first Origin whitewash since 1995. This feat solidified Queensland's position as a powerhouse in State of Origin history.

The 2010 NRL season was also notable for its record-breaking attendance figures. The league set a new record for total season average attendance, with 17,367 fans per game, and a record total season aggregate attendance of 3,490,778. These numbers highlighted the growing popularity of the NRL and the increasing engagement of fans with the sport. The high attendance figures were a testament to the exciting and competitive nature of the matches throughout the season.

During the 2010 finals series, fans witnessed one of the most thrilling games in modern NRL history. The second qualifying match between the Wests Tigers and the Sydney Roosters went into extra time, becoming the first McIntyre system final to do so. This match, dubbed the "One Hundred Minute Epic," was widely regarded as one of the greatest games of the era. It showcased the intensity and drama that NRL finals football can deliver, leaving fans on the edge of their seats until the very end.

The grand finale of the 2010 season was the NRL Grand Final, played between the St. George Illawarra Dragons and the Sydney Roosters. The Dragons emerged victorious with a commanding 32–8 win. This victory was particularly significant as it marked the first premiership for the St. George Illawarra Dragons in their eleven-year history as a joint venture club. Additionally, it was the first premiership for the St. George part of the joint venture in 31 years, making it a historic and emotional win for the club and its supporters.

The success of the All Stars Match, the State of Origin series, and the record-breaking attendance figures all contributed to a landmark year for the NRL in 2010. These achievements underscored the league's ability to innovate, engage fans, and deliver high-quality rugby league action. The events of 2010 also highlighted the deep connection between the NRL and the communities it serves, particularly through the celebration of the Indigenous All Stars and the ongoing commitment to reconciliation.

The triumphs and milestones of the 2010 season left an indelible mark on the history of the NRL. The year's events demonstrated the league's growth, the increasing popularity of the sport, and the ability to create memorable and historic moments. As the NRL moved forward, the achievements of 2010 provided a strong foundation for continued success and further engagement with fans and communities across Australia and beyond.

The 2010 NRL season was a defining year that showcased the league's capacity for innovation, record-breaking achievements, and the creation of historic moments. The successes of the All Stars Match, State of Origin series, and the NRL Grand Final highlighted the sport's growing popularity and the deep connections between the league and its fans. The events of 2010 will be remembered as a pivotal chapter in the history of the NRL, setting the stage for continued growth and success in the years to come.

The 2010 season was a remarkable chapter in the history of the NRL, characterized by numerous achievements, innovations, and significant milestones that left an enduring impact on the league. From the inaugural All Stars Match to the thrilling State of Origin series and the memorable Grand Final, each event contributed to a season that will be remembered for its contributions to the sport and its fanbase.

The All Stars Match, held in conjunction with the Sorry Day reconciliation anniversary, was more than just a game; it was a powerful statement of unity and inclusion. By celebrating the Aboriginal community's contributions to rugby league, the NRL demonstrated its commitment to diversity and reconciliation. The success of this event not only entertained fans but also reinforced the league's role in promoting social causes and strengthening community ties.

The 29th State of Origin series was another highlight of the 2010 season, showcasing the fierce rivalry between Queensland and New South Wales. The historic live free-to-air 3D TV broadcast brought a new dimension to the viewing experience, captivating audiences with cutting-edge technology. Queensland's unprecedented fifth consecutive series win, achieved with a clean sweep, solidified their dominance in the State of Origin. This victory was a testament to the skill, determination, and teamwork of the Queensland players, and it added another chapter to the storied history of the series.

Attendance records set during the 2010 season were a clear indication of the NRL's growing popularity. With an average of 17,367 fans per game and a total season aggregate attendance of 3,490,778, the league demonstrated its ability to attract and engage a broad audience. These record-breaking figures reflected the fans' passion for the sport and their commitment to supporting their teams. The high attendance numbers also underscored the importance of providing a top-quality experience for fans, both in stadiums and through broadcast coverage.

The 2010 finals series delivered some of the most thrilling and memorable moments of the season. The second qualifying match between the Wests Tigers and the Sydney Roosters, known as the "One Hundred Minute Epic," captivated fans with its intensity and drama. The match's extra-time battle exemplified the high stakes and excitement of NRL finals football, leaving an indelible impression on all who witnessed it. This game will be remembered as one of the greatest in modern NRL history, showcasing the sport's ability to produce unforgettable moments.

The grand finale of the season, the 2010 NRL Grand Final, was a fitting climax to a year of incredible highs. The St. George Illawarra Dragons' victory over the Sydney Roosters was a momentous occasion for the club and its supporters. Winning their first premiership as a joint venture club and the first for the St. George part in 31 years, the Dragons' triumph was a celebration of perseverance, dedication, and excellence. The Grand Final's record-breaking margin of victory further highlighted the Dragons' dominance and skill.

The successes of the 2010 season extended beyond the field, reflecting the NRL's broader impact on the sport and its community. The league's ability to innovate with events like the All Stars Match, embrace cutting-edge technology in broadcasting, and engage fans through record attendance figures demonstrated its forward-thinking approach. The 2010 season set a benchmark for future seasons, providing a blueprint for continued growth and success.

The achievements of 2010 also underscored the importance of strong leadership and vision within the NRL. The league's ability to navigate challenges, seize opportunities, and deliver a compelling product to fans was a testament to the efforts of players, coaches, administrators, and everyone involved in the sport. The season's successes were a collective effort, reflecting the dedication and passion of the entire rugby league community.

As the NRL looked to the future, the 2010 season provided a solid foundation for further expansion, innovation, and engagement. The events of this landmark year demonstrated the league's potential to reach new heights and continue captivating audiences. The lessons learned and the milestones achieved in 2010 would guide the NRL in its ongoing journey to promote and develop rugby league, ensuring its place as a premier sporting competition.

The 2010 NRL season was a defining chapter in the league's history, marked by record-breaking achievements, thrilling matches, and significant milestones. The All Stars Match, State of Origin series, record attendance figures, and the memorable Grand Final all contributed to a year of unprecedented success. These events highlighted the NRL's ability to innovate, engage, and inspire, setting the stage for continued growth and excellence in the years to come. The 2010 season will be remembered as a pivotal moment in the history of the NRL, a year that showcased the best of rugby league and its enduring appeal to fans around the world.

Part Three: 2010–2019: The Rise of the ARLC and a New Era of Dominance

Chapter 16: The Establishment of the ARLC and the 2011 Season

In December 2010, a significant moment arrived for rugby league in Australia. The Australian Rugby League (ARL) and News Corporation reached an agreement on a constitutional framework, paving the way for an independent commission to govern the sport. This new body, known as the Australian Rugby League Commission (ARLC), marked a shift from joint control to a more centralized and independent governance structure. The negotiations were extensive and intricate, addressing key issues like sponsorship, media rights, funding for state bodies, support for the Melbourne Storm, and the ownership and management of clubs.

The establishment of the ARLC was seen as a crucial step toward ensuring the sport's sustainability and growth. This new governance structure aimed to provide a unified direction, free from conflicts of interest that had previously plagued the administration of the league. The transition was not without its challenges, but the consensus was that it would lead to a more prosperous future for rugby league in Australia.

The 2011 season was notable not just for the administrative changes but also for the thrilling on-field action. The Manly-Warringah Sea Eagles and the New Zealand Warriors contested the Grand Final, showcasing the high level of competition within the

NRL. The Warriors, participating in their second Grand Final, faced a determined Sea Eagles side.

Under the guidance of head coach Des Hasler, the Manly-Warringah Sea Eagles demonstrated their prowess and strategic acumen throughout the season. Their journey to the Grand Final was marked by consistent performances, strong teamwork, and a solid defensive record. On the day of the Grand Final, Manly executed their game plan to perfection, securing a 24-10 victory over the Warriors.

This win was significant for Manly, marking their second premiership under Des Hasler's leadership. The Sea Eagles' success was a testament to their resilience and ability to perform under pressure. The match was a display of tactical brilliance and physical endurance, captivating fans and reinforcing the league's popularity.

The Warriors, despite their loss, were commended for their tenacity and the skill they brought to the competition. Their journey to the Grand Final was inspiring, highlighting the increasing competitiveness of teams outside of New South Wales and Queensland. The Warriors' presence in the final underscored the growing international appeal of the NRL, particularly in New Zealand, where rugby league continued to gain a strong following.

Off the field, the ARLC began its work, focusing on creating a strategic vision for the sport's future. One of the early tasks was to address the financial stability of all clubs, ensuring that teams had the resources necessary to compete at the highest level. This involved negotiating new sponsorship deals and broadcasting rights that would bring additional revenue to the league.

The commission also prioritized grassroots development, recognizing that the future of the sport depended on nurturing young talent. Initiatives were launched to increase participation at junior levels, improve coaching standards, and provide better facilities for training and development. These efforts aimed to create a robust pipeline of players who could one day star in the NRL.

As the 2011 season concluded, the NRL and its newly established commission looked to the future with optimism. The changes in governance promised a more streamlined and efficient administration, capable of driving the sport forward. The success of the season, both in terms of viewership and competitive quality, set a strong foundation for the years to come.

The establishment of the ARLC and the achievements of the 2011 season marked a new chapter in the history of rugby league in Australia. With a solid governance structure and a clear vision for growth, the sport was poised to enter a new era of success and stability. The 2011 Grand Final, with its thrilling conclusion and showcase of talent, served as a fitting end to a transformative year for the NRL.

The 2011 season was a pivotal year for the National Rugby League, both on and off the field. The establishment of the Australian Rugby League Commission (ARLC) marked a significant step towards a more unified and independent governance structure. This change was anticipated to bring about a new era of stability and growth for the sport, addressing long-standing issues related to sponsorship, media rights, and the financial health of clubs.

The path to creating the ARLC was not straightforward. It involved extensive negotiations to resolve key matters, including the funding of state bodies, support for clubs like the Melbourne Storm, and ensuring fair representation within the new body. These discussions highlighted the complexities of transitioning from a joint governance model to an independent commission. However, the agreement reached in December 2010 set the stage for a promising future for rugby league in Australia.

On the field, the 2011 season did not disappoint. It featured intense competition, culminating in a memorable Grand Final between the Manly-Warringah Sea Eagles and the New Zealand Warriors. Manly's victory was a testament to their skill, strategy, and determination, securing their second premiership under the leadership of coach Des Hasler. The Sea Eagles' performance throughout the season showcased their resilience and ability to excel under pressure, earning them deserved recognition as champions.

The New Zealand Warriors, despite their loss, made a significant impact on the season. Their journey to the Grand Final demonstrated the growing competitiveness of teams outside the traditional strongholds of New South Wales and Queensland. The Warriors' success brought increased attention to rugby league in New Zealand, contributing to the sport's expanding international appeal. Their presence in the final underscored the NRL's status as a premier competition, capable of attracting talent and fans from across the region.

As the ARLC began its work, it focused on creating a strategic vision for the future of rugby league. One of the key priorities was to ensure the financial stability of all clubs, providing them with the resources needed to compete effectively. This involved negotiating new sponsorship deals and broadcasting rights, which would bring additional revenue to the league. The commission also placed a strong emphasis on grassroots development, recognizing the importance of nurturing young talent. Initiatives were launched to increase participation at junior levels, improve coaching standards, and enhance facilities for training and development.

The 2011 season also saw the reintroduction of Monday Night Football and two Friday night games, both of which turned out to be ratings successes. This innovation in scheduling provided fans with more opportunities to engage with the sport, contributing to the overall popularity of the NRL. The weather conditions during the middle of the season, particularly the cyclonic conditions in Sydney and Newcastle, posed challenges for some games, but the league managed to maintain a high level of excitement and competition throughout.

Looking ahead, the NRL and its newly established commission were well-positioned to drive the sport forward. The changes in governance promised a more streamlined and efficient administration, capable of addressing the evolving needs of the league. The success of the 2011 season, in terms of both viewership and competitive quality, set a strong foundation for future growth. The ARLC's strategic initiatives aimed at enhancing the financial stability of clubs and developing grassroots talent were expected to contribute significantly to the sport's long-term success.

The conclusion of the 2011 season marked the beginning of a new chapter in the history of rugby league in Australia. The establishment of the ARLC and the achievements of the season signaled a bright future for the sport. With a solid governance structure and a clear vision for growth, rugby league was poised to enter a new era of success and stability. The 2011 Grand Final, with its thrilling conclusion and showcase of talent, served as a fitting end to a transformative year for the NRL.

The 2011 season will be remembered as a landmark year for rugby league. The establishment of the ARLC provided the sport with a strong and independent governance framework, while the on-field action captivated fans and showcased the high level of competition within the NRL. The success of the Manly-Warringah Sea Eagles and the strong performance of the New Zealand Warriors highlighted the depth of talent in the league. As the ARLC continued its work, the future of rugby league in Australia looked brighter than ever, promising continued growth and excitement for fans and players alike.

Chapter 17: Establishing the ARLC

On 10 February 2012, a major change took place in the world of rugby league. The Australian Rugby League Commission (ARLC) took full control of the game. This new independent commission replaced the former state-based boards and took over from the previous NRL partnership, which included the ARL board and News Limited. The formation of the ARLC was a significant move towards unifying and strengthening the governance of rugby league in Australia. Peter V'landys AM was appointed as the Chairman, a position he continues to hold.

The ARLC's primary aim was to ensure the growth and sustainability of rugby league at all levels. By taking control of the game, the commission sought to streamline operations, reduce bureaucracy, and provide clear direction for the future. The new structure allowed for more consistent and efficient decision-making processes, benefiting both the professional and grassroots levels of the sport. This change was welcomed by many within the rugby league community, who saw it as a necessary step towards modernizing and improving the game.

The 2012 NRL season was the first under the new commission's governance. This season saw a high level of competition and excitement, culminating in a thrilling Grand Final. The Canterbury-Bankstown Bulldogs faced off against the Melbourne Storm. This was the first time since 2008 that the top two teams of the regular season contested the Grand Final. The match was eagerly anticipated by fans, as both teams had shown remarkable form throughout the season.

The Grand Final was a hard-fought battle. Both teams displayed exceptional skill and determination, making for an intense and captivating game. In the end, the Melbourne Storm emerged victorious, defeating the Canterbury-Bankstown Bulldogs with a score of 14-4. This victory marked the Storm's second premiership and was particularly significant as it came after the team had two previous premierships stripped due to salary cap breaches. The win was seen as a form of redemption and a testament to the team's resilience and hard work.

The success of the Melbourne Storm in 2012 highlighted the competitive nature of the NRL. Despite the challenges and controversies of the past, the team managed to regroup and perform at the highest level. Their victory was celebrated by fans and acknowledged by critics as a well-deserved achievement. The 2012 season also demonstrated the effectiveness of the new governance structure, with the ARLC providing the necessary support and oversight to ensure a fair and competitive league.

Beyond the Grand Final, the 2012 season was filled with memorable moments and impressive performances from various teams and players. The introduction of the ARLC brought renewed focus on the development of young talent and the importance of maintaining high standards both on and off the field. Initiatives were introduced to improve player welfare, enhance coaching techniques, and promote the sport in new and innovative ways.

One of the key achievements of the ARLC in its inaugural year was the negotiation of a new television rights deal. This deal brought in significant revenue, which was then reinvested into the game. The increased funding allowed for better facilities, improved training programs, and greater support for grassroots rugby league. This investment was crucial in ensuring the long-term growth and sustainability of the sport.

As the 2012 season came to a close, there was a sense of optimism and excitement within the rugby league community. The establishment of the ARLC marked the beginning of a new era, one that promised greater unity, professionalism, and success for the game. The achievements of the season, both on and off the field, set a strong foundation for the future. The ARLC's commitment to transparency, integrity, and growth was evident, and the positive impact of these changes was felt across all levels of rugby league.

The establishment of the Australian Rugby League Commission in 2012 was a transformative moment for the sport. The new governance structure brought about significant improvements in the management and operation of rugby league in Australia. The success of the Melbourne Storm in the Grand Final was a fitting end to a season that marked the beginning of a new and promising chapter for the NRL. With the ARLC at the helm, the future of rugby league looked brighter than ever, with the potential for continued growth and success on both the national and international stages.

The 2012 season under the new Australian Rugby League Commission (ARLC) was a pivotal year for rugby league in Australia. This season marked the beginning of a new era, characterized by significant governance reforms, enhanced competitiveness, and increased professionalism. The establishment of the ARLC brought much-needed unity and direction to the sport, ensuring its growth and sustainability for the future.

One of the most notable achievements of the ARLC in its first year was the successful negotiation of a lucrative television rights deal. This deal not only provided a substantial financial boost to the league but also allowed for greater investment in the development of the sport. Funds from the deal were used to improve facilities, enhance training programs, and support grassroots rugby league initiatives. This investment was crucial in building a strong foundation for the future, ensuring that young talent had the resources and opportunities needed to excel.

The 2012 season saw the introduction of several new initiatives aimed at improving the overall quality and appeal of the game. The return of Monday Night

Football and the addition of a second Friday night game proved to be ratings successes, attracting more viewers and increasing the sport's popularity. The reduction in the number of byes per team also made for a more consistent and competitive season, with every team playing more regularly and fans getting to see their favorite teams in action more often.

The Grand Final of the 2012 season was a highlight, with the Melbourne Storm defeating the Canterbury-Bankstown Bulldogs 14-4. This victory was significant not only because it was the Storm's second premiership but also because it came after the team had faced severe penalties for salary cap breaches. The win was a testament to the team's resilience and determination, showcasing their ability to overcome adversity and perform at the highest level. This victory was celebrated widely and was a moment of redemption for the Melbourne Storm, reinforcing their status as one of the top teams in the NRL.

The season also saw the return of the South Sydney Rabbitohs to finals football for the first time in decades. This was a momentous occasion for the club and its supporters, who had endured years of hardship and struggle. The Rabbitohs' return to form was a symbol of the positive changes brought about by the new governance structure and the renewed focus on supporting and developing all clubs within the league.

Off the field, the ARLC worked tirelessly to promote the sport and engage with the community. Various marketing campaigns and community outreach programs were launched to increase the sport's visibility and attract new fans. These efforts were successful in raising the profile of rugby league and building a stronger, more connected community of supporters. The ARLC's commitment to transparency and integrity also helped restore public trust in the sport, ensuring that fans could enjoy the game with confidence in its fairness and professionalism.

The ARLC's first year in control was not without its challenges. The transition to the new governance structure required significant adjustments and there were some teething problems along the way. However, the overall impact of the changes was overwhelmingly positive. The ARLC's leadership brought a new level of stability and direction to the sport, laying the groundwork for continued success and growth in the years to come.

As the 2012 season drew to a close, there was a palpable sense of optimism and excitement within the rugby league community. The changes implemented by the ARLC had already begun to bear fruit, and the future looked bright for the sport. The successes of the season, both on and off the field, demonstrated the potential of the new governance structure and the positive impact it could have on the game.

The 2012 season under the Australian Rugby League Commission was a transformative year for rugby league in Australia. The establishment of the ARLC brought about significant improvements in governance, competitiveness, and professionalism, setting a strong foundation for the future. The season's successes, including the Melbourne Storm's Grand Final victory and the return of the South Sydney Rabbitohs to finals football, were highlights that showcased the positive impact of these changes. With the ARLC at the helm, the future of rugby league in Australia looked brighter than ever, with the potential for continued growth and success on both the national and international stages.

Chapter 18: The 2013 Season: Resurgence and Controversy

The 2013 NRL season was a rollercoaster of triumphs and tribulations, marked by the resurgence of two of rugby league's most historic clubs: the Sydney Roosters and the South Sydney Rabbitohs. Both teams showcased exceptional performance throughout the season, finishing first and second on the ladder respectively. Their return to dominance was a nostalgic nod to the early days of the sport and a promising sign for the future of these iconic clubs.

The Sydney Roosters, under the leadership of coach Trent Robinson, had a standout season. Their strong defense and dynamic attack saw them clinch the minor premiership, finishing at the top of the table. This achievement was a testament to their hard work and strategic gameplay throughout the season. Players like Sonny Bill Williams and Mitchell Pearce played crucial roles, consistently delivering high-caliber performances that thrilled fans and intimidated opponents.

Similarly, the South Sydney Rabbitohs had a remarkable season, finishing in second place. Coached by Michael Maguire, the Rabbitohs displayed resilience and skill, making them one of the most formidable teams of the season. Key players like Greg Inglis and John Sutton led by example, inspiring their teammates and fans alike. The Rabbitohs' success was a significant milestone, reflecting the club's rich history and its ongoing commitment to excellence.

However, the 2013 season was not without its controversies. The Cronulla-Sutherland Sharks found themselves at the center of a major scandal when they were caught using performance-enhancing substances dating back to 2011. The Australian Sports Anti-Doping Authority (ASADA) investigation brought to light the extent of the doping practices within the club. This scandal was a significant setback for the NRL, casting a shadow over the sport's integrity and leading to widespread scrutiny and criticism.

The NRL's response to the doping scandal was swift and decisive. The league implemented stricter anti-doping measures and increased penalties for violations. These actions were crucial in restoring public trust and ensuring the integrity of the competition. The league also provided support and education to clubs and players to prevent future incidents, emphasizing the importance of clean and fair play.

Despite the off-field controversies, the 2013 season concluded with an exciting Grand Final. The Sydney Roosters faced off against the Manly-Warringah Sea Eagles in a thrilling match. The Grand Final was a highly anticipated event, with both teams showcasing their best skills and strategies. The Roosters emerged victorious with a 26-18 win, claiming their 13th premiership. This victory was a fitting end to their outstanding season and a significant achievement for the club.

The 2013 Grand Final was more than just a game; it was a celebration of the resilience and spirit of rugby league. Fans from all over Australia tuned in to witness the culmination of a season filled with highs and lows. The Roosters' victory was a testament to their dedication and hard work, and it provided a sense of closure and triumph amidst the season's challenges.

Off the field, the NRL continued to focus on growing the sport and engaging with the community. Various initiatives were launched to promote rugby league at the grassroots level and support the development of young talent. The league also worked on enhancing the fan experience, with improved facilities and increased access to games through various media platforms.

As the 2013 season drew to a close, there was a renewed sense of optimism and excitement for the future of rugby league. The successes of the Sydney Roosters and South Sydney Rabbitohs, along with the league's commitment to integrity and growth, set a positive tone for the seasons to come. The lessons learned and the challenges overcome during the 2013 season would undoubtedly shape the future of the sport, ensuring its continued success and popularity.

The 2013 NRL season was a significant chapter in the history of rugby league in Australia. The resurgence of foundation clubs, the handling of the Cronulla-Sutherland Sharks scandal, and the thrilling Grand Final all contributed to a memorable and impactful season. The achievements and challenges of 2013 laid the groundwork for the future, highlighting the resilience, passion, and integrity that define the sport of rugby league.

The 2013 NRL season was a memorable and transformative year for rugby league in Australia. Marked by the resurgence of the Sydney Roosters and South Sydney Rabbitohs, the season brought a renewed sense of excitement and nostalgia for fans of the sport. The impressive performances of these foundation clubs showcased their determination and skill, cementing their places as powerhouses in the league.

The Sydney Roosters' journey to the top of the ladder was a testament to their hard work, strategic planning, and exceptional gameplay. Their minor premiership win highlighted the team's consistency and dominance throughout the season. Key players like Sonny Bill Williams and Mitchell Pearce played pivotal roles, demonstrating their talent and leadership on the field. The Roosters' success was a source of inspiration for fans and a reminder of the club's storied history and ongoing commitment to excellence.

Similarly, the South Sydney Rabbitohs' strong performance in 2013 was a significant achievement.

Finishing second on the ladder, the Rabbitohs showed resilience and determination under the guidance of coach Michael Maguire. The leadership of players like Greg Inglis and John Sutton was instrumental in the team's success, and their performances brought joy and pride to Rabbitohs supporters. The Rabbitohs' resurgence was a heartwarming narrative, reflecting the club's rich heritage and its passionate fanbase.

However, the season was not without its challenges. The Cronulla-Sutherland Sharks scandal brought to light the issue of performance-enhancing substances in the sport, casting a shadow over the NRL. The ASADA investigation revealed the extent of doping practices within the Sharks, leading to significant repercussions for the club and the league. This scandal was a stark reminder of the importance of maintaining the integrity of the sport and the need for stringent anti-doping measures.

In response to the doping scandal, the NRL took decisive action to restore public trust and ensure the sport's integrity. The implementation of stricter anti-doping policies and increased penalties for violations were essential steps in addressing the issue. The league's commitment to clean and fair play was evident, and efforts were made to educate players and clubs on the importance of adhering to these standards.

Despite the off-field controversies, the 2013 season concluded with a thrilling Grand Final between the

Sydney Roosters and the Manly-Warringah Sea Eagles. The Roosters' 26-18 victory was a fitting end to their outstanding season, securing their 13th premiership. The Grand Final was the most-watched television show in Australia in 2013, reflecting the widespread interest and passion for rugby league. The Roosters' triumph was a moment of celebration for the club and its supporters, marking the culmination of a season filled with hard work and dedication.

Off the field, the NRL continued to focus on growing the sport and engaging with the community. Various initiatives were launched to promote rugby league at the grassroots level, supporting the development of young talent and encouraging participation in the sport. The league also worked on enhancing the fan experience, with improved facilities and increased access to games through various media platforms. These efforts were crucial in ensuring the continued popularity and success of rugby league in Australia.

As the 2013 season drew to a close, there was a sense of optimism and excitement for the future of the NRL. The successes and challenges of the season provided valuable lessons and insights, shaping the direction of the sport in the years to come. The resilience, passion, and commitment demonstrated by players, clubs, and fans alike were testaments to the enduring spirit of rugby league.

The 2013 NRL season was a significant chapter in the history of rugby league in Australia. The resurgence of foundation clubs, the handling of the Cronulla-Sutherland Sharks scandal, and the thrilling Grand Final all contributed to a memorable and impactful year. The achievements and challenges of 2013 laid the groundwork for the future, highlighting the resilience, passion, and integrity that define the sport of rugby league. As the NRL continues to evolve and grow, the lessons learned from the 2013 season will undoubtedly play a crucial role in shaping the future of the sport, ensuring its continued success and popularity for years to come.

Chapter 19: The 2014 Season – Auckland Nines and the Rabbitohs' Triumph

The 2014 NRL season was notable for several significant events and changes, starting with the introduction of the Auckland Nines. This new tournament format, held at Eden Park in Auckland, brought excitement and a fresh dynamic to the league. Featuring nine players per side and played over two days, the Auckland Nines was a fast-paced, high-energy competition that quickly became a fan favorite. The inaugural tournament was a success, showcasing the skills of the players in a new and thrilling way.

Despite the excitement of the Auckland Nines, the 2014 season was also overshadowed by the fallout from the ASADA scandal. The Cronulla-Sutherland Sharks were hit with a hefty one million dollar fine for their involvement in the doping scandal that had come to light in previous years. The league's decision to impose such a substantial penalty reflected its commitment to maintaining the integrity of the sport. Additionally, Sharks' head coach Shane Flanagan was suspended for the entire 2014 season, a significant blow to the club's prospects.

As the season progressed, teams battled it out for a spot in the finals, with the competition proving as fierce as ever. The South Sydney Rabbitohs, one of the league's oldest and most storied clubs, emerged as a dominant force. Under the leadership of coach Michael Maguire, the Rabbitohs displayed remarkable consistency and determination, capturing the hearts of their supporters. Key players such as Greg Inglis, Sam Burgess, and Adam Reynolds played pivotal roles in the team's success, demonstrating skill and leadership on the field.

The 2014 Grand Final was highly anticipated, with the South Sydney Rabbitohs facing off against the Canterbury-Bankstown Bulldogs. For South Sydney, this grand final appearance was particularly significant as it was their first since 1971. The long wait added a layer of emotion and anticipation for Rabbitohs fans, who had remained loyal through decades of ups and downs. The Bulldogs, on the other hand, were also a formidable opponent, known for their strong defense and tactical play.

The grand final itself was a spectacular event, held at ANZ Stadium in Sydney. The atmosphere was electric, with fans from both sides filling the stadium and millions more watching on television. The Rabbitohs started strong and maintained their momentum throughout the game. Their powerful performance was highlighted by the exceptional play of Sam Burgess, who famously played with a fractured cheekbone sustained in the opening minutes of the match. His bravery and resilience became one of the defining moments of the game.

South Sydney's victory was decisive, with a final score of 30–6. The win ended a 43-year premiership drought for the Rabbitohs, bringing immense joy and relief to their fans. The scenes of celebration that followed were unforgettable, with players and supporters alike reveling in the long-awaited triumph. The win was a testament to the team's hard work, dedication, and the strategic acumen of coach Michael Maguire. It was also a significant moment in rugby league history, as one of the game's foundation clubs returned to the pinnacle of success.

In addition to the grand final victory, the 2014 season saw several other noteworthy achievements and milestones. The Auckland Nines set a new standard for pre-season competitions, showcasing the versatility and skill of NRL players. The league's handling of the ASADA scandal, while challenging, demonstrated a firm commitment to integrity and fairness, reinforcing the importance of clean sport.

Off the field, the NRL continued to engage with the community through various initiatives and programs aimed at promoting the sport and supporting grassroots development. Efforts to grow the game at the junior level were bolstered by increased funding and resources, ensuring a strong pipeline of talent for the future. The league also made strides in enhancing the fan experience, with improved stadium facilities and greater access to games through digital platforms.

The 2014 NRL season was a mix of innovation, triumph, and challenge. The introduction of the Auckland Nines added a new dimension to the game, while the South Sydney Rabbitohs' historic premiership victory provided a fitting climax to a memorable year. Despite the setbacks and controversies, the league emerged stronger, with a renewed focus on integrity, community engagement, and the continued growth of rugby league in Australia. As the NRL looked ahead to future seasons, the lessons and successes of 2014 would undoubtedly play a crucial role in shaping the path forward.

The 2014 NRL season was a remarkable year in the history of the league, filled with both triumphs and challenges that left an indelible mark on the sport. The introduction of the Auckland Nines was a significant milestone, bringing a fresh and exciting format that captivated fans and showcased the athleticism and versatility of the players. This new tournament not only added a new dimension to the pre-season but also set a high standard for future competitions, proving to be a resounding success.

The season was also marked by the repercussions of the ASADA scandal, with the Cronulla-Sutherland Sharks receiving a substantial fine and the suspension of their head coach Shane Flanagan. This scandal served as a stark reminder of the importance of integrity and clean sport, prompting the NRL to take decisive action to uphold the values of the game. The handling of the scandal, though challenging, demonstrated the league's commitment to maintaining the credibility and fairness of rugby league.

On the field, the South Sydney Rabbitohs' journey to the grand final was a story of resilience, determination, and exceptional teamwork. After decades of struggle, their triumphant return to the grand final and subsequent victory were momentous occasions for the club and its loyal supporters. The sight of Sam Burgess playing through a fractured cheekbone epitomized the spirit and toughness of the Rabbitohs, earning him admiration and respect across the sporting world.

The grand final itself was a spectacle of high-quality rugby league, with the Rabbitohs dominating the Canterbury-Bankstown Bulldogs to claim a decisive 30-6 victory. This win not only ended a 43-year premiership drought for South Sydney but also reaffirmed the club's status as one of the most storied and beloved teams in the league. The celebrations that followed were a testament to the deep connection between the Rabbitohs and their fans, creating unforgettable memories for everyone involved.

Beyond the grand final, the 2014 season saw several other significant achievements. The Auckland Nines provided a thrilling start to the year, while the league's robust response to the ASADA scandal reinforced its commitment to integrity. The success of the All Stars Match highlighted the importance of promoting inclusivity and celebrating the rich cultural heritage of rugby league, particularly its strong ties with the Aboriginal community.

The record attendance figures and increased viewership indicated the growing popularity of the NRL, underscoring the league's efforts to enhance the fan experience. The introduction of new initiatives and programs aimed at promoting grassroots development and community engagement ensured that the sport continued to thrive at all levels. These efforts were crucial in nurturing young talent and fostering a strong sense of community around rugby league.

Moreover, the league's ongoing digital transformation made games more accessible to fans, providing multiple platforms for engagement and interaction. This shift not only broadened the league's reach but also created a more inclusive and connected fan base, further solidifying the NRL's position as a premier sporting competition.

The 2014 NRL season was a year of innovation, resilience, and celebration. The introduction of the Auckland Nines and the triumphant return of the South Sydney Rabbitohs were standout moments that highlighted the dynamic and unpredictable nature of rugby league. Despite the challenges posed by the ASADA scandal, the league's steadfast commitment to integrity and fairness shone through, reinforcing the values that underpin the sport.

As the NRL moved forward, the lessons and successes of the 2014 season served as a foundation for continued growth and development. The league's dedication to promoting inclusivity, enhancing the fan experience, and supporting grassroots development ensured a bright future for rugby league in Australia. The 2014 season will be remembered not only for the Rabbitohs' historic victory but also for the significant strides made in advancing the sport and reinforcing its place in the hearts of fans across the nation.

Chapter 20: The 2015 NRL Season

The 2015 NRL season was unforgettable, marked by the return of Queensland powerhouses, the North Queensland Cowboys and the Brisbane Broncos. Both teams showcased outstanding performances throughout the season, finishing in the top four and earning the right to contest the Grand Final. This was a significant moment for Queensland rugby league fans, as it was the first all-Queensland NRL Grand Final in the history of the competition.

The Grand Final between the Cowboys and the Broncos is often hailed as the greatest grand final of all time. The match was played at an electrifying pace, with both teams demonstrating incredible skill, determination, and resilience. From the opening whistle, it was clear that neither side was willing to give an inch, resulting in a closely fought contest that kept fans on the edge of their seats.

As the game progressed, the intensity only increased. The Broncos held a slim lead heading into the final minutes of the match, but the Cowboys were not ready to concede defeat. With the full-time siren about to sound, the Cowboys launched a final desperate attack. In a moment that will forever be etched in NRL history, Kyle Feldt scored a try in the corner as the siren sounded, leveling the scores and setting up a potential match-winning conversion for Johnathan Thurston.

Thurston, one of the game's greatest players, had the chance to seal the victory for his team. The stadium fell silent as he lined up the conversion from the sideline. However, in a dramatic twist, the ball struck the post and bounced away, sending the match into golden point extra time. This was the first time in NRL history that a Grand Final had been decided by golden point, adding to the drama and excitement of the occasion.

Golden point began with both teams vying for field position to set up a match-winning field goal. The tension was palpable as every play carried immense pressure. The Broncos received the kick-off, but disaster struck when Ben Hunt dropped the ball, handing the Cowboys a golden opportunity. With the composure and skill that had defined his career, Thurston calmly slotted a field goal to win the match 17–16, securing the Cowboys' first-ever NRL Premiership.

The victory was a testament to the Cowboys' perseverance and belief. Thurston's heroics were celebrated, but the win was truly a team effort, with every player contributing to the historic achievement. The scenes of jubilation that followed the field goal were unforgettable, as players, coaches, and fans alike celebrated a momentous victory that had been years in the making.

The 2015 Grand Final was more than just a game; it was a showcase of everything that makes rugby league special. The skill, athleticism, and sportsmanship on display were exemplary, and the match served as a fitting climax to a thrilling season. The drama and excitement of the Grand Final captured the imagination of fans across the country and around the world, reinforcing the NRL's reputation for producing some of the most compelling sporting contests.

The success of the 2015 season was not limited to the Grand Final. Throughout the year, the competition saw increased attendance, higher television ratings, and greater engagement from fans. The return of Monday Night Football and the inclusion of two Friday night games were well-received, providing more opportunities for fans to enjoy live rugby league. The overall quality of the matches, combined with the league's efforts to promote the sport, ensured that rugby league continued to grow in popularity.

The 2015 NRL season will be remembered as one of the most exciting and memorable in the history of the competition. The all-Queensland Grand Final, the dramatic conclusion in golden point, and the Cowboys' historic victory were highlights that captured the essence of rugby league. The season showcased the best of the sport, from the skill and dedication of the players to the passion and loyalty of the fans. As the NRL looked ahead, the achievements of 2015 set a high standard for future seasons and left an enduring legacy for the game.

The 2015 NRL season's conclusion was nothing short of spectacular, and it left an indelible mark on the history of rugby league. The dramatic Grand Final between the North Queensland Cowboys and the Brisbane Broncos encapsulated the spirit of the sport and highlighted the intense rivalry and passion that drives the NRL. The epic showdown and the unforgettable moments that defined the match have ensured that the 2015 season will be remembered for generations to come.

Firstly, the rise of the North Queensland Cowboys to their maiden premiership was a story of perseverance and determination. The Cowboys had faced numerous challenges and setbacks over the years, but their journey to the top was a testament to their resilience. Johnathan Thurston, the team's inspirational leader, played a pivotal role throughout the season, guiding his team with skill and poise. His performance in the Grand Final, especially under the immense pressure of golden point, showcased his extraordinary talent and solidified his status as one of the greatest players in NRL history.

The all-Queensland Grand Final was also a significant milestone for the NRL, as it demonstrated the growing strength and popularity of rugby league outside of New South Wales. The Broncos, a team with a rich history and a strong following, provided formidable opposition and contributed to the high-quality contest. The game captivated audiences across Australia, with record television ratings and an electric atmosphere at ANZ Stadium, reflecting the widespread appeal of the sport.

The dramatic conclusion of the Grand Final, with Kyle Feldt's last-minute try and Thurston's golden point field goal, provided a fitting climax to an extraordinary season. These moments of high drama and skill exemplified the excitement and unpredictability that make rugby league so compelling. The emotional celebrations that followed the Cowboys' victory highlighted the deep connection between the players, the club, and their loyal supporters. It was a moment of triumph that united fans and showcased the power of sport to inspire and bring people together.

Throughout the 2015 season, the NRL continued to grow and evolve. The introduction of Monday Night Football and the inclusion of two Friday night games were innovative changes that enhanced the viewing experience for fans. These adjustments, along with the overall increase in match quality, contributed to higher attendance and television ratings, reflecting the league's successful efforts to engage and entertain its audience.

The season also saw significant achievements off the field. The NRL's commitment to community engagement and grassroots development was evident in various initiatives aimed at promoting the sport and supporting local clubs. These efforts helped to strengthen the foundation of rugby league and ensure its continued growth and success. The league's focus on player welfare and professional development further demonstrated its dedication to maintaining high standards and supporting the athletes who make the sport possible.

The success of the 2015 season and the thrilling Grand Final provided a strong platform for the future of the NRL. The memorable moments and achievements of the year inspired a new generation of players and fans, fostering a sense of excitement and anticipation for what lies ahead. The Cowboys' victory and the Broncos' valiant performance underscored the competitiveness and depth of talent in the league, promising more thrilling contests in the years to come.

The 2015 NRL season will be remembered as one of the most remarkable in the history of the competition. The dramatic Grand Final, the rise of the North Queensland Cowboys, and the continued growth and evolution of the league were defining features of a truly extraordinary year. The season showcased the best of rugby league, from the skill and determination of the players to the passion and loyalty of the fans. As the NRL moves forward, the achievements and memories of 2015 will continue to inspire and shape the future of the sport, ensuring that rugby league remains a beloved and celebrated part of Australian culture.

Chapter 21: Triumphs and Milestones – The 2016 NRL Season

The 2016 NRL season was a year of remarkable achievements and dramatic moments that captivated rugby league fans across Australia. As the season progressed, the competition intensified, showcasing the depth of talent and resilience of the teams. The Melbourne Storm, known for their consistent performance, secured the minor premiership, continuing their dominance from previous years. The Canberra Raiders made a notable return to the top four for the first time since 2003, marking a significant milestone in their recent history. Meanwhile, the Cronulla-Sutherland Sharks, alongside the North Queensland Cowboys, completed the top four, setting the stage for a highly competitive finals series.

The 2016 season continued a trend of suspense and excitement, with the minor premiership once again not being decided until the final round. This was the fourth consecutive year in which the outcome of the minor premiership was uncertain until the very end, underscoring the competitive nature of the NRL. The consistency of the Melbourne Storm throughout the season was impressive, reflecting their well-rounded squad and effective strategies. However, the competition remained fierce, with several teams proving themselves as strong contenders.

The Grand Final of 2016 was a historic match, pitting the Melbourne Storm against the Cronulla-Sutherland Sharks. For the Sharks, it was their fourth Grand Final appearance, a testament to their long-standing presence in the competition. For the Storm, it was their seventh Grand Final, reinforcing their status as one of the NRL's most successful clubs. The anticipation for this match was immense, as both teams had demonstrated their capabilities throughout the season.

The Grand Final proved to be a thrilling encounter, with the game remaining tightly contested until the final whistle. The Melbourne Storm and the Cronulla-Sutherland Sharks both displayed impressive defensive and attacking skills, making for an enthralling spectacle. The match was a showcase of rugby league's finest attributes, with both teams executing their strategies effectively under pressure.

In the dying moments of the game, the Cronulla-Sutherland Sharks clinched their first premiership in a dramatic finish. The 14–12 victory was a momentous occasion, ending a 49-year premiership drought for the Sharks. The achievement was celebrated passionately by the team and their supporters, marking a historic triumph for the club. The win was a culmination of years of hard work and perseverance, and it was a fitting reward for the club's dedication to the sport.

The Melbourne Storm, despite their loss, were commendable throughout the season and the Grand Final. Their performance in 2016 continued to highlight their status as one of the NRL's elite teams. The match against the Sharks was a testament to their strength and resilience, even in the face of a challenging opponent. The Storm's ability to maintain their high standards of play throughout the season was impressive, and they remained a formidable force in the competition.

The 2016 season also reinforced the excitement and unpredictability of the NRL. The close contests, dramatic finishes, and the high level of competition all contributed to a memorable year for rugby league. The Grand Final was a fitting end to a season full of exceptional performances and significant milestones.

The 2016 NRL season was a landmark year in the history of the competition. The Melbourne Storm's return to the top, the Canberra Raiders' resurgence, and the Cronulla-Sutherland Sharks' historic premiership were key highlights. The season showcased the best of rugby league, from thrilling games and intense rivalries to the remarkable achievements of the teams. The Grand Final, with its dramatic conclusion and the Sharks' long-awaited victory, was a fitting conclusion to an extraordinary season. As the NRL moved forward, the events of 2016 would continue to resonate, shaping the future of the competition and inspiring future generations of players and fans.

The 2016 NRL season was a year that left a profound impact on the rugby league landscape, reflecting both the enduring appeal of the sport and the high level of competition that characterizes the National Rugby League. This chapter captures the essence of a season marked by significant achievements, intense rivalries, and a dramatic Grand Final that would be remembered for years to come.

The Melbourne Storm's dominance throughout the 2016 season was a testament to their strength and consistency. Securing the minor premiership was no small feat, and the Storm's performance was a clear indication of their capacity to compete at the highest level. The team's ability to navigate the challenges of the season and maintain their top position was impressive and showcased their tactical prowess and depth of talent.

The Canberra Raiders' return to the top four was a story of resurgence and determination. After a lengthy absence from the upper echelons of the competition, the Raiders' reemergence as a top contender was a significant achievement. Their performance throughout the season demonstrated their growth and potential, signaling a promising future for the club. The Raiders' presence in the top four added to the competitive nature of the finals series and highlighted the evolving dynamics of the NRL.

The Cronulla-Sutherland Sharks and the North Queensland Cowboys rounded out the top four, contributing to a highly competitive finals series. For the Sharks, the 2016 season was especially momentous as it marked the culmination of years of effort and ambition. The team's performance was a reflection of their resilience and commitment to success. The Cowboys, similarly, continued to be a formidable presence in the league, showcasing their ability to compete at the highest level.

The Grand Final of 2016 was a dramatic and memorable event that captured the essence of rugby league's excitement and unpredictability. The clash between the Melbourne Storm and the Cronulla-Sutherland Sharks was a highly anticipated match, with both teams showcasing their strengths and vying for the ultimate prize. The intensity of the game and the skill of the players made for an enthralling spectacle that kept fans on the edge of their seats.

The Cronulla-Sutherland Sharks' victory in the Grand Final was a historic moment, ending a 49-year premiership drought. This triumph was not just a victory on the field but a significant achievement for the club and its supporters. The win was a testament to the Sharks' perseverance and dedication, and it was celebrated with great enthusiasm by the team and their fans. The moment was a highlight of the season and a fitting reward for the club's long journey.

The Melbourne Storm, despite falling short in the Grand Final, continued to demonstrate their high level of performance and professionalism. Their journey throughout the 2016 season was marked by excellence and resilience, and their contribution to the season's excitement and quality was undeniable. The Storm's ability to remain competitive and maintain their standards was a reflection of their strength as a club.

Overall, the 2016 NRL season was a landmark year that showcased the best aspects of rugby league. The combination of strong performances, dramatic finishes, and historic achievements made for a memorable season. The Grand Final, with its thrilling conclusion and the Sharks' long-awaited victory, was a fitting end to a remarkable year. As the NRL moved forward, the events of the 2016 season would be remembered as a defining chapter in the competition's history, influencing future seasons and continuing to inspire players, teams, and fans alike.

Chapter 22: The Dawn of the NRL Women's League and the 2017 Women's Rugby League World Cup

The 2017 Women's Rugby League World Cup was a landmark event for women's rugby league, marking the fifth staging of the tournament and setting the stage for the future of the sport. Held in Australia from November 16 to December 2, 2017, this World Cup was a significant milestone in the development of women's rugby league. The competition not only showcased the talent of female rugby players but also highlighted the growing importance of women's rugby on the global stage.

The tournament was hosted across two key venues: Southern Cross Group Stadium in Sydney and Brisbane Stadium in Brisbane. The Southern Cross Group Stadium was used for the pool and semi-final matches, while the grand final was played at Brisbane Stadium. This setup allowed for a broad audience to engage with the tournament, increasing its visibility and impact. The final was particularly notable as it was played as part of a double-header with the men's final, a testament to the rising profile of women's rugby league.

The competition saw participation from five automatically qualified teams: Australia, New Zealand, England, Papua New Guinea, and Canada.

These teams were chosen based on their past performances and established rugby league programs. The automatic qualification of these teams underscored their strong rugby league traditions and the high level of competition expected at the World Cup.

A round-robin tournament was initially planned to determine the sixth and final team. This tournament was to feature the Cook Islands, Fiji, Samoa, and Tonga. Unfortunately, due to various logistical issues, Fiji, Samoa, and Tonga withdrew at short notice. As a result, the Cook Islands were automatically included as the sixth team, ensuring that the World Cup maintained its intended competitive format.

The tournament's structure featured two pools, each containing three teams. The top two teams from each pool advanced to the semi-finals, creating a competitive pathway for the teams to reach the final. Each team played three pool games, including an additional inter-pool game to ensure a comprehensive competitive process. This format was designed to test the teams' abilities and determine the best contenders for the semi-finals.

The success of the 2017 Women's Rugby League World Cup had a profound impact on the sport. The visibility and excitement generated by the tournament demonstrated the potential and popularity of women's rugby league. In response to this success, a national women's league was established, with its inaugural season commencing in September 2018. This new league featured four clubs aligned with existing NRL teams, marking a significant step forward in the development of women's rugby league.

The creation of the national women's league was a direct result of the World Cup's success and the growing interest in women's rugby league. It provided a structured and competitive environment for female players to showcase their skills and develop their careers. The alignment with existing NRL clubs also helped integrate women's rugby league into the broader rugby league community, fostering greater support and recognition.

The 2017 Women's Rugby League World Cup not only celebrated the achievements of female rugby players but also laid the groundwork for future growth in the sport. The establishment of the national women's league was a pivotal moment, reflecting the increasing importance of women's rugby league and its potential to become a major force in the rugby league landscape. As the league continued to develop, the impact of the World Cup and the subsequent growth of the women's game would be felt across the rugby league world, inspiring a new generation of players and fans.

The 2017 Women's Rugby League World Cup was more than just a tournament; it was a historic event that heralded a new era for women's rugby league. The decision to hold the tournament in Australia and the subsequent success it achieved were pivotal in raising the profile of the women's game. The World Cup not only showcased the elite level of women's rugby league but also demonstrated its growing popularity and the immense talent that exists within the sport. The attention and enthusiasm generated by the tournament set the stage for the future development of women's rugby league on both a national and international scale.

The competition itself was a resounding success. The format of having two pools with three teams each allowed for a rigorous and competitive series of matches. This format ensured that each team faced a variety of opponents, enhancing the overall quality of the games and giving fans a chance to see the best teams from around the world compete. The addition of an inter-pool game for each team was a particularly effective way to increase the level of competition and ensure that every team had a fair opportunity to advance to the semi-finals.

The logistical challenges faced by the round-robin tournament, particularly the withdrawal of Fiji, Samoa, and Tonga, were unfortunate but did not detract from the overall success of the World Cup. The automatic qualification of the Cook Islands allowed the tournament to proceed smoothly and maintain its competitive integrity. This flexibility in the qualification process highlighted the importance of ensuring the World Cup could go ahead as planned, despite unforeseen circumstances.

The grand final, held at Brisbane Stadium and played as part of a double-header with the men's final, was a fitting culmination of the World Cup. The large attendance and high level of excitement surrounding the final demonstrated the growing interest in women's rugby league and its ability to draw significant crowds. The decision to play the final as a double-header with the men's final was a strategic move that not only showcased the women's game but also integrated it into the broader rugby league calendar, enhancing its visibility and appeal.

The introduction of the national women's league in September 2018 was a direct outcome of the World Cup's success. This new league, comprising four clubs aligned with existing NRL teams, provided a structured and competitive platform for female players. It marked a significant step forward in the development of women's rugby league, offering players more opportunities to compete at a high level and gain recognition for their skills. The alignment with established NRL clubs also helped integrate the women's league into the wider rugby league community, fostering greater support and investment in the women's game.

The national women's league was a crucial development that built on the momentum generated by the World Cup. It provided a foundation for the growth and professionalization of women's rugby league, offering a pathway for players to develop their careers and for the sport to reach new audiences. The league's success has since become a testament to the growing importance and popularity of women's rugby league in Australia and beyond.

In retrospect, the 2017 Women's Rugby League World Cup was a watershed moment for the sport. It highlighted the incredible talent and dedication of female rugby players and set the stage for the future growth of women's rugby league. The establishment of the national women's league was a natural and necessary progression, reflecting the increasing recognition and support for women's rugby league. As the sport continues to evolve and expand, the impact of the World Cup and the subsequent developments will be felt for years to come, inspiring future generations of players and fans and ensuring that women's rugby league remains a vibrant and integral part of the rugby league landscape.

Part Four: 2020–2021: Resilience in Crisis and New Horizons

Chapter 23: Navigating the Pandemic

On 22 March 2020, the National Rugby League (NRL) faced an unprecedented challenge as it continued to play games amidst the COVID-19 pandemic. The NRL was one of the last major sports leagues in the world to proceed with its season despite global disruptions. At the outset, the NRL's decision to carry on with matches drew significant criticism. The pandemic had already prompted widespread changes across various sectors, and the league's determination to persist was met with a mixture of disbelief and concern from fans, media, and public figures alike.

The initial plan to keep the season going came under heavy scrutiny as COVID-19 restrictions began tightening across Australia. As the virus spread and new restrictions were imposed, the NRL faced mounting pressure to reconsider its position. On 23 March 2020, just a day after the NRL's initial announcement, Queensland's government decided to close its borders. This decision forced the NRL to suspend the season indefinitely. The move was a drastic measure, reflecting the gravity of the pandemic's impact on public and economic health.

Suspending the season was not merely a logistical challenge but also a financial one. The league, clubs, and associated stakeholders faced the prospect of severe economic fallout. With matches postponed, the usual revenue streams from gate receipts, sponsorships, and broadcasting rights were jeopardized. Concerns mounted that some teams might not withstand the financial strain without the usual income generated from games and associated activities.

The uncertainty surrounding the NRL's financial stability during the pandemic led to intense deliberations about how to manage the league's survival and the well-being of its teams. There were fears that the crisis could lead to the collapse of some teams, threatening the integrity and future of the competition. The league's governing bodies, along with team owners and administrators, had to navigate these treacherous waters carefully, making critical decisions about player contracts, financial support, and operational adjustments.

As the pandemic continued to evolve, so did the NRL's response. The league implemented a range of health and safety protocols to ensure that when matches did resume, they could be conducted with minimal risk. These measures included stringent testing, biosecurity plans, and adjustments to the game schedule to accommodate the evolving situation. The NRL's ability to adapt became a crucial factor in its efforts to weather the storm.

When the NRL eventually resumed its season, it did so under a cloud of uncertainty but also with a renewed sense of determination. The league faced the challenge of not only resuming play but also ensuring that it could complete the season while adhering to public health guidelines. The successful resumption of the season was a testament to the resilience and adaptability of the NRL in the face of one of the most significant crises in modern history.

The impact of COVID-19 on the NRL was profound, affecting every aspect of the league, from player welfare and financial stability to fan engagement and game-day operations. The experience underscored the importance of flexibility and preparedness in the face of global challenges. The NRL's journey through the pandemic would have lasting implications, shaping how the league approached future challenges and opportunities.

In the end, the NRL's response to the COVID-19 pandemic highlighted its capacity to overcome adversity and adapt to rapidly changing circumstances. While the pandemic presented numerous challenges, it also provided the league with valuable lessons about resilience, collaboration, and the need for robust contingency planning. The league's ability to navigate this crisis laid a foundation for its recovery and future growth in the years to come.

The 2020 NRL season's ordeal amid the COVID-19 pandemic is a profound chapter in the league's history, marked by extraordinary challenges and significant adjustments. As one of the last major sports leagues to initially continue playing, the NRL's decision was met with both admiration and criticism. The pandemic forced the league to confront issues of public health, financial stability, and operational continuity in ways it had never experienced before.

The immediate suspension of the season, prompted by Queensland's border closures, illustrated the severity of the crisis. This abrupt halt revealed the precarious balance the NRL had to maintain between continuing operations and safeguarding the health of players, staff, and fans. The financial impact of the shutdown was substantial, exposing the vulnerabilities inherent in a sports league dependent on live attendances and commercial revenue. The prospect of some teams potentially folding underscored the gravity of the situation, highlighting the interconnected nature of sports, economics, and public health.

In response to the pandemic, the NRL had to quickly pivot and adapt. Implementing comprehensive health and safety protocols became paramount. These measures, including regular testing and biosecurity plans, were essential not just for the league's immediate survival but also for its longer-term viability. The rigorous approach to ensuring a safe return to play reflected a broader commitment to maintaining the integrity of the competition while prioritizing the well-being of everyone involved.

The successful resumption of the season was a remarkable achievement. It demonstrated the league's resilience and the effectiveness of its crisis management strategies. Despite the disruptions and the uncertainty, the NRL managed to resume play and complete the season, which was a testament to the dedication and adaptability of all stakeholders. The league's ability to navigate these turbulent times showcased its strength and determination, providing a beacon of hope during a period of global uncertainty.

However, the pandemic's impact was not limited to immediate operational and financial concerns. It also prompted a reevaluation of how the league operates and plans for future crises. The experience underscored the importance of having robust contingency plans and being able to quickly adapt to changing circumstances. The lessons learned from the pandemic are likely to influence how the NRL approaches future challenges, ensuring that it is better prepared for any similar events that may arise.

The pandemic also highlighted the crucial role of sports in providing a sense of normalcy and continuity during times of crisis. For many fans, the return of the NRL provided a much-needed distraction and a source of connection in an otherwise disorienting period. This reinforced the value of sports in society, not only as a form of entertainment but also as a community-building force.

As the league moved forward from the pandemic, it faced the task of rebuilding and strengthening its foundations. The financial and operational adjustments made during the pandemic provided insights into the league's resilience and areas for improvement. The ability to navigate such a crisis is a testament to the NRL's strength and adaptability, qualities that will serve it well in the years ahead.

The 2020 NRL season amidst the COVID-19 pandemic was a period of significant challenge and transformation. The league's response to the crisis highlighted its resilience, adaptability, and commitment to its stakeholders. While the pandemic presented numerous obstacles, it also provided valuable lessons and opportunities for growth. The experience of navigating through such a global crisis has fortified the NRL, preparing it for future challenges and ensuring its continued relevance and success in the ever-evolving landscape of professional sports.

Chapter 24: Return to Play Amidst Controversy

On 9 April 2020, the Australian Rugby League (ARL) Commission, under the leadership of Wayne Pearce, made a landmark announcement: the NRL would return to action on 28 May. This decision was pivotal, as it marked a significant moment in sports history during the COVID-19 pandemic. The announcement was met with both anticipation and skepticism, as the league faced intense scrutiny from various quarters.

The announcement was immediately met with heavy criticism from the New South Wales Government and health officials. Premier Gladys Berejiklian expressed her concerns, stating that she had not approved the NRL's return. The health officials, grappling with the ongoing pandemic, were wary of the implications of bringing back live sports amidst the crisis. They feared that resuming the NRL might undermine public health efforts and potentially lead to a spike in COVID-19 cases.

In response to the criticism, the NRL released documents showing that they had secured approval from NSW Police Commissioner Mick Fuller. This approval was crucial, as it allowed the league to continue its operations without crowds in attendance. The decision to proceed with the season under these conditions was a testament to the NRL's commitment to resuming play while adhering to health and safety guidelines.

The NRL kicked off on 28 May with a highly anticipated match between the Parramatta Eels and the Brisbane Broncos. The game was played behind closed doors at Suncorp Stadium, marking a departure from the usual atmosphere of packed stadiums. Despite the lack of a live audience, the match drew significant attention and achieved impressive television ratings. In fact, it recorded the highest TV ratings for a regular-season game since 2014, showcasing the enduring popularity of the league even in challenging times.

The league's return was notable not only for its timing but also for its broader implications. The NRL became the first sport in Australia to return to play after a suspension, and it was also the first globally to resume a season that had been previously halted due to the pandemic. This early return underscored the NRL's resilience and its ability to navigate the complexities of operating under extraordinary circumstances.

The decision to resume the competition two weeks ahead of other sports was a strategic move that highlighted the NRL's proactive approach. It demonstrated the league's determination to provide entertainment and maintain continuity during a period of global uncertainty. The successful restart of the season was a significant achievement, reflecting both the league's operational capabilities and the strong support of its stakeholders.

Returning to play amidst such a high level of scrutiny and controversy required meticulous planning and strict adherence to health protocols. The NRL implemented comprehensive measures to ensure the safety of players, staff, and officials. This included regular COVID-19 testing, biosecurity protocols, and strict hygiene practices. The league's commitment to these measures was crucial in maintaining public trust and ensuring the integrity of the competition.

The successful resumption of the NRL also had a positive impact on the broader sports community. It provided a sense of normalcy and offered fans a much-needed distraction from the challenges posed by the pandemic. The league's ability to return to play and deliver a season amidst such adversity was a testament to its resilience and adaptability.

The return of the NRL on 28 May 2020 was a landmark moment in the league's history. Despite facing significant criticism and logistical challenges, the NRL managed to resume play successfully and achieve impressive television ratings. The decision to return early highlighted the league's resilience and commitment to providing entertainment during a global crisis. The experience of navigating the pandemic has strengthened the NRL, preparing it for future challenges and reaffirming its position as a leading sports league in Australia and beyond.

The return of the NRL on 28 May 2020 stands as a defining moment in the league's history, reflecting both its resilience and the broader context of sports amid a global pandemic. The decision to resume play, despite significant challenges and criticism, demonstrated the NRL's determination to navigate an unprecedented situation. This chapter marks a crucial juncture not only for the league but for sports worldwide, showcasing how a major competition can adapt and persevere through extraordinary circumstances.

The controversy surrounding the NRL's return was considerable. The criticism from the New South Wales Government and health officials underscored the complexity of balancing public health concerns with the desire to revive live sports. Premier Gladys Berejiklian's concerns highlighted the tension between maintaining safety and supporting the economic and emotional needs of the sports community. The scrutiny faced by the NRL was a reminder of the broader implications of sports in society, especially during times of crisis.

The league's ability to secure approval from NSW Police Commissioner Mick Fuller and proceed with its plans was a significant achievement. It not only addressed the immediate concerns but also set a precedent for how sports organizations could operate under restrictive conditions. The approval demonstrated the NRL's commitment to adhering to health protocols and ensuring a safe environment for all involved. This was a crucial step in regaining the confidence of both stakeholders and the public.

The opening match between the Parramatta Eels and the Brisbane Broncos, held behind closed doors, was emblematic of the new reality facing sports. The absence of a live audience transformed the experience, yet the high television ratings underscored the enduring appeal of rugby league. The NRL's ability to deliver a successful and engaging broadcast without the traditional game-day atmosphere was a testament to its adaptability and the dedication of its fans.

The league's early return to play, ahead of other sports, highlighted its role as a pioneer in navigating the challenges posed by the pandemic. Being the first major sport to resume its season was both a strategic advantage and a symbol of resilience. It provided a template for other sports organizations and demonstrated how sports could play a role in providing normalcy and entertainment during difficult times.

Implementing rigorous health and safety measures was essential in the NRL's return. The league's commitment to regular COVID-19 testing, biosecurity protocols, and hygiene practices ensured that the season could proceed with minimal risk. These measures not only protected players and staff but also set a standard for how sports could operate safely during a pandemic. The NRL's successful management of these protocols reinforced its position as a leading example of crisis management in the sports industry.

The broader impact of the NRL's return extended beyond the immediate context of the pandemic. It offered a sense of continuity and normalcy for fans who were eager for live sports. The league's ability to deliver a season despite the challenges provided a valuable distraction and emotional support for many people. This positive impact on the community highlighted the role of sports as a source of joy and unity during times of adversity.

Looking forward, the experiences and lessons learned from navigating the pandemic will undoubtedly influence the NRL's approach to future challenges. The league's resilience and adaptability during this period will serve as a foundation for addressing any future uncertainties. The successful return to play also demonstrated the strength of the rugby league community and its ability to rally together in times of need.

The return of the NRL on 28 May 2020 was a landmark moment that showcased the league's resilience, adaptability, and commitment to its stakeholders. Despite facing significant controversy and challenges, the NRL managed to resume play successfully and achieve impressive television ratings. This chapter not only highlights the league's ability to navigate a global crisis but also reaffirms its enduring role as a leading sports competition in Australia. The lessons learned from this period will undoubtedly shape the future of the NRL and continue to influence the broader sports industry.

Chapter 25: The Expansion to the Dolphins

In October 2021, a significant announcement was made about the future of the National Rugby League (NRL). After months of speculation and discussions, the NRL and the Australian Rugby League Commission (ARLC) revealed that the competition would expand to include a new team. This team, known as the Dolphins, would join the league for the 2023 season. The introduction of the Dolphins marked a major development in the NRL's history, adding a new dimension to the competition and reflecting the league's continued growth and evolution.

The Dolphins, based in the far northern suburb of Redcliffe near Brisbane, were chosen to be the 17th team in the NRL. This decision was influenced by several factors, including the strategic importance of expanding the league into Queensland, a region with a strong rugby league following. The Dolphins' inclusion aimed to build on the existing passion for the sport in Queensland and to capitalize on the growing interest in rugby league in the northern areas of the state.

The announcement of the Dolphins as the new team was the result of a lengthy and thorough selection process. The ARLC and the NRL conducted an extensive review of potential expansion candidates, considering factors such as financial stability, community support, and the ability to contribute to the overall growth of the league. The Dolphins emerged as the preferred choice due to their strong local support, solid financial backing, and their commitment to developing a competitive and successful team.

The Dolphins' entry into the NRL was seen as a strategic move to further expand the league's footprint in Queensland. The state had already proven to be a strong rugby league market, with a history of successful teams and passionate fans. By adding a new team based in Redcliffe, the NRL aimed to tap into this existing enthusiasm and create new opportunities for fans and players alike.

The introduction of the Dolphins was expected to bring several benefits to the NRL. Firstly, it would increase the overall competitiveness of the league by adding another strong team. The Dolphins were anticipated to contribute to a more dynamic and unpredictable competition, enhancing the overall quality of the games. Secondly, the expansion was expected to boost the league's revenue through increased sponsorship opportunities, television rights, and matchday attendance.

The arrival of the Dolphins also signaled a new era for rugby league in Queensland. The team's presence was anticipated to strengthen the league's connection with the local community and to encourage more young players to take up the sport. By establishing a new club in the region, the NRL hoped to inspire the next generation of rugby league stars and foster a deeper connection between the sport and its supporters.

In preparation for the Dolphins' debut in the NRL, significant work was undertaken to ensure the team was ready for the challenge. This included the development of a competitive roster, the construction of suitable facilities, and the establishment of a strong support network. The Dolphins were expected to bring a fresh energy and perspective to the league, with a focus on building a successful and sustainable team.

The expansion to include the Dolphins was part of the NRL's broader strategy to grow the sport and reach new audiences. It reflected the league's commitment to continuous improvement and its ambition to remain at the forefront of Australian sports. By adding a new team and expanding the competition, the NRL aimed to enhance the overall appeal of the league and to provide more opportunities for fans and players.

The announcement of the Dolphins as the 17th team in the NRL represented a significant milestone for the league. The expansion to include a new team in Queensland highlighted the NRL's ongoing efforts to grow the sport and connect with new audiences. As the Dolphins prepared for their debut season in 2023, the league looked forward to the new challenges and opportunities that this expansion would bring, continuing its tradition of innovation and progress in Australian rugby league.

The decision to admit the Dolphins as the 17th team in the NRL marked a pivotal moment in the league's history. This expansion not only signaled a new chapter for rugby league in Australia but also underscored the NRL's commitment to growth and innovation. The inclusion of the Dolphins was the culmination of years of planning, strategic thinking, and a recognition of the sport's expanding appeal.

The introduction of the Dolphins, based in Redcliffe, Queensland, represented more than just the addition of a new team; it was a significant step toward expanding the NRL's reach and influence. Queensland, with its rich rugby league heritage and passionate fan base, was a natural choice for expansion. By establishing a team in Redcliffe, the NRL aimed to tap into an already enthusiastic market and foster a deeper connection with the region's rugby league community.

The expansion reflected the league's broader vision of increasing its footprint across Australia. The NRL's strategic focus on Queensland was not only about tapping into new fan bases but also about reinforcing the league's position in a state that had consistently demonstrated strong support for the sport. The Dolphins were expected to bring fresh energy to the competition, contributing to a more dynamic and competitive league.

The process leading up to the Dolphins' admission was thorough and deliberate. The ARLC and NRL undertook a comprehensive review of potential expansion candidates, weighing various factors such as financial viability, community support, and the ability to enhance the league's overall quality. The Dolphins emerged as a strong candidate due to their robust local backing and financial stability, making them a suitable choice for expansion.

As the Dolphins prepared for their debut in the 2023 season, the league anticipated several benefits from their inclusion. The addition of a new team was expected to elevate the overall standard of the competition, bringing new challenges and opportunities for existing teams. The Dolphins' presence was anticipated to stimulate greater fan engagement, increase sponsorship deals, and generate additional revenue for the NRL.

The expansion also had significant implications for grassroots rugby league in Queensland. By establishing a new team, the NRL aimed to inspire young players and strengthen the sport's presence at the community level. The Dolphins were set to become a key player in nurturing local talent and promoting rugby league throughout the region.

The strategic placement of the Dolphins in Redcliffe, a suburb known for its passion for rugby league, was a calculated move to maximize the team's impact. The team's establishment was expected to create a sense of local pride and further solidify the sport's connection with its fans. The Dolphins were poised to become a central figure in Queensland's rugby league landscape, fostering a renewed sense of excitement and anticipation among supporters.

In the broader context of the NRL's growth, the Dolphins' admission highlighted the league's ongoing commitment to innovation and progress. The expansion reflected a forward-thinking approach, with the NRL continually seeking ways to enhance the competition and connect with new audiences. The inclusion of the Dolphins was a testament to the league's dedication to evolving and adapting to the changing landscape of Australian sport.

The expansion to include the Dolphins as the 17th team in the NRL was a landmark development for the league. It represented a significant investment in the future of rugby league, emphasizing the NRL's dedication to growth, community engagement, and the enhancement of the competition. As the Dolphins prepared for their inaugural season, the NRL looked forward to the new opportunities and challenges that lay ahead, embracing the excitement and potential that this expansion brought to the sport.

Part Five: The Evolution of the Game – Season Structure and Format

Chapter 26: Gearing Up – The NRL Pre-season Journey

The NRL pre-season typically begins in February and ends in early March. During this time, clubs organise trial matches to test playing combinations and get their squads ready for the upcoming season. These trials are essential for coaches to see how new players fit into the team and to fine-tune strategies.

Some clubs have traditional pre-season matches that are played for trophies. For example, Easts (Sydney Roosters) and Wests (Wests Tigers) compete for the Foundation Cup, while South Sydney Rabbitohs and St. George Illawarra Dragons battle for the Charity Shield. These matches not only prepare teams but also excite fans for the upcoming season.

The trials are often held in cities and towns that don't usually host NRL matches. This approach helps to promote rugby league in regional areas and gives fans in those locations a chance to see their favorite teams and players up close. It's a way to spread the love of the game beyond the big cities.

In the past, a World Sevens rugby league tournament was held during the pre-season. This was a fast-paced, shortened version of the game that featured teams from around the world. However, it was scrapped due to concerns about player injuries. The fast and intense nature of the Sevens format was seen as too risky for players before the regular season.

In 2023, the NRL introduced the NRL Pre-season Challenge to create a more structured pre-season for each club. This new competition added a competitive edge to the pre-season, making the games more meaningful for both players and fans. It also helped clubs better prepare for the grueling regular season by providing more consistent and high-quality opposition.

The pre-season is not just about games. It's also a crucial period for player conditioning and injury rehabilitation. Clubs use this time to get their players in peak physical condition. Training sessions are intense, focusing on building strength, endurance, and agility. Players who are returning from injuries also use this time to get back to full fitness.

Off the field, the pre-season is a busy time for club administration. New sponsorship deals are signed, and marketing campaigns are launched to engage fans and build excitement for the new season. Merchandise sales typically spike as fans gear up with the latest team apparel and memorabilia.

Finally, the pre-season is a time for new players, especially rookies, to integrate into the team. This is a crucial period for team bonding, where new players build relationships with their teammates and coaching staff. Team-building activities and training camps are often organized to foster a strong team spirit and unity.

The NRL pre-season is a vital period that sets the stage for the regular season. It combines trial matches, conditioning, team bonding, and off-field activities to ensure that teams are fully prepared for the challenges ahead. With the introduction of the NRL Pre-season Challenge, this period has become even more structured and competitive, benefiting both players and fans.

The NRL pre-season is a crucial period for clubs as they prepare for the upcoming season. It begins in February and ends in early March, a window where teams focus on fine-tuning their strategies, assessing player combinations, and building team cohesion. Although it might seem like a mere formality to some, the pre-season sets the stage for what is to come in the grueling months ahead.

During this time, clubs often organize trial matches. These matches serve multiple purposes: they provide coaches with the opportunity to test different playing combinations, give new players a chance to prove their worth, and allow the team to build chemistry on the field. While these matches are not as intense as regular-season games, they are critical for identifying strengths and weaknesses that need to be addressed.

Some clubs also play for specific trophies during the pre-season. For instance, Easts and Wests compete for the Foundation Cup, while South Sydney and St. George Illawarra vie for the Charity Shield. These matches not only serve as preparation but also bring a competitive edge to the pre-season, adding excitement for both players and fans.

The pre-season trials are often held in cities and towns that do not regularly host NRL matches. This strategy helps to promote the sport in different regions, giving local fans the chance to see their favorite teams in action up close. It also allows clubs to connect with a broader fan base and build support in various communities.

In the past, the NRL hosted a World Sevens rugby league football tournament during the pre-season. However, this event was scrapped due to concerns about player injuries. The high-intensity nature of sevens rugby posed a risk to players, and clubs preferred to focus on traditional trial matches to ensure their squads remained healthy and ready for the regular season.

In 2023, the NRL introduced the Pre-season Challenge, a more structured approach to pre-season activities. This initiative aimed to provide each club with a consistent and competitive pre-season experience. The Pre-season Challenge included a series of matches that allowed teams to test their skills against various opponents, ensuring they were well-prepared for the rigors of the upcoming season.

The pre-season is also a time for new signings to integrate into their new teams. For players who have transferred from other clubs or leagues, this period is crucial for adapting to new systems and building rapport with teammates. Coaches use this time to assess how new additions fit into their plans and to make any necessary adjustments before the season starts.

Fitness and conditioning are key focuses during the pre-season. Clubs put their players through rigorous training programs to ensure they are in peak physical condition. This period often includes intense fitness drills, strength training, and conditioning exercises designed to enhance players' endurance, strength, and agility. A well-conditioned team is better equipped to handle the demands of the long NRL season.

Team bonding activities are also an integral part of the pre-season. These activities help build camaraderie and trust among players, which can translate into better on-field performance. Whether it's team-building exercises, social outings, or training camps, these activities aim to create a strong sense of unity within the squad.

The NRL pre-season is much more than a series of trial matches and training sessions. It is a critical period of preparation that sets the foundation for the entire season. Clubs use this time to refine their strategies, assess player combinations, build team cohesion, and promote the sport in different regions. With the introduction of the Pre-season Challenge, the NRL has provided a more structured and competitive pre-season experience, ensuring that teams are ready to hit the ground running when the regular season begins. The importance of this period cannot be overstated, as it plays a significant role in shaping the success of teams throughout the year.

Chapter 27: The All Stars Spectacle

The All Stars match, introduced in 2010, has become a celebrated event in the NRL preseason. This unique game brings together top players from different teams, offering fans a thrilling spectacle before the regular season kicks off. The match isn't just about showcasing skills; it's also a platform for celebrating cultural heritage and unity within the rugby league community.

The teams for the All Stars match are selected through public voting. Fans have the chance to vote for their favorite players, making this game a true representation of the public's choices. This voting process adds an element of excitement and engagement for fans, who eagerly await the announcement of the final squads. The selected players then come together to compete for the prestigious Arthur Beetson Trophy, named in honor of the legendary rugby league player.

In addition to the competitive aspect, the All Stars match has a strong cultural significance. It serves as a celebration of Indigenous culture and heritage, with the Australian Indigenous All Stars team representing the rich history and contributions of Aboriginal and Torres Strait Islander players to the sport. The match often features traditional performances and ceremonies, highlighting the importance of cultural pride and recognition.

The All Stars match was temporarily removed from the NRL calendar in 2018 due to the World Cup being played the previous year. The decision was made to prevent excessive player workload and ensure that athletes had adequate rest and recovery time. However, the match made a triumphant return in 2019, much to the delight of fans and players alike.

In 2019, the All Stars match was hosted in Melbourne, featuring the Australian Indigenous All Stars against the New Zealand Maori All Stars. This addition of the Maori All Stars brought a new dimension to the game, celebrating the cultural heritage of New Zealand's Indigenous people. The match was a thrilling contest, showcasing the skills and talents of players from both teams and reinforcing the spirit of unity and respect.

The All Stars match isn't just a game; it's an event that brings communities together. It provides an opportunity for fans to see their favorite players in a different light, playing alongside rivals and representing something bigger than their individual clubs. The camaraderie and sportsmanship displayed during the match set a positive example for the broader rugby league community.

Off the field, the All Stars match has a significant impact as well. Proceeds from the game often go towards various community programs and initiatives, particularly those aimed at supporting Indigenous communities. This charitable aspect of the match highlights the NRL's commitment to giving back and making a positive difference in society.

In recent years, the All Stars match has continued to evolve. The introduction of women's teams in the All Stars concept has added another layer of excitement and inclusivity. The women's All Stars match showcases the talents of female players and promotes the growth of women's rugby league, inspiring young girls to pursue the sport.

The All Stars match has firmly established itself as a highlight of the NRL preseason. It brings together top players, celebrates cultural heritage, and promotes unity and respect within the rugby league community. With its unique blend of competition and cultural significance, the All Stars match continues to captivate fans and make a lasting impact both on and off the field. As the NRL moves forward, the All Stars match will undoubtedly remain a cherished tradition, symbolizing the spirit of rugby league and its ability to bring people together.

The All Stars match, with its inception in 2010, has grown to become a cornerstone of the NRL preseason, embodying a rich blend of competition, cultural celebration, and community impact. As we conclude this chapter, it is essential to reflect on the multifaceted significance of this event and its enduring legacy within the rugby league landscape.

From the outset, the All Stars match captivated fans by providing a unique platform for the best players in the league to compete in an exhilarating contest. The public voting process, which allows fans to choose the players, adds an element of excitement and engagement, making the game a true representation of the supporters' voice. This democratic selection process fosters a sense of involvement and ownership among the fans, enhancing their connection to the game and its stars.

The cultural dimension of the All Stars match cannot be overstated. By featuring the Australian Indigenous All Stars and, since 2019, the New Zealand Maori All Stars, the game serves as a powerful tribute to the Indigenous heritage of both Australia and New Zealand. The inclusion of traditional performances, ceremonies, and cultural symbols during the match highlights the importance of acknowledging and celebrating the contributions of Indigenous peoples to the sport. This cultural celebration extends beyond the field, promoting awareness and respect for Indigenous cultures among the broader rugby league community and the public.

The decision to temporarily remove the All Stars match from the calendar in 2018 due to the World Cup was a testament to the NRL's commitment to player welfare. By prioritizing the health and well-being of players, the league demonstrated a responsible approach to managing player workloads. The match's return in 2019 was met with enthusiasm, reaffirming its importance and the excitement it generates among fans and players alike.

The 2019 match in Melbourne, featuring the Australian Indigenous All Stars against the New Zealand Maori All Stars, marked a significant evolution in the event's history. This cross-cultural contest added a new layer of depth and intrigue, celebrating the heritage of both nations' Indigenous communities. The game showcased the talents and skills of players from diverse backgrounds, reinforcing the themes of unity and mutual respect.

The All Stars match also serves as a powerful symbol of community and social responsibility. The proceeds from the game often support various community programs and initiatives, particularly those benefiting Indigenous communities. This charitable aspect underscores the NRL's commitment to making a positive impact off the field, using the platform of rugby league to drive meaningful change and support important causes.

In recent years, the inclusion of women's teams in the All Stars concept has further enriched the event. The women's All Stars match highlights the growing prominence of women's rugby league and provides a platform for female athletes to showcase their talents on a grand stage. This development promotes gender inclusivity and inspires young girls to pursue their passion for rugby league, contributing to the sport's growth and diversity.

As we look to the future, the All Stars match is poised to remain a cherished tradition within the NRL. Its unique blend of high-level competition, cultural celebration, and community impact ensures that it will continue to captivate fans and make a lasting difference. The match embodies the spirit of rugby league, bringing people together, celebrating diversity, and fostering a sense of unity and pride.

The All Stars match stands as a testament to the enduring power of sport to unite, inspire, and uplift. It celebrates the rich cultural heritage of Indigenous communities, engages fans in a unique and democratic selection process, and supports important social causes. As the NRL evolves, the All Stars match will undoubtedly continue to play a vital role in shaping the future of rugby league, leaving an indelible mark on the sport and its community.

Chapter 28: Nines Fever: The High-Octane Rugby League Extravaganza

In 2014, the NRL introduced a thrilling new format to the rugby league calendar: the NRL Nines. This inaugural tournament brought together all sixteen NRL clubs for a fast-paced, exciting version of the game. Held at Eden Park in Auckland, New Zealand, the NRL Nines quickly became a fan favorite, showcasing the skills and speed of rugby league in a unique way.

The NRL Nines format features teams of nine players, playing shorter matches. This structure encourages a faster, more dynamic style of play, with plenty of tries and spectacular plays. Fans loved the high-energy games and the chance to see their favorite players in a different light. The tournament was an instant hit, drawing large crowds and significant television audiences.

Alongside the men's tournament, women's nines games were also featured. Initially, these games were played between the Australian and New Zealand national women's teams. This inclusion highlighted the growing popularity and skill level of women's rugby league. In later tournaments, teams from the NRL Women's (NRLW) competition also participated, further promoting the women's game and providing more opportunities for female players to shine on a big stage.

Despite its popularity, the NRL Nines faced challenges. By 2018, the tournament was removed from the calendar due to concerns about player workload. The intense NRL season, combined with representative duties, meant that players were at risk of burnout and injury. The decision to pause the NRL Nines was made to prioritize player health and well-being.

However, the tournament made a comeback in 2020. Fans were thrilled to see the NRL Nines return, bringing back the excitement and unique spectacle of the event. The 2020 tournament was a success, reaffirming the appeal of this fast-paced version of rugby league. Unfortunately, the challenges of managing player workload persisted, and the NRL Nines has not been played since then for the same reason.

The NRL Nines is a testament to the innovation and adaptability of rugby league. It shows how the sport can evolve and introduce new formats to keep fans engaged and entertained. The tournament's success demonstrates that there is a strong appetite for different styles of rugby league, and the NRL Nines provided a perfect blend of entertainment and high-level competition.

The inclusion of women's games in the NRL Nines also played a significant role in promoting gender equality in rugby league. It gave female players a platform to showcase their talents and helped raise the profile of the women's game. This move was in line with the NRL's broader efforts to support and develop women's rugby league, contributing to the growth and popularity of the sport.

Looking to the future, the NRL Nines remains a beloved concept among fans. There is hope that it may return to the calendar once again when player workload concerns can be adequately addressed. The excitement and unique format of the NRL Nines have left a lasting impression, and its potential for future success is undeniable.

The NRL Nines brought a fresh and exciting dimension to rugby league. It showcased the sport's ability to innovate and adapt, providing fans with thrilling, fast-paced action. Despite challenges related to player workload, the NRL Nines made a significant impact and highlighted the growing importance of women's rugby league. As the NRL continues to evolve, the legacy of the NRL Nines serves as a reminder of the sport's capacity to captivate and entertain audiences in new and exciting ways.

The NRL Nines tournament was introduced in 2014 as a thrilling, fast-paced addition to the rugby league calendar. The inaugural event at Eden Park in Auckland showcased a new format that captured the excitement of the sport in a condensed, high-energy version. With all sixteen NRL clubs participating, the tournament quickly became a fan favorite.

The inclusion of women's nines games between the Australian and New Zealand national women's teams added another layer of excitement. Later tournaments saw the involvement of NRLW teams, further promoting women's rugby league. The Nines format, with its shorter halves and reduced number of players on the field, created an environment where speed, skill, and creativity were on full display. This format allowed for more open play and higher-scoring games, making it a unique spectacle for fans.

However, despite its popularity, the Nines tournament faced challenges. Player workload became a significant concern, leading to the tournament's removal from the calendar after 2018. The intense physical demands of the regular NRL season, combined with the additional strain of the Nines, made it difficult to sustain the tournament annually. The 2020 revival brought back some of the excitement, but the same issues eventually led to its hiatus once more.

The NRL Nines showcased the sport in a way that was both familiar and fresh. The fast-paced nature of the games, combined with the festive atmosphere of the tournament, made it a highlight for fans. Players had the opportunity to display their skills in a different context, and teams could experiment with new strategies and lineups. The tournament also provided a platform for lesser-known players to shine and make a name for themselves.

The absence of the Nines from the calendar has been felt by fans and players alike. While the regular NRL season offers its own thrills, the Nines brought a unique energy and excitement that is hard to replicate. The possibility of its return remains a topic of discussion, as fans hope for another chance to experience the high-octane action that the tournament provided.

The NRL Nines was a groundbreaking addition to the rugby league landscape. It demonstrated the versatility and excitement of the sport in a new format, captivating audiences and providing unforgettable moments. Despite the challenges that led to its hiatus, the legacy of the Nines lives on, and the possibility of its return continues to spark anticipation among fans. The tournament's brief but impactful history highlights the potential for innovation in rugby league and the enduring appeal of the sport's most dynamic elements.

Chapter 29: The World Club Challenge: NRL vs. Super League Showdown

The World Club Challenge is a special pre-season match where the champion of the National Rugby League (NRL) faces off against the champion of the Super League. The first match took place in 1976 and was played occasionally through the late 80s and 90s. In 1997, there was a one-off Super League tournament. Since 2000, it has been a regular annual fixture, showcasing a battle between the best teams from Australia and the UK.

This match is more than just a game; it's a clash of rugby league cultures. The NRL, known for its fast-paced, hard-hitting style, and the Super League, celebrated for its skillful and expansive play, bring their best to this contest. Fans from both hemispheres eagerly await the game, which often promises thrilling moments and fierce competition.

In 2015, the World Club Challenge was expanded into the World Club Series. This new format included two exhibition games before the main Challenge game. The expanded series ran from 2015 to 2017 and featured the league champions joined by two invited teams from each league, creating a three-game series. Each invited team played a single game leading up to the main Challenge match.

The World Club Series was exciting and drew significant attention. However, in 2017, the format was scaled back to include only one invited team from each league. The NRL cited reasons such as tight schedules, distant travel, and long seasons as challenges for maintaining the expanded series. Despite the reduction, the games remained highly competitive and entertaining.

In 2018, the World Club Series was canceled, reverting to the original single match format. This change was made to focus on the quality and intensity of the main Challenge game. Since then, the World Club Challenge has continued as a single, highly anticipated match each year.

The World Club Challenge holds a special place in the rugby league calendar. It provides an opportunity for the champions of the NRL and the Super League to test their skills against each other. The game often attracts large crowds and high television ratings, reflecting its importance to fans and players alike.

Over the years, the World Club Challenge has produced memorable moments and legendary performances. Teams and players cherish the chance to compete for international bragging rights. Winning the Challenge is a prestigious achievement, adding to the club's legacy and history.

The World Club Challenge is a highlight of the rugby league year. It brings together the best of the NRL and the Super League, creating a spectacle of high-quality rugby. The game's rich history, competitive spirit, and international appeal make it a beloved event for fans around the world. As the tradition continues, the World Club Challenge remains a testament to the global reach and excitement of rugby league.

The World Club Challenge is a special pre-season match where the champion of the National Rugby League (NRL) faces off against the champion of the Super League. The first match took place in 1976 and was played occasionally through the late 80s and 90s. In 1997, there was a one-off Super League tournament. Since 2000, it has been a regular annual fixture, showcasing a battle between the best teams from Australia and the UK.

This match is more than just a game; it's a clash of rugby league cultures. The NRL, known for its fast-paced, hard-hitting style, and the Super League, celebrated for its skillful and expansive play, bring their best to this contest. Fans from both hemispheres eagerly await the game, which often promises thrilling moments and fierce competition.

In 2015, the World Club Challenge was expanded into the World Club Series. This new format included two exhibition games before the main Challenge game. The expanded series ran from 2015 to 2017 and featured the league champions joined by two invited teams from each league, creating a three-game series. Each invited team played a single game leading up to the main Challenge match.

The World Club Series was exciting and drew significant attention. However, in 2017, the format was scaled back to include only one invited team from each league. The NRL cited reasons such as tight schedules, distant travel, and long seasons as challenges for maintaining the expanded series. Despite the reduction, the games remained highly competitive and entertaining.

In 2018, the World Club Series was canceled, reverting to the original single match format. This change was made to focus on the quality and intensity of the main Challenge game. Since then, the World Club Challenge has continued as a single, highly anticipated match each year.

The World Club Challenge holds a special place in the rugby league calendar. It provides an opportunity for the champions of the NRL and the Super League to test their skills against each other. The game often attracts large crowds and high television ratings, reflecting its importance to fans and players alike.

Over the years, the World Club Challenge has produced memorable moments and legendary performances. Teams and players cherish the chance to compete for international bragging rights. Winning the Challenge is a prestigious achievement, adding to the club's legacy and history.

The World Club Challenge is a highlight of the rugby league year. It brings together the best of the NRL and the Super League, creating a spectacle of high-quality rugby. The game's rich history, competitive spirit, and international appeal make it a beloved event for fans around the world. As the tradition continues, the World Club Challenge remains a testament to the global reach and excitement of rugby league.

Chapter 30: Premiership Rounds: The Heart of NRL Action

The NRL premiership season is the heart of rugby league in Australia, bringing thrilling matches and intense competition week after week. As a winter sport, the season kicks off in early March and runs for 27 weeks until the start of September. This extended season allows fans to enjoy rugby league throughout the winter months, with games played every weekend.

Each round of the regular season features a carefully planned schedule of matches. Typically, one match is played on Thursday night, two on Friday night, three on Saturday, and two on Sunday. This spread of games ensures that fans have multiple opportunities to watch their favorite teams in action, whether live at the stadium or on television.

The structure of the competition is straightforward but competitive. Teams receive two competition points for a win and one point for a draw. If a team has a bye week, they also receive two points. A loss, however, yields no points. This points system keeps the ladder rankings dynamic and ensures that every match can significantly impact a team's standing.

Teams on the ladder are first ranked by their total competition points. If two or more teams have the same number of points, the match points differential, which is the difference between points scored and points conceded, is used to separate them. If the teams are still tied, points percentage comes into play, further refining the rankings.

The goal of every team during the regular season is to secure a spot at the top of the ladder. The club that finishes the season with the highest ranking is declared the minor premiers. This title is a prestigious achievement, marking a team's consistent excellence throughout the gruelling season.

The NRL regular season is not just about competition; it's also about showcasing the best of rugby league talent. Players strive to deliver their best performances, knowing that every match is an opportunity to impress fans, selectors, and sponsors. The season also sees the emergence of young talent, with rookies making their mark alongside seasoned veterans.

Throughout the premiership rounds, fans are treated to a variety of exciting matchups. Rivalries, both old and new, ignite passions and add extra spice to the fixtures. Games between traditional rivals like the Sydney Roosters and South Sydney Rabbitohs often draw large crowds and generate intense media coverage.

The regular season also features special themed rounds, such as Indigenous Round, which celebrates the contributions of Indigenous players and culture to rugby league. These themed rounds add depth and meaning to the season, highlighting the sport's rich heritage and its role in the broader community.

As the season progresses, the stakes get higher, and the competition intensifies. Teams not only fight for wins but also for better positioning on the ladder, aiming to secure a favorable draw in the finals series. The premiership rounds build anticipation and excitement, setting the stage for the thrilling conclusion of the season in the finals.

The NRL premiership rounds are the backbone of the rugby league season. They offer fans a steady stream of high-quality matches and keep the competition alive and engaging from March to September. The regular season is a marathon, not a sprint, requiring teams to perform consistently and strategically. As the foundation of the NRL calendar, the premiership rounds embody the spirit, skill, and passion that make rugby league one of Australia's most beloved sports.

The premiership rounds form the backbone of the NRL season, where the foundations for success are laid and the character of teams is tested. These 27 weeks of competition are a marathon, requiring endurance, resilience, and strategic brilliance from every club involved. It's during this period that the groundwork is set for the drama of the finals, with every match carrying significant weight.

Throughout the premiership rounds, the consistency of performance is paramount. Teams must navigate a grueling schedule, managing player fitness and form while adapting to the evolving dynamics of the competition. This phase of the season is a true test of a team's depth and ability to withstand the pressures that come with a long campaign. The regular season's length means that even early losses can be recovered from, provided the team can find form and momentum.

Fans play an integral role during these rounds, bringing their passion and energy to every game, whether in the stadiums or watching from home. The NRL premiership rounds are not just about the players on the field; they are a community event, uniting supporters across cities and regions. The themed rounds, such as the Indigenous Round, highlight the sport's cultural significance and its role in promoting inclusivity and respect.

As teams compete for points, the ladder becomes a focal point of discussion and analysis. Each victory, draw, or loss can shift positions, creating an ever-changing landscape of competition. The battle for the top eight spots is fierce, with clubs striving to secure their place in the finals. The minor premiership, awarded to the team finishing first on the ladder, is a coveted title, reflecting a season of sustained excellence.

The unpredictability of the premiership rounds adds to the excitement. Upsets and surprise performances keep the competition alive, reminding everyone that on any given day, any team can triumph. This unpredictability fuels hope and determination, driving teams to push their limits and fans to stay engaged throughout the season.

Community engagement during the premiership rounds cannot be overstated. Matches taken to regional areas bring the sport closer to fans who might not otherwise have the chance to see live NRL action. These games foster a deeper connection between the clubs and their broader supporter base, enhancing the sport's reach and impact.

Media coverage during this period is extensive, with in-depth analysis, player interviews, and expert commentary keeping fans informed and entertained. The role of the media in building narratives around the season's unfolding drama is crucial, as it helps to sustain interest and excitement from the first round to the last.

As the season progresses, the pressure intensifies. Teams jostling for finals spots must maintain their form, while those aiming for the minor premiership push themselves to achieve consistent results. The closing rounds of the season are often the most thrilling, as every match can determine the final standings and set the stage for the finals series.

The conclusion of the premiership rounds marks a significant milestone in the NRL season. It signals the end of the marathon and the beginning of the sprint, where the best teams of the season face off in the finals. The experiences and lessons learned during the premiership rounds are invaluable as teams prepare for the high-stakes environment of knockout rugby league.

In reflecting on the premiership rounds, it's clear that they are a vital and vibrant part of the NRL journey. They shape the narrative of the season, provide a platform for showcasing talent, and engage fans in a shared experience of highs and lows. The journey through these rounds is filled with memorable moments, both for the teams and their supporters, making it an essential chapter in the story of any NRL season.

Chapter 31: Rugby League Las Vegas

In 2024, the NRL launched an exciting new event called Rugby League Las Vegas. This annual event, held at Allegiant Stadium in Las Vegas, showcases the sport of rugby league and aims to expand its audience in the United States. It features two Round 1 NRL matches, and starting in 2025, a Round 1 Super League game as well. The event is contracted to continue until 2028, bringing thrilling rugby league action to a new and enthusiastic fan base.

The creation of Rugby League Las Vegas was driven by the NRL's desire to grow the sport beyond its traditional strongholds in Australia and New Zealand. By introducing rugby league to the American market, the NRL hopes to attract new fans and generate greater international interest in the competition. The choice of Las Vegas, a city known for its entertainment and sports events, adds a unique and exciting element to the NRL calendar.

The inaugural event in March 2024 featured the Brisbane Broncos, Manly Warringah Sea Eagles, South Sydney Rabbitohs, and Sydney Roosters. These teams played two thrilling matches, with Manly Warringah defeating South Sydney and Sydney triumphing over Brisbane. The games drew a crowd of over 40,000 spectators, the largest attendance for any rugby league event in the United States at the time. The matches were also broadcast on Fox Sports in the

United States, with Australian viewership surpassing 1.6 million.

Despite the success in stadium attendance, TV viewing figures in the United States were relatively low, with only 61,000 viewers. However, this was still an improvement over previous NRL broadcasts in the state. The event also included a Colonial Cup match between the national men's teams of the United States and Canada, which ended in a thrilling 16–16 draw, showcasing the growing interest and potential for rugby league in North America.

In July 2024, the NRL announced that the 2025 Rugby League Las Vegas event would feature the Canberra Raiders, Cronulla-Sutherland Sharks, New Zealand Warriors, and Penrith Panthers. Additionally, the event would include an opening round match of the United Kingdom's Super League, with Wigan Warriors facing Warrington Wolves. This marked the first regular-season Super League game held in the United States. An ashes test match between the Australia and England women's national sides was also added to the event, highlighting the inclusion and promotion of women's rugby league.

The involvement of Super League in the 2025 event came after Wigan's CEO, Kris Radlinski, watched the 2024 event on TV and sent a speculative email to the organizers. This collaboration between the NRL and Super League not only enhances the appeal of Rugby League Las Vegas but also strengthens the global rugby league community by bringing together top teams from both competitions.

Rugby League Las Vegas represents a significant step forward for the sport, providing a platform for international exposure and growth. The event offers fans in the United States a chance to experience the excitement and intensity of live rugby league, while also giving players the opportunity to showcase their skills on a global stage. The inclusion of both NRL and Super League teams creates a diverse and competitive environment, further elevating the status of the event.

As Rugby League Las Vegas continues to evolve, it is poised to become a major highlight of the rugby league calendar. The combination of top-tier matches, a vibrant location, and a growing fan base makes it a must-watch event for rugby league enthusiasts worldwide. The NRL's commitment to expanding the sport's reach and engaging new audiences ensures that Rugby League Las Vegas will remain an integral part of the rugby league landscape for years to come.

Rugby League Las Vegas is a groundbreaking initiative that brings the thrill of rugby league to new audiences in the United States. With its exciting matches, international collaboration, and commitment to growth, the event is set to make a lasting impact on the sport. As the NRL and Super League teams compete in this unique and dynamic setting, fans can look forward to witnessing history in the making at Rugby League Las Vegas.

The introduction of Rugby League Las Vegas marks a transformative moment in the history of rugby league. This event signifies the NRL's bold vision to globalize the sport and tap into new markets, particularly in the United States. The choice of Las Vegas, a city synonymous with entertainment and sporting spectacles, is a strategic move to attract a diverse audience and provide an unforgettable experience for both new and seasoned rugby league fans.

The inaugural event in 2024 set a high standard, showcasing the competitive spirit and high-octane action that rugby league is known for. The involvement of prominent NRL teams like the Brisbane Broncos, Manly Warringah Sea Eagles, South Sydney Rabbitohs, and Sydney Roosters ensured that the matches were of the highest quality. The attendance of over 40,000 spectators at Allegiant Stadium was a testament to the event's appeal and the potential for growth in the American market.

The broadcast of the matches on Fox Sports in the United States, despite modest viewing figures, represented a crucial step in increasing the sport's visibility. The substantial viewership in Australia highlighted the global interest in this landmark event. The inclusion of the Colonial Cup match between the United States and Canada added an international flavor, further emphasizing the event's significance in promoting rugby league across North America.

Looking ahead to 2025, the expansion of Rugby League Las Vegas to include the Canberra Raiders, Cronulla-Sutherland Sharks, New Zealand Warriors, and Penrith Panthers, as well as the addition of a Super League match between Wigan Warriors and Warrington Wolves, underscores the event's growing stature. The inclusion of an ashes test match between the Australian and England women's teams demonstrates a commitment to promoting women's rugby league and fostering gender equality in the sport.

The collaboration between the NRL and Super League not only enriches the event but also strengthens the ties between the two premier rugby league competitions. This partnership enhances the global appeal of Rugby League Las Vegas and provides fans with a unique opportunity to witness the best of both leagues in a single, thrilling event.

Rugby League Las Vegas is more than just a series of matches; it is a celebration of the sport's heritage, its dynamic present, and its promising future. The event's ability to draw large crowds, generate significant media attention, and create memorable moments on and off the field is a testament to its success. It serves as a beacon for the potential of rugby league to captivate audiences around the world and inspire a new generation of fans.

As the event continues to evolve, its impact on the global rugby league landscape will only grow. The

NRL's commitment to innovation and expansion is evident in the ambitious plans for Rugby League Las Vegas. By bringing the sport to a new and enthusiastic audience, the NRL is paving the way for a bright and exciting future for rugby league.

Rugby League Las Vegas represents a bold and visionary step forward for the sport. The event's success in its inaugural year and the plans for its expansion in 2025 and beyond highlight the NRL's dedication to growing the sport on a global scale. With its combination of top-tier matches, international collaboration, and a vibrant host city, Rugby League Las Vegas is set to become a cornerstone of the rugby league calendar and a catalyst for the sport's continued growth and development.

Chapter 32: Magic Round Extravaganza

In 2019, the NRL introduced an exciting new event called Magic Round. This unique event features all 16 NRL teams playing their matches over one weekend at Suncorp Stadium in Brisbane. Magic Round was created to bring a festival atmosphere to rugby league and give fans a chance to see all their favorite teams in action at one venue. From its inception, it has been a huge success and has become a highly anticipated annual event.

Magic Round is more than just a series of games; it's a celebration of rugby league. Fans from all over Australia, and even from overseas, travel to Brisbane to be part of this special weekend. The stadium is packed with passionate supporters, all wearing their team colors and creating a vibrant, festive atmosphere. The event has something for everyone, from thrilling matches to family-friendly activities and entertainment.

The idea behind Magic Round was to give fans a unique experience and to showcase the best of rugby league in one place. It also allows teams to connect with fans outside their home regions. For many fans, it's a chance to see teams and players they might not usually get to watch live. The excitement of seeing multiple games in one weekend adds to the allure of Magic Round.

Each year, Magic Round kicks off on a Friday and runs through to Sunday. The schedule is carefully planned to ensure that every match gets its moment in the spotlight. This means there are games throughout the day and into the evening, giving fans plenty of action to enjoy. The event also includes special activities like fan zones, player meet-and-greets, and live music, making it a true festival of rugby league.

Magic Round has had a positive impact on the local economy as well. Brisbane benefits from the influx of visitors who come for the weekend, boosting tourism and local businesses. Hotels, restaurants, and shops see increased activity, and the city embraces the event with special promotions and activities. It's a win-win situation for both the NRL and Brisbane.

The success of Magic Round has led to discussions about expanding the concept. There have been talks about potentially taking Magic Round to other cities or even other countries. The idea is to spread the excitement of rugby league to new audiences and to continue growing the sport's popularity. While Brisbane remains the home of Magic Round, the future possibilities are exciting.

Magic Round has quickly become a highlight of the NRL season. It's a time when fans, players, and the entire rugby league community come together to celebrate the sport they love. The atmosphere is electric, the games are thrilling, and the memories made are unforgettable. It's a testament to the creativity and innovation of the NRL in finding new ways to engage fans and promote the sport.

In conclusion, Magic Round is a groundbreaking event that has added a new dimension to the NRL season. It brings together all 16 teams in one place, creating a festival-like atmosphere that celebrates rugby league. From its successful launch in 2019, it has grown into a beloved annual tradition. With its unique format, exciting games, and vibrant atmosphere, Magic Round is a shining example of the NRL's commitment to providing fans with unforgettable experiences and growing the sport's reach.

Magic Round has revolutionized the NRL experience, making it a standout event that fans eagerly anticipate each year. The concept of bringing all 16 teams together to play in one stadium over a single weekend has created a unique and electrifying atmosphere that resonates with both die-hard rugby league enthusiasts and casual fans. The success of Magic Round can be attributed to several key factors that have contributed to its popularity and enduring appeal.

Firstly, the concentration of matches over three days provides an unparalleled viewing experience. Fans have the opportunity to watch multiple games back-to-back, creating a non-stop festival of rugby league. This intense schedule not only maximizes entertainment but also ensures that each game is played in front of a passionate and diverse crowd, adding to the excitement and energy in the stadium.

Secondly, the location of Suncorp Stadium in Brisbane has proven to be an ideal setting for Magic Round. The city's strong rugby league culture and enthusiastic fan base provide a perfect backdrop for the event. Brisbane's hospitality and vibrant atmosphere make it a welcoming destination for fans traveling from all over the country and beyond. The economic boost to the local economy through tourism and increased business activity during Magic Round weekend is another significant benefit.

The festival-like atmosphere of Magic Round extends beyond the matches themselves. The NRL has successfully integrated a variety of entertainment options and fan engagement activities into the event. From interactive fan zones and live music performances to player meet-and-greets and autograph sessions, there is something for everyone. These additional attractions enhance the overall experience, making Magic Round a family-friendly event that appeals to a wide audience.

Moreover, Magic Round has provided a platform for teams to reach out to their supporters in a new and exciting way. The event allows clubs to connect with fans who might not have the opportunity to attend home games regularly. This increased visibility and engagement help strengthen the bond between teams and their supporters, fostering a sense of community and loyalty.

The innovation and success of Magic Round have also sparked discussions about potential expansions and adaptations of the concept. There is interest in exploring the possibility of hosting Magic Round in other cities or even internationally. This would not only help spread the excitement of rugby league to new audiences but also showcase the sport on a global stage. The NRL's willingness to think outside the box and embrace new ideas demonstrates its commitment to growing the game and reaching new markets.

Magic Round has also served as a reminder of the resilience and adaptability of the NRL. Despite the challenges posed by the COVID-19 pandemic, the league has managed to maintain the spirit and excitement of Magic Round, even when faced with restrictions and uncertainties. This determination to keep the event alive underscores the importance of Magic Round in the NRL calendar and its significance to the rugby league community.

Magic Round has quickly established itself as a highlight of the NRL season. Its innovative format, festive atmosphere, and ability to bring together fans from all walks of life have made it a beloved tradition. The event's success is a testament to the NRL's vision and commitment to enhancing the fan experience and promoting the sport. As Magic Round continues to evolve and potentially expand, it promises to remain a key fixture in the rugby league calendar, celebrating the passion and excitement that define the game.

Chapter 33: Themed Rounds

Themed rounds have become an essential part of the NRL premiership season, adding variety and special significance to certain weeks throughout the year. These themed rounds not only celebrate the rich history and diverse community of rugby league but also raise awareness for important causes. They bring a unique atmosphere to the games and engage fans in meaningful ways.

One of the most significant themed rounds is the ANZAC Round. Held annually around April 25th, this round pays tribute to the Australian and New Zealand Army Corps (ANZAC) and honors the sacrifices made by soldiers in both countries. During ANZAC Round, teams and fans participate in ceremonies and observances, including moments of silence and special pre-game rituals. The matches are often played with extra intensity, reflecting the spirit of bravery and camaraderie associated with ANZAC Day.

Heritage Round is another beloved themed week, where teams and fans celebrate the history and traditions of rugby league. Players wear retro jerseys that harken back to earlier eras, and the games are often accompanied by displays of historical memorabilia. Heritage Round provides a nostalgic look back at the evolution of the sport and highlights the rich legacy of the NRL and its clubs.

Women in League Round is a significant event that celebrates the contributions of women to the sport of rugby league. This round recognizes the roles played by female players, coaches, administrators, and volunteers. It also promotes the growth of women's rugby league and encourages greater female participation at all levels of the game. The Women in League Round is marked by special events and initiatives aimed at empowering and honoring women in the sport.

Retro Round is a fan-favorite themed week that embraces the styles and cultures of past decades. Teams don throwback jerseys, and stadiums are decorated with vintage memorabilia. Fans often participate by wearing retro clothing and accessories, creating a fun and nostalgic atmosphere. Retro Round not only pays homage to the history of the game but also fosters a sense of community among supporters who share a love for rugby league's past.

Beanies for Brain Cancer Round is a themed week dedicated to raising awareness and funds for brain cancer research. Spearheaded by the Mark Hughes Foundation, this round encourages fans to purchase and wear special beanies, with proceeds going towards brain cancer research. The NRL community comes together to support this important cause, demonstrating the sport's commitment to making a positive impact beyond the field.

Rivalry Round adds an extra layer of excitement to the season by featuring matches between traditional rivals. These games are often highly anticipated and draw large crowds, as teams compete for bragging rights and special trophies. Rivalry Round intensifies the competitive spirit of the NRL and showcases some of the most thrilling and passionate contests of the season.

In 2022, the NRL introduced additional themed rounds to further celebrate diversity and inclusivity within the sport. Pride Round was created to honor and respect LGBTQI players and fans, promoting a message of acceptance and equality. Unfortunately, the round faced challenges when seven Manly players boycotted the game, refusing to wear the specially designed jerseys. The resulting controversy and negative publicity led to the decision not to hold a Pride Round in 2023. Instead, the NRL chose to focus on other themed rounds that had been well-received.

Multicultural Round is another important themed week that celebrates the diverse backgrounds and cultures represented in rugby league. This round highlights the contributions of players from various ethnicities and promotes the values of inclusion and respect. Special events and activities are organized to showcase different cultures, creating a vibrant and welcoming atmosphere for all fans.

In addition to these major themed rounds, the NRL season features various special trophies awarded during specific matches. These trophies add an extra element of competition and honor the history and traditions of rivalries. Teams and fans alike take pride in competing for these coveted awards, which often carry historical and sentimental value.

Themed rounds play a crucial role in enhancing the NRL premiership season, adding depth and meaning to the games. They provide opportunities to celebrate the sport's heritage, honor important contributions, and raise awareness for significant causes. By incorporating these themed weeks, the NRL creates a richer and more engaging experience for players, fans, and the wider community.

Themed rounds have become an integral part of the NRL season, bringing more than just competition to the sport. They create a platform for celebration, remembrance, awareness, and community engagement. Each themed round offers a unique opportunity to highlight various aspects of rugby league and its significance beyond the game.

The ANZAC Round stands out as one of the most poignant themed rounds. It is a solemn reminder of the sacrifices made by soldiers from Australia and New Zealand. This round is marked by ceremonies that honor their bravery and commitment, connecting the sport to a deeper sense of national pride and history. The emotional weight of ANZAC Round adds a layer of respect and gratitude, making the matches played during this period feel particularly meaningful.

Heritage Round allows the NRL community to reflect on the rich history of the sport. By donning retro jerseys and celebrating the traditions of rugby league, players and fans alike pay homage to the past. This round serves as a bridge between generations, connecting today's game with its roots and reminding everyone of the journey the sport has taken. It is a celebration of legacy, showcasing the evolution of rugby league while honoring its origins.

Women in League Round is a powerful testament to the contributions of women in rugby league. It highlights the importance of female participation and celebrates the roles women play, both on and off the field. This round promotes gender equality and encourages more women to get involved in the sport. It is a celebration of empowerment and progress, recognizing the invaluable impact women have had and continue to have in rugby league.

Retro Round adds a fun and nostalgic element to the season. By embracing styles and cultures from past decades, this round brings a sense of playfulness and community spirit. It allows fans to reminisce and enjoy the simpler times of rugby league, creating a festive atmosphere that everyone can enjoy. Retro Round is a reminder of the sport's enduring appeal and the joy it brings to its supporters.

Beanies for Brain Cancer Round is a heartfelt initiative that combines the love of rugby league with a critical cause. By raising awareness and funds for brain cancer research, this round demonstrates the sport's commitment to making a positive impact. The widespread support from the NRL community during this round highlights the compassion and solidarity within the sport, showing that rugby league is more than just a game.

Rivalry Round intensifies the competitive spirit of the NRL by focusing on traditional rivalries. These matchups are often highly anticipated and bring out the best in teams and fans. The energy and passion during Rivalry Round are unmatched, making it one of the most exciting periods of the season. It celebrates the fierce competition and storied histories between rival clubs, adding an extra layer of excitement to the premiership rounds.

In 2022, the NRL's attempt to introduce a Pride Round was met with challenges, illustrating the complexities of promoting inclusivity in sports. While the intention was to celebrate and respect LGBTQI players, the boycott by Manly players and subsequent negative publicity highlighted the need for continued dialogue and education. Despite this setback, the NRL's commitment to inclusivity remains strong, as evidenced by the continued focus on other themed rounds.

Multicultural Round is another significant themed week, celebrating the diverse backgrounds of players and fans. It showcases the cultural richness within rugby league and promotes values of inclusion and respect. This round is a vibrant celebration of diversity, reflecting the broad appeal of rugby league and its ability to bring people from different backgrounds together.

Themed rounds, with their unique focuses and celebrations, enrich the NRL season. They provide moments of reflection, joy, and community spirit, enhancing the overall experience for everyone involved. Whether through honoring history, promoting important causes, or celebrating diversity, these rounds contribute to the tapestry of rugby league, making it more than just a sport but a unifying force that brings people together.

As the NRL continues to evolve, themed rounds will undoubtedly remain a vital part of the premiership season. They serve as powerful reminders of the sport's impact both on and off the field, creating lasting memories and fostering a sense of belonging within the rugby league community. Through these special weeks, the NRL not only entertains but also educates, inspires, and connects with its diverse and passionate fan base.

Chapter 34: Mid-Season Representative Rounds

NRL players don't just compete for their club teams in the premiership rounds. They also get selected to play in various representative competitions held during the season. These mid-season representative rounds usually happen from mid-April to mid-July each year. During this time, players have the chance to showcase their skills on bigger stages, representing their state or country in different matches.

One of the major events during this period is the annual Anzac Test between Australia and New Zealand. This match is typically played in early to mid-April and holds significant importance as it commemorates the Anzac spirit. The rivalry between the two teams is intense, and the match draws a lot of attention from rugby league fans. It is a prestigious event that highlights the talent and competitive spirit of both nations.

Another exciting match during this period is the New South Wales City vs. Country Origin game. Played on the same weekend as the Anzac Test, this game pits players from the city against those from the country areas of New South Wales. It is a showcase of regional pride and provides an opportunity for players to demonstrate their abilities in hopes of being selected for higher honors, such as the State of Origin series.

The mid-season representative rounds also feature test matches between Pacific Island Nations. These games are usually played on the same weekend as the Anzac Test and the City vs. Country Origin match. The matches involve teams from the Cook Islands, Fiji, Papua New Guinea, Samoa, and Tonga. These contests include the Melanesian Cup and Polynesian Cup, adding to the excitement and diversity of the representative rounds. These games are crucial for the development and recognition of rugby league talent in the Pacific region.

Arguably the most anticipated event during the mid-season representative rounds is the State of Origin series. This three-match series, held from June to July, is a fierce competition between New South Wales and Queensland. The rivalry is intense, and the matches are known for their high skill level, physicality, and passionate fan support. State of Origin games are often considered some of the toughest and most entertaining in rugby league, with players giving their all to bring pride to their state.

In addition to these scheduled matches, players from outside Oceania may travel back to their home countries for training camps or national team matches. This period provides an opportunity for international players to represent their countries and contribute to the growth of rugby league globally. It is a time for players to reconnect with their roots and bring their experience and skills to their national teams.

The mid-season representative rounds are not just about the matches themselves but also about the stories and moments that unfold. They bring a different level of excitement to the NRL season, as players get to wear different jerseys and play for different causes. The rounds highlight the depth of talent in rugby league and the passion that players have for representing their state or country.

Fans eagerly look forward to these rounds as they provide a break from the regular premiership competition and offer a different type of spectacle. The representative rounds bring a mix of pride, rivalry, and camaraderie, making them a special part of the rugby league calendar. They remind everyone of the broader impact of the sport and the honor that comes with representing one's region or nation.

The mid-season representative rounds are a vibrant and essential part of the NRL season. They offer players the chance to shine on bigger stages and bring excitement and diversity to the sport. Whether it's the Anzac Test, the City vs. Country Origin match, the Pacific Island Nation tests, or the State of Origin series, these rounds add depth and richness to the rugby league experience. They celebrate the sport's heritage, its international reach, and the incredible talent of its players.

The mid-season representative rounds are a highlight of the NRL calendar, offering fans a break from club competition to focus on the pride and passion of state and national representation. This chapter explored the various competitions and matches that make up this exciting period, showcasing the diversity and depth of rugby league talent.

The Anzac Test between Australia and New Zealand stands out as a significant fixture, honoring the Anzac spirit while providing a stage for intense competition. This match is more than just a game; it is a commemoration of history and a display of the fierce rivalry between two rugby league powerhouses.

Similarly, the New South Wales City vs. Country Origin match offers a unique opportunity for players to showcase their skills and for fans to celebrate regional pride. This match serves as a vital stepping stone for players aiming to make their mark in the prestigious State of Origin series.

The inclusion of test matches between Pacific Island Nations adds an extra layer of excitement to the representative rounds. These games not only highlight the growing prominence of rugby league in the Pacific but also bring unique styles and thrilling matches to the forefront, enriching the overall rugby league experience.

The State of Origin series remains the pinnacle of the mid-season representative rounds. The fierce rivalry between New South Wales and Queensland captivates fans and players alike, producing some of the most intense and memorable matches in rugby league. The series exemplifies the spirit of competition and the deep-seated pride each state holds.

These rounds are more than just a collection of matches; they are a celebration of rugby league's heritage and international reach. Players get the chance to return to their roots, contributing to the sport's development on a global scale. This period fosters the growth of rugby league worldwide, allowing players to share their experiences and skills with their national teams.

The representative rounds highlight the importance of state and national pride, with players representing their regions and countries, carrying the hopes and aspirations of their supporters. This sense of pride and responsibility often brings out the best in players, resulting in performances that inspire and create lasting memories.

The mid-season representative rounds are a vital and exhilarating part of the NRL season. They provide a unique blend of competition, showcasing the sport's heritage, diversity, and the extraordinary talent of its players. From the Anzac Test and City vs. Country Origin match to the Pacific Island Nation tests and the State of Origin series, these rounds offer a rich and varied rugby league experience. They celebrate the broader impact of rugby league and the honor of representing one's region or nation, adding depth and richness to the rugby league calendar. As the NRL continues to grow, the mid-season representative rounds will undoubtedly remain a cherished and essential part of the sport.

Chapter 35: Finals Series

The finals series is the climax of the NRL season, where the eight highest-placed teams battle it out for the ultimate prize. This thrilling competition begins at the end of the regular season, with the top eight teams competing over four weeks in September. The excitement builds as teams aim to secure their place in the grand final, the pinnacle event of the NRL calendar.

The finals series is structured to ensure a fair and competitive pathway to the grand final. From 1998 to 2011, the NRL used the McIntyre final eight system. However, with the establishment of the Australian Rugby League Commission (ARLC) in 2012, the format was changed to the current system, which is considered fairer for teams finishing in the top four.

In the first week of the finals, the top four teams play each other in qualifying finals, while the bottom four teams face off in elimination finals. The winners of the qualifying finals earn a week off and move directly to the preliminary finals. The losers of the qualifying finals get a second chance and play the winners of the elimination finals in the semi-finals.

The second week, known as the semi-finals, determines which teams will progress to the preliminary finals. The losers of the elimination finals are knocked out, while the winners face the losers of the qualifying finals. This stage is crucial, as it decides the final four teams that will compete in the preliminary finals.

In the third week, the preliminary finals, the top two teams from the qualifying finals return to the field. They play against the winners of the semi-finals, with the victors earning a coveted spot in the grand final. The intensity and stakes are incredibly high, as only two teams can advance.

The grand final, usually held on the first Sunday of October, is the most anticipated event of the NRL season. It is a spectacle that attracts fans from all over the world, eager to see which team will be crowned the champions. The atmosphere is electric, with passionate supporters cheering their teams on in a display of loyalty and excitement.

The grand final is more than just a game; it's a celebration of rugby league. From the pre-match entertainment to the final whistle, every moment is packed with emotion and drama. The players leave everything on the field, knowing that they are playing for their club's honor and the ultimate glory.

Winning the grand final is the dream of every NRL player and fan. It represents the culmination of a season's hard work, determination, and perseverance. The victorious team is etched into the history books, remembered as the best of the best. The grand final trophy is a symbol of excellence, pride, and achievement.

The finals series is the highlight of the NRL season. It showcases the best teams in a thrilling, high-stakes competition that captures the hearts of fans. The journey from the regular season to the grand final is filled with intense matches, unforgettable moments, and the pure excitement of rugby league at its finest. The finals series not only determines the champion but also highlights the skill, dedication, and spirit of the teams and players who make the NRL one of the most exciting sports leagues in the world.

The finals series of the NRL is an extraordinary showcase of skill, determination, and passion. The journey through the finals is a test of a team's strength, strategy, and endurance. Each match carries immense weight, with players pushing their limits to ensure victory for their clubs. The thrill of the finals captures the essence of rugby league, drawing fans into a whirlwind of emotions and excitement.

The shift from the McIntyre final eight system to the current format under the ARLC reflects a commitment to fairness and competitiveness. This change has allowed teams finishing in the top four to have a more equitable path to the grand final. The structure ensures that every match is critical, with no room for complacency, and rewards consistent performance throughout the season.

Week one of the finals sets the stage for the drama to unfold. The qualifying and elimination finals create immediate tension, with teams fighting to either secure a week off or avoid elimination. The results of these matches lay the groundwork for the semi-finals, where the stakes are raised even higher. The semi-finals are a battleground where dreams are either kept alive or shattered, and only the strongest advance.

The preliminary finals are the penultimate test. The best teams face off in a high-stakes environment, knowing that a win will secure them a spot in the grand final. The intensity of these matches is unparalleled, with players giving everything they have to ensure their team reaches the final showdown. The preliminary finals often produce some of the most memorable moments in NRL history, as teams fight with everything on the line.

The grand final is the pinnacle of the NRL season, a grand spectacle that unites fans from all corners. It is more than just a match; it is a celebration of the sport, a culmination of months of hard work, and a chance to etch a team's name in history. The grand final is a day of high emotion, where every pass, tackle, and try is magnified, and the atmosphere is electric.

Winning the grand final is the ultimate achievement in rugby league. It is the goal that every player dreams of and every fan hopes for. The moment when the final whistle blows and the champions are crowned is one of pure joy and triumph. The grand final trophy represents the highest honor, a testament to a season of excellence, dedication, and teamwork.

The finals series also highlights the resilience and spirit of the teams. It showcases their ability to rise to the occasion, to perform under pressure, and to overcome challenges. The journey to the grand final is arduous, and only the most determined teams make it through. The finals series celebrates not just the winners but all the teams that have shown incredible skill and heart throughout the season.

The NRL finals series is a breathtaking display of rugby league at its best. It is a journey filled with intense competition, dramatic moments, and the ultimate pursuit of glory. The finals series brings out the best in the teams and players, creating unforgettable memories for fans. It is a testament to the passion, skill, and dedication that define the NRL and make it one of the most thrilling sports leagues in the world.

Chapter 36: Grand Final

The NRL Grand Final is the pinnacle of rugby league in Australia, an event that captivates fans across the nation. It determines the season's premiers and is one of the most significant sporting events in the country. Held annually at Sydney's Stadium Australia since 1999, except for 2021 when it was moved to Brisbane's Suncorp Stadium due to the COVID pandemic, the Grand Final attracts massive crowds and an extensive television audience.

The first Grand Final at Stadium Australia set a record for the highest attendance at an Australian rugby league game, with 107,999 people filling the stands. This record-setting event marked the beginning of a new era for the NRL Grand Final, establishing it as a must-see spectacle in Australian sports.

Traditionally, the Grand Final was played on Sunday afternoons, but the scheduling has shifted over the years. In 2001, the start time was moved to 8 pm, and then to 7 pm in subsequent years. From 2008, a compromise was reached to balance the preferences of the official broadcaster, Nine Network, and fans who enjoyed afternoon kick-offs. As a result, the Grand Final now begins at 5 pm AEST, providing an optimal viewing experience for all.

The week leading up to the Grand Final is filled with anticipation and excitement, highlighted by the NRL Grand Final Breakfast. This event is attended by both competing teams, numerous guests, and is broadcast live on Australian television. It sets the stage for the big game, building anticipation and adding to the grandeur of the occasion.

The Grand Final itself is not just about the match; it's an all-encompassing event. The day starts with an opening ceremony featuring live entertainment and the singing of the national anthem by renowned Australasian and international artists. One of the most memorable moments of the pre-game festivities is the delivery of the NRL trophy to the field by an Australian Army helicopter, a tradition that adds to the drama and excitement.

As the final whistle blows and the Grand Final concludes, the winning team is celebrated in a presentation ceremony. Each player on the victorious team is awarded a premiership ring, a symbol of their hard-earned triumph. The player deemed to be the man-of-the-match receives the prestigious Clive Churchill Medal, recognizing their outstanding performance. The Prime Minister of Australia typically presents the trophy to the winning captain, adding a touch of national significance to the event.

The NRL Grand Final is more than just a game; it's a celebration of the sport, a culmination of a season's worth of hard work, dedication, and passion. The atmosphere is electric, with fans from all over the country coming together to witness the crowning of the champions. The match itself is a showcase of the best rugby league has to offer, with high stakes and intense competition ensuring a thrilling experience for all.

In 2010, the Government of New South Wales secured the rights to host the Grand Final at Stadium Australia until 2022, investing $45 million to ensure that this iconic event remains in Sydney. This deal highlights the importance of the Grand Final not only to rugby league but also to the cultural and sporting landscape of Australia.

Stadium Australia, located in Sydney, has become synonymous with the NRL Grand Final. With a highest attendance of 107,999 and an average attendance of around 80,000, it provides the perfect backdrop for this epic showdown. The stadium's impressive capacity and state-of-the-art facilities ensure that every Grand Final is a memorable experience for players and fans alike.

The NRL Grand Final is the ultimate celebration of rugby league, a showcase of the sport's finest talent, and a testament to the dedication and passion of everyone involved. From the opening ceremony to the final presentation, every moment is designed to create an unforgettable experience. The Grand Final is not just the end of the season; it's the culmination of a journey, a moment of triumph that will be remembered for years to come.

The NRL Grand Final is more than just the culmination of a rugby league season; it is an event that embodies the spirit and passion of the sport. Every year, fans from all over Australia and beyond eagerly await this marquee event, which has become a tradition deeply embedded in the nation's sporting culture. The grandeur and excitement that surround the Grand Final are unparalleled, making it a significant highlight in the Australian sporting calendar.

The evolution of the Grand Final, from its traditional afternoon time slot to the prime-time evening spectacle, reflects the changing dynamics and increasing popularity of the event. This shift has allowed for a broader audience to experience the magic of the Grand Final, whether they are watching from the stands at Stadium Australia or from their homes across the globe. The blend of entertainment, tradition, and high-stakes competition creates an atmosphere that is both electric and unforgettable.

Stadium Australia, with its impressive capacity and modern facilities, provides the perfect stage for this grand event. The record attendance of 107,999 in 1999 set the standard for what has become an annual celebration of rugby league. The stadium's ability to host such a large number of fans adds to the spectacle, ensuring that each Grand Final is a memorable experience for everyone involved. The return of the Grand Final to Sydney year after year reaffirms the city's position as the heart of Australian rugby league.

The NRL Grand Final Breakfast is another cherished tradition that adds to the excitement of Grand Final week. This event, attended by the competing teams and numerous guests, is broadcast live, allowing fans to share in the anticipation and build-up to the big game. It is a time for reflection, celebration, and recognition of the hard work and dedication that have brought the teams to this point.

The pre-game ceremonies, including the delivery of the NRL trophy by an Australian Army helicopter and performances by renowned musical acts, enhance the sense of occasion. These elements contribute to the unique atmosphere of the Grand Final, setting it apart from regular season matches and other sporting events. The combination of tradition and modern spectacle ensures that each Grand Final is a special event that resonates with fans of all ages.

The presentation ceremony at the conclusion of the Grand Final is a moment of triumph and celebration. The awarding of premiership rings to the winning team, the presentation of the Clive Churchill Medal to the man-of-the-match, and the handing over of the trophy by the Prime Minister all contribute to the sense of achievement and recognition for the victors. These traditions honor the skill, determination, and teamwork that are required to reach the pinnacle of the sport.

The securing of the Grand Final at Stadium Australia until 2022 for $45 million underscores the importance of this event not only to the sport of rugby league but also to the cultural and economic landscape of New South Wales. This investment ensures that Sydney remains the focal point for the Grand Final, continuing to draw fans and generate excitement year after year.

The NRL Grand Final is a testament to the enduring appeal of rugby league. It brings together fans, players, and communities in a celebration of the sport they love. The memories created at each Grand Final, from thrilling matches to unforgettable performances, contribute to the rich tapestry of rugby league history. The event stands as a symbol of excellence, passion, and the unifying power of sport.

The NRL Grand Final is much more than a game; it is an iconic event that captures the hearts and minds of millions. It showcases the very best of rugby league, celebrating the achievements of the season while providing a platform for extraordinary performances and unforgettable moments. The traditions, the spectacle, and the sheer excitement of the Grand Final ensure that it remains a highlight of the sporting year, a true festival of rugby league that will continue to inspire and entertain for generations to come.

Chapter 37: Post-Season Internationals

Once the NRL premiership concludes, the rugby league season doesn't end there. For many players, the focus shifts to representing their countries in various international competitions. These post-season internationals are a crucial part of the rugby league calendar, providing thrilling matches and showcasing the sport's global reach.

One of the most significant international events is the Rugby League World Cup, held every four years. This tournament brings together teams from around the world to compete for the ultimate prize in rugby league. It features intense competition and showcases the skills and talents of players on an international stage. The World Cup is a highlight for fans and players alike, offering a unique opportunity to see the best teams from different nations go head-to-head.

Another important international competition is the Four Nations tournament. This event features Australia, New Zealand, England, and an additional qualifier. The Four Nations provides high-quality matches and fierce rivalries, making it a must-watch for rugby league enthusiasts. The inclusion of a fourth team adds an element of unpredictability and excitement, as emerging nations get the chance to compete against the sport's powerhouses.

The Prime Minister's XIII match is an annual fixture played in Papua New Guinea. This match typically sees an Australian team, often composed of NRL stars, take on the Papua New Guinea national team. It's a unique event that not only promotes rugby league in Papua New Guinea but also fosters goodwill and development within the sport. The passionate local crowds make this match a vibrant and memorable occasion.

In addition to the traditional formats, the Rugby League World Cup 9s offers a fast-paced and exhilarating version of the game. This tournament features teams from around the world competing in a shortened format that emphasizes speed, skill, and excitement. The World Cup 9s is a relatively new addition to the rugby league calendar but has quickly gained popularity for its entertaining style and the opportunity it provides for smaller nations to compete on a global stage.

Test matches between Australia and New Zealand are always highly anticipated. These two nations have a storied rivalry in rugby league, and their clashes are characterized by intense competition and high-quality play. Post-season test matches allow players from both countries to represent their national teams and continue their rivalry beyond the domestic season.

The Rugby League Pacific Championship is another important event in the post-season calendar. This tournament features teams from Pacific Island nations such as Fiji, Samoa, Tonga, and Papua New Guinea. It highlights the talent and passion for rugby league in the Pacific region and provides valuable international experience for the participating teams. The Pacific Championship is a celebration of the sport's growth and popularity in this part of the world.

Tours to European rugby league countries are also a part of the post-season schedule. These tours allow teams from Australia and New Zealand to compete against European national teams, promoting rugby league in Europe and providing competitive matches for both sides. Hosting tours of European rugby league national teams in Australia or New Zealand further strengthens the global ties within the sport.

Post-season internationals are a vital and exciting part of the rugby league calendar. They offer players the chance to represent their countries and fans the opportunity to see high-quality international matches. Whether it's the World Cup, the Four Nations, the Prime Minister's XIII match, the World Cup 9s, test matches between Australia and New Zealand, the Pacific Championship, or tours to and from Europe, these events showcase the best of rugby league on a global stage. They highlight the sport's growth, foster international rivalries, and provide unforgettable moments for players and fans alike. The post-season internationals ensure that the excitement and passion of rugby league continue long after the NRL premiership has concluded.

The post-season internationals in rugby league offer a remarkable extension to the sport's competitive calendar, bringing with them a unique blend of cultural exchange, intense rivalry, and global outreach. These events ensure that the excitement of rugby league does not end with the NRL premiership but instead continues to captivate audiences worldwide, fostering a sense of global community and shared passion for the game.

The Rugby League World Cup stands as the pinnacle of international competition, embodying the sport's rich history and its future aspirations. Held every four years, it gathers the best teams from around the globe, creating a stage where emerging talents can shine and established stars can affirm their legacies. The World Cup not only celebrates athletic excellence but also highlights the sport's ability to bring together diverse cultures and nations under a common banner.

The Four Nations tournament further enhances the international rugby league scene by featuring Australia, New Zealand, England, and a qualifier, ensuring high-stakes matches that draw significant attention. This competition is a testament to the sport's competitive spirit, showcasing thrilling games that resonate with fans and players alike. The inclusion of a fourth team adds an element of unpredictability, making each tournament unique and eagerly anticipated.

The Prime Minister's XIII match in Papua New Guinea is more than just a game; it's a symbol of rugby league's role in community building and international relations. This annual fixture, played with fervor and passion, underscores the sport's influence in fostering goodwill and development in regions where rugby league is not just a game but a way of life. The electrifying atmosphere and the engagement of local communities make this match a highlight of the post-season.

The Rugby League World Cup 9s brings a fresh and exhilarating dimension to the sport. Its fast-paced, high-energy format is designed to captivate both traditional fans and new audiences. By emphasizing speed and skill, the World Cup 9s showcases a different facet of rugby league, making it an appealing addition to the international calendar and providing smaller nations a platform to compete and shine on a global stage.

Test matches between Australia and New Zealand remain a cornerstone of the international rugby league, with their historic rivalry adding layers of drama and intensity to every encounter. These matches are not only about national pride but also about showcasing the highest level of rugby league. The fierce competition and the storied history between these two nations ensure that their clashes are always must-watch events, drawing viewers from across the world.

The Rugby League Pacific Championship celebrates the sport's growth in the Pacific region, highlighting the incredible talent and passion found in nations such as Fiji, Samoa, Tonga, and Papua New Guinea. This championship is a testament to the sport's expanding footprint, providing valuable competitive experience for Pacific teams and promoting rugby league's inclusivity and diversity.

Tours to European rugby league countries, as well as hosting European teams in Australia or New Zealand, play a crucial role in promoting the sport's global reach. These tours offer invaluable opportunities for players to experience different styles of play and for fans to witness the sport's international appeal. They foster cultural exchange and strengthen the bonds within the rugby league community, demonstrating the sport's ability to transcend geographical boundaries.

In essence, the post-season internationals encapsulate the spirit of rugby league—competitive, inclusive, and globally connected. They provide a platform for players to achieve international glory, for fans to experience world-class rugby league, and for the sport to grow and thrive on a global scale. These events ensure that the excitement of rugby league extends beyond the domestic season, keeping the passion for the sport alive year-round and contributing to its enduring legacy. Through these international competitions, rugby league continues to inspire, unite, and entertain, solidifying its place as a beloved global sport.

Part Six: The Warriors on the Field

Chapter 38: The Icons of Rugby League

National Rugby League (NRL) footballers are among Australasia's most famous athletes, commanding multimillion-dollar playing contracts and sponsorship deals. Each club in the NRL has a "top squad" of twenty-five players who are signed under a salary cap. For the most part, the players who play in NRL matches are sourced from these top squads. During a season, the need may arise for a club to use players outside these 25, in which case players are usually sourced from the club's corresponding NRL Under-20s team or a feeder club in the New South Wales Cup or Queensland Cup.

The salary cap ensures that all teams have an equal chance to compete by limiting the total amount a club can spend on player salaries. This system helps maintain a competitive balance within the league. Each club's top squad comprises a mix of seasoned veterans and promising young talents. The journey to becoming an NRL player often begins at a young age, with many players starting in junior rugby league programs and progressing through the ranks.

Training and preparation are key aspects of an NRL player's life. The pre-season is an intense period where players undergo rigorous physical conditioning, skills training, and team-building exercises. This preparation is crucial for the grueling season ahead, which demands peak physical fitness and mental resilience. Players must also adhere to strict dietary and lifestyle regimens to maintain their performance levels throughout the season.

In addition to their on-field responsibilities, NRL players are often involved in community and charity work. Many players take part in programs aimed at promoting healthy lifestyles, supporting underprivileged communities, and raising awareness for various social causes. This community engagement helps to strengthen the bond between the players and their fans, fostering a sense of loyalty and support.

The role of an NRL player extends beyond just playing the game. They are often seen as role models and ambassadors for the sport. Their conduct both on and off the field can significantly impact their careers and the reputation of their clubs. The NRL has strict codes of conduct and disciplinary measures to ensure players maintain high standards of behavior.

Player development is an ongoing process, with clubs investing heavily in coaching and support staff to help players reach their full potential. This includes not only physical training but also psychological support, career advice, and educational opportunities. Many players pursue further education or vocational training to prepare for life after rugby league, understanding the importance of having a career beyond their playing days.

Injuries are an unfortunate but inevitable part of a rugby league player's career. The physical nature of the sport means that players are at constant risk of injury. Clubs have dedicated medical and physiotherapy teams to manage player health and recovery. Injury management is critical to a player's longevity in the sport, with many clubs employing cutting-edge techniques and technologies to aid in rehabilitation.

The transition from player to retiree can be challenging. Many former players stay involved in the sport through coaching, commentary, or administrative roles. The NRL and its clubs provide support programs to help players transition to life after rugby league, ensuring they have the skills and resources needed to succeed in their post-playing careers.

NRL players are more than just athletes; they are influential figures in their communities, ambassadors for the sport, and role models for aspiring young players. Their journey from junior leagues to the professional stage is marked by dedication, hard work, and a passion for the game. The structures in place within the NRL, from the salary cap to player development programs, ensure that the league remains competitive and that its players are supported both on and off the field.

The chapter on NRL players highlights the multifaceted lives of these athletes, showing that their impact goes far beyond the field. NRL footballers are not only recognized for their athletic prowess but also for their significant roles as public figures and community leaders. The strict salary cap system ensures a level playing field, making the competition fair and exciting for fans. This system also requires clubs to be strategic in managing their squads, balancing the inclusion of experienced players with the development of emerging talents.

Training and preparation are essential elements of an NRL player's career. The rigorous pre-season workouts and continuous skill development are crucial for maintaining high performance levels throughout the season. Players' commitment to their physical conditioning, coupled with their dedication to strict dietary and lifestyle practices, showcases the discipline required to compete at the highest level. This dedication is evident in their resilience and ability to perform under pressure week after week.

Off the field, NRL players contribute significantly to their communities. Their involvement in charitable activities and social causes demonstrates their commitment to giving back and using their platform for good. This connection with the community helps build a loyal fan base and strengthens the relationship between players and supporters. The positive influence of these athletes extends beyond the game, inspiring many and contributing to various societal improvements.

Conduct and behavior are critical aspects of an NRL player's career. The league's strict codes of conduct ensure that players maintain professionalism, both on and off the field. This professionalism is crucial in shaping the public's perception of the sport and maintaining the integrity of the league. Players understand that their actions can have far-reaching consequences, and many take their roles as role models very seriously.

The support structures within the NRL are designed to help players achieve their best. The investment in coaching, psychological support, and career advice reflects the comprehensive approach to player development. These programs ensure that players are well-rounded individuals, prepared for both the demands of their sport and life after their playing careers. The focus on education and career training underscores the importance of preparing for a future beyond rugby league.

Injuries are a reality of professional sports, and the NRL's approach to injury management is critical for player longevity. The advanced medical and rehabilitation support available to players ensures that they receive the best care possible, allowing them to recover and return to the field. This focus on health and recovery is vital in a sport as physically demanding as rugby league, where the risk of injury is ever-present.

The transition from playing to retirement can be challenging, but the NRL provides support to help players navigate this phase. Many former players stay connected to the sport through various roles, contributing their knowledge and experience to the next generation. The support programs offered by the league ensure that players have the resources and skills needed to succeed in their post-playing careers, emphasizing the league's commitment to its athletes' long-term well-being.

NRL players are extraordinary individuals who excel not only in their sport but also in their contributions to society. Their journey from junior leagues to professional rugby showcases dedication, hard work, and a passion for the game. The comprehensive support systems within the NRL ensure that players are well-prepared for the challenges they face, both during and after their playing careers. The chapter underscores the importance of these athletes as role models, community leaders, and ambassadors for the sport, highlighting the enduring impact of their contributions on and off the field.

Chapter 39: The Rise of Polynesian Influence in the NRL

In recent years, the National Rugby League (NRL) has seen a significant rise in the number of Polynesian players, making a powerful impact on the sport. This shift in player demographics has not only influenced the style of play but has also reshaped the cultural landscape of the league. The increase in Polynesian players reflects broader social changes and the growing presence of Pacific Island communities in Australia and New Zealand. The 2011 season marked a milestone, with 35% of NRL players and over 45% of NRL Under-20s players being of Polynesian descent. This trend has only continued to grow, solidifying the role of Polynesian athletes in the sport.

The physicality and unique playing style brought by Polynesian players have become a defining feature of modern NRL games. Known for their strength, speed, and agility, these players have introduced a new level of intensity to the sport. Their influence is particularly evident in the forward pack, where their power and athleticism dominate the field. This has led to changes in team strategies, with coaches adapting their game plans to leverage the strengths of their Polynesian players. The dynamic and explosive style of play associated with Polynesian athletes has added excitement and unpredictability to NRL matches, attracting fans and contributing to the league's growing popularity.

The rise of Polynesian players in the NRL has also brought about a greater cultural diversity within the league. These players have introduced their rich traditions, values, and customs to the sport, creating a more inclusive and vibrant environment. Cultural practices, such as pre-game rituals and the celebration of important milestones, have become more visible and respected within the league. The presence of Polynesian players has fostered a sense of community and brotherhood among teams, with players often drawing strength from their shared cultural heritage. This cultural diversity has enhanced the league's appeal, resonating with a broader audience and encouraging the participation of young athletes from similar backgrounds.

However, the rise of Polynesian players has also led to discussions about the declining presence of Indigenous players in the NRL. In the 1990s, Indigenous players made up 21% of the league, but by the 2009 season, this figure had dropped to 11%. Some have suggested that the increase in Polynesian players has contributed to this decline, as the competition for spots in NRL teams has intensified. The decline in Indigenous representation has sparked conversations about the need for targeted programs to support and develop Indigenous talent. The NRL has recognized this issue and has implemented initiatives aimed at encouraging greater participation and providing pathways for Indigenous athletes to succeed in the sport.

Despite these challenges, the NRL continues to celebrate the contributions of both Polynesian and Indigenous players. Events like the Indigenous Round and the Pacific Tests highlight the rich cultural diversity within the league and honor the unique contributions of these communities. These events serve as a reminder of the importance of inclusivity and respect for all cultures within the sport. They also provide a platform for players to showcase their heritage and connect with fans on a deeper level, reinforcing the league's commitment to diversity.

The impact of Polynesian players extends beyond the field, with many becoming influential figures in their communities. They serve as role models and ambassadors for the sport, inspiring young athletes to pursue their dreams and giving back through various charitable initiatives. The success of Polynesian players in the NRL has also had a ripple effect, encouraging greater participation in rugby league in Pacific Island nations. This has led to the growth of the sport in these regions and increased the level of competition in international rugby league.

The rise of Polynesian players in the NRL has brought about significant changes to the league, both on and off the field. Their influence has transformed the style of play, introduced greater cultural diversity, and created new opportunities for young athletes. While the decline in Indigenous players remains a concern, the NRL's commitment to inclusivity and support for all players ensures that the league remains a place where talent from all backgrounds can thrive. The continued success of Polynesian players is a testament to their hard work, dedication, and passion for the sport, and their legacy will undoubtedly continue to shape the future of the NRL for years to come.

The increasing presence of Polynesian players in the NRL represents more than just a shift in the sport's demographics; it highlights the evolving identity of rugby league in Australasia. The impact of these players extends beyond their physical prowess on the field—they bring a unique blend of culture, spirit, and resilience that has significantly enriched the league. Their influence is felt in every aspect of the game, from the way teams approach their strategies to the cultural dynamics within locker rooms. This transformation has not only brought a fresh and exciting energy to the NRL but has also broadened the league's appeal to a more diverse audience.

However, the rise of Polynesian players has also brought about complex challenges, particularly concerning the representation of Indigenous players. As the competition for spots in NRL teams intensifies, the decline in Indigenous players has raised important questions about equity and opportunity within the sport. The NRL's efforts to address this issue through targeted programs and initiatives reflect a commitment to fostering inclusivity and ensuring that the league remains a platform where all talented athletes can thrive. This balance between celebrating the rise of Polynesian players and addressing the concerns around Indigenous representation is crucial for the future of the sport.

The cultural contributions of Polynesian players have added a new dimension to the NRL, making the league a vibrant and culturally rich environment. These players have brought their traditions and values into the spotlight, creating a sense of unity and respect within teams. The visibility of Polynesian culture in the league has also provided an important connection for fans from similar backgrounds, further enhancing the NRL's role as a community-focused sport. The recognition and celebration of this cultural diversity through events and rituals are not just about acknowledging the past but also about paving the way for a more inclusive future.

While the success of Polynesian players in the NRL is commendable, it also underscores the importance of providing opportunities for all players, regardless of their background. The league's ongoing efforts to support Indigenous players and other underrepresented groups are vital to maintaining a fair and competitive environment. The stories of these players, their journeys, and their achievements serve as powerful reminders of what can be accomplished when talent is nurtured and given the opportunity to flourish. Their presence in the NRL is a testament to the league's growing inclusivity and the broader social changes occurring in Australasia.

The rise of Polynesian players has also had a profound impact on the sport globally. Their success in the NRL has inspired young athletes in Pacific Island nations, encouraging greater participation and investment in rugby league in these regions. This has contributed to the sport's growth and the emergence of new talent on the international stage. The ripple effect of their influence is a powerful example of how the NRL can play a role in shaping the future of rugby league worldwide. The legacy of these players will likely continue to influence the sport for generations to come, as they inspire the next wave of talent from both Polynesian and Indigenous backgrounds.

The evolution of the NRL with the rise of Polynesian players is a story of cultural enrichment, increased competition, and the ongoing challenge of inclusivity. The league's response to these changes, through its commitment to diversity and support for all players, will define its future. The contributions of Polynesian players are not just a chapter in the NRL's history; they are an integral part of its identity, shaping the sport in ways that go beyond the scoreboard. As the NRL moves forward, the lessons learned from this period will be essential in ensuring that the league remains a place where every player, regardless of background, can achieve greatness.

Chapter 40: Trailblazers and Champions: The Legacy of Indigenous Players in the NRL

The story of Indigenous Australians in rugby league is one of immense pride, resilience, and extraordinary achievement. George Green, the first Indigenous player to compete in the New South Wales Rugby League (NSWRL), broke barriers when he debuted in 1909. His pioneering journey paved the way for countless Indigenous players to follow, each contributing to the rich history of the sport. These athletes have not only excelled on the field but have also become symbols of inspiration and empowerment for Indigenous communities across Australia.

Arthur Beetson stands as one of the most iconic figures in Australian sports history. In 1973, he became the first Aboriginal person to captain an Australian national team in any sport, a milestone that transcended rugby league and made a significant impact on the nation's consciousness. Beetson's leadership, skill, and passion for the game set a standard that many Indigenous players aspired to emulate. His legacy is felt to this day, with the Arthur Beetson Medal being awarded to the best Indigenous player in the NRL, a fitting tribute to a trailblazer who changed the game forever.

The contributions of Indigenous players to the NRL are not limited to individual achievements. The presence of Indigenous athletes has brought a unique cultural element to the sport, enriching the league with traditions, stories, and values that resonate deeply within the broader Australian society. These players have often been at the forefront of initiatives promoting cultural awareness and reconciliation, using their platform to advocate for social justice and equality. The annual Indigenous Round in the NRL is a testament to this influence, celebrating the contributions of Indigenous players and culture to the game.

Johnathan Thurston and Greg Inglis are two of the most celebrated Indigenous players in recent NRL history. Thurston, known for his leadership and clutch performances, and Inglis, renowned for his power and skill, have left indelible marks on the sport. Both players have been instrumental in their teams' successes and have earned numerous accolades, including representing Australia in international competitions. Their careers are shining examples of what can be achieved through talent, hard work, and dedication, and they serve as role models for young Indigenous athletes aspiring to reach the highest levels of rugby league.

Despite the significant representation of Indigenous players in the NRL, the journey has not been without its challenges. Discrimination, both overt and subtle, has been a reality for many Indigenous athletes throughout the history of the sport. However, the resilience and determination of these players to succeed, regardless of the obstacles, have been key in breaking down barriers and fostering a more inclusive environment within the league. The progress made in recent years is a reflection of the growing recognition of the importance of diversity and inclusion in sports.

The statistics reveal the remarkable impact of Indigenous players in the NRL. With Indigenous Australians making up 35% of the roster for the Kangaroos and a significant percentage of players in the State of Origin series, their influence is undeniable. These figures are even more striking when compared to the fact that only 2.3% of the Australian population identified as Indigenous in the 2006 census. This disproportionate representation highlights the immense talent and contribution of Indigenous players to the sport, underscoring the NRL's role as a platform for showcasing the best of Indigenous athleticism.

Beyond the numbers, the stories of these players carry a deeper significance. They reflect the power of sport to bring people together, to bridge cultural divides, and to inspire future generations. The success of Indigenous players in the NRL is not just a testament to their skill and dedication, but also a reflection of the strength and vitality of Indigenous culture. These athletes have become ambassadors for their communities, embodying the spirit of their ancestors while forging new paths for those who will follow in their footsteps.

As the NRL continues to evolve, the legacy of Indigenous players will remain a cornerstone of the sport's history. Their contributions have shaped the game in profound ways, from the playing field to the broader cultural landscape. The ongoing efforts to support and celebrate Indigenous players ensure that their impact will be felt for years to come, inspiring future generations of athletes and reminding us all of the enduring power of rugby league as a force for positive change.

The journey of Indigenous players in the NRL is a powerful narrative of resilience, talent, and cultural pride that has profoundly shaped the landscape of rugby league. From George Green's pioneering debut in 1909 to the celebrated careers of legends like Arthur Beetson, Johnathan Thurston, and Greg Inglis, Indigenous athletes have not only excelled on the field but have also become symbols of inspiration for their communities and beyond. Their stories reflect the transformative power of sport, offering a testament to how rugby league has provided a platform for Indigenous players to showcase their immense skills, while also advocating for broader social justice and cultural recognition.

The influence of Indigenous players goes beyond their athletic achievements. Through their presence and success, they have brought attention to important issues affecting Indigenous communities, helping to foster greater understanding and respect within the sport and wider society. The annual Indigenous Round in the NRL is a significant example of this impact, serving as a celebration of the cultural heritage that these players bring to the game. This event highlights the importance of acknowledging and honoring the contributions of Indigenous athletes, who have not only entertained but also educated and united fans from all backgrounds.

Despite the undeniable successes, the path has not been easy for many Indigenous players. They have had to overcome numerous challenges, including discrimination and the pressure of being role models in a society that has not always been welcoming or inclusive. Yet, their determination to excel and their commitment to their communities have made them powerful advocates for change. Their stories are a reminder of the importance of perseverance, and they continue to inspire new generations of players who look up to them as heroes both on and off the field.

The statistical representation of Indigenous players in the NRL is remarkable, especially considering their relatively small percentage of the overall Australian population. This overrepresentation in the sport speaks volumes about the natural talent, passion, and dedication found within Indigenous communities. It also highlights the NRL's role in providing opportunities for these players to reach the highest levels of competition, proving that rugby league is not just a game, but a vehicle for personal and community empowerment.

As the NRL moves forward, the legacy of Indigenous players will remain a vital part of its history and future. Their contributions have not only shaped the game itself but have also influenced the cultural and social fabric of rugby league. These players have shown that the sport can be a powerful force for positive change, bringing people together and promoting values of equality, respect, and unity. Their impact will be felt for generations to come, as they continue to inspire young athletes to dream big and strive for greatness.

The story of Indigenous players in the NRL is one of triumph, not just in terms of victories on the field, but in the broader context of their role in society. They have helped to break down barriers, challenge stereotypes, and promote a more inclusive and understanding community. Through their hard work and dedication, they have earned their place among the greatest in the sport, and their legacy will endure as a beacon of hope and inspiration for all who follow in their footsteps.

In reflecting on the achievements of Indigenous players, it is clear that they have enriched the NRL in countless ways. Their contributions have been instrumental in making rugby league not just a sport, but a celebration of cultural diversity and human potential. As we look to the future, the continued recognition and support of Indigenous players will be essential in ensuring that rugby league remains a sport that values and celebrates the contributions of all its players, regardless of their background.

The journey of Indigenous players in the NRL is far from over. As the sport continues to evolve, so too will the role of these athletes in shaping its future. Their stories will continue to be told, their achievements celebrated, and their legacy honored, ensuring that the rich history of Indigenous participation in rugby league remains an integral part of the game for generations to come.

Chapter 41: Celebrating Indigenous Heritage in the NRL

The strong connection between Indigenous Australians and rugby league is celebrated in many ways, but one of the most significant is the annual All Stars match. This game, held during the NRL preseason, brings together a team of Indigenous Australian players to compete against a team made up of non-Indigenous players, selected through public voting. The All Stars match is more than just a game; it's a powerful symbol of the respect and recognition that the NRL has for the contributions of Indigenous players to the sport. It also serves as an opportunity to highlight and honor the rich cultural heritage that these players bring to the game.

The concept of the All Stars match was pioneered by former player Preston Campbell, who saw the potential of the game to unite people and celebrate Indigenous culture. The match has become a much-anticipated event in the NRL calendar, drawing attention from fans across Australia and beyond. The excitement and pride that surround the game are palpable, and it provides a platform for Indigenous players to showcase their talents while also representing their communities. The game is not only a celebration of rugby league but also a celebration of identity, culture, and the shared history between Indigenous Australians and the sport.

One of the unique aspects of the All Stars match is the Preston Campbell Medal, awarded to the man of the match. This medal, named after the game's founder, is a prestigious honor that carries deep significance for the recipient. It represents not just excellence on the field, but also a commitment to the values of respect, unity, and cultural pride that the All Stars match embodies. For the players, winning this medal is a moment of great personal and cultural pride, and it serves as a reminder of the important role that Indigenous players play in the NRL.

In addition to the All Stars match, the Indigenous Leadership Group is another initiative that has had a profound impact on the game. This group, consisting of the elite Indigenous players in the NRL, plays a crucial role in promoting Indigenous culture and supporting younger players as they navigate their careers in the sport. The Leadership Group hosts regular multi-day camps where all Indigenous NRL players are invited to learn more about their culture, connect with their heritage, and support one another. These camps are not just about rugby league; they are about building a strong sense of community and identity among the players.

The formation of the Indigenous Leadership Group was another idea championed by Preston Campbell, who recognized the need for a platform where Indigenous players could come together, share their experiences, and support each other. The group has become an integral part of the NRL, helping to ensure that Indigenous players feel valued and supported both on and off the field. The camps organized by the group provide a safe space for players to discuss the challenges they face, celebrate their successes, and learn more about their cultural roots.

Through the All Stars match and the Indigenous Leadership Group, the NRL has made significant strides in recognizing and celebrating the contributions of Indigenous players. These initiatives have helped to foster a greater understanding and appreciation of Indigenous culture within the sport and have provided important opportunities for Indigenous players to connect with their heritage. The NRL's commitment to these programs reflects its broader commitment to inclusivity and respect for all players, regardless of their background.

The impact of the All Stars match and the Indigenous Leadership Group extends beyond the rugby league field. These initiatives have helped to raise awareness of Indigenous culture among the wider public and have provided a platform for important conversations about the role of sport in promoting social justice and cultural recognition. The NRL's support for these programs demonstrates the power of sport to bring people together and to promote values of respect, unity, and understanding.

As the NRL continues to evolve, the All Stars match and the Indigenous Leadership Group will remain vital components of the league's efforts to celebrate and support its Indigenous players. These initiatives have not only enriched the game of rugby league but have also had a lasting impact on the broader community. Through these programs, the NRL has shown that it is possible to honor the past, celebrate the present, and build a future where all players, regardless of their background, are valued and respected for their contributions to the sport.

The initiatives like the All Stars match and the Indigenous Leadership Group represent more than just events or gatherings within the NRL—they symbolize a deep and ongoing commitment to honoring the cultural heritage and contributions of Indigenous Australians to the sport. These efforts reflect a broader movement within the NRL to embrace diversity, inclusivity, and respect for all players, regardless of their background. By creating spaces where Indigenous players can celebrate their identity and connect with their culture, the NRL not only enriches the lives of these athletes but also educates and inspires the broader rugby league community.

The significance of the All Stars match goes beyond the game itself. It stands as a powerful reminder of the impact that sport can have in bridging cultural divides and fostering a sense of unity among people from different backgrounds. The match serves as a celebration of the unique talents and perspectives that Indigenous players bring to the field, and it allows fans to engage with and appreciate the rich cultural traditions that are interwoven with the sport. Through this annual event, the NRL has successfully created a platform where cultural pride and athletic excellence go hand in hand.

The Indigenous Leadership Group further strengthens this connection by providing ongoing support and mentorship to Indigenous players throughout their careers. By fostering a sense of community and offering opportunities for personal and cultural growth, the Leadership Group plays a crucial role in helping players navigate the challenges of professional sport while staying connected to their roots. The camps and gatherings organized by the group are not just about improving performance on the field—they are about building resilience, fostering a strong sense of identity, and ensuring that Indigenous players have the support they need to succeed both in their careers and in life.

These initiatives also have a ripple effect beyond the immediate rugby league community. They challenge stereotypes, promote understanding, and encourage a greater appreciation for the diversity that exists within the sport. By celebrating Indigenous culture through high-profile events like the All Stars match, the NRL sends a powerful message about the importance of inclusivity and respect for all players. This, in turn, helps to create a more welcoming and supportive environment for future generations of athletes.

The ongoing success of these programs demonstrates the NRL's commitment to making a positive impact both on and off the field. By prioritizing cultural awareness and providing platforms for Indigenous players to shine, the league is helping to build a stronger, more inclusive community. The lessons learned and the connections made through these initiatives will have a lasting impact, not just on the players involved but on the broader rugby league community and Australian society as a whole.

As the NRL continues to evolve, it will be crucial to maintain and expand these efforts to ensure that the sport remains a place where all players can thrive, regardless of their background. The achievements of the All Stars match and the Indigenous Leadership Group provide a solid foundation upon which future initiatives can be built. By continuing to celebrate diversity and promote inclusivity, the NRL can ensure that the sport remains a powerful force for good in the lives of its players and fans.

In the end, the success of these programs highlights the importance of collaboration, respect, and understanding in creating a more inclusive and supportive environment within the NRL. The league's commitment to these values is not just about enhancing the game—it's about making a meaningful contribution to society as a whole. As the NRL moves forward, the legacy of the All Stars match and the Indigenous Leadership Group will continue to inspire and guide the league's efforts to promote cultural pride, unity, and respect for all players.

Chapter 42: The Legacy of Preston Campbell and the All Stars Match

Preston Campbell is more than just a former rugby league player—he is a visionary who has left a lasting impact on the sport through his ideas and initiatives. One of his most significant contributions is the creation of the All Stars match, a game that celebrates the rich cultural heritage of Indigenous Australians and promotes unity within the rugby league community. The All Stars match, first held in 2010, quickly became a highlight of the NRL calendar, bringing together the best Indigenous players to face off against a team of non-Indigenous stars selected by public vote.

The All Stars match is more than just a game; it is a celebration of culture, identity, and pride. It gives Indigenous players a unique platform to showcase their talents while honoring their heritage. For many players, participating in the All Stars match is a deeply personal and meaningful experience. It allows them to connect with their roots, celebrate their culture, and inspire the next generation of Indigenous athletes. The match also serves as a powerful reminder to the broader rugby league community of the important contributions Indigenous players have made to the sport over the years.

One of the most prestigious awards in the All Stars match is the Preston Campbell Medal, named after the man who made the game possible. This medal is awarded to the player judged to be the best on the field, and it carries a special significance because it represents not just individual excellence but also the spirit of the game and the values that Campbell sought to promote. Winning the Preston Campbell Medal is an honor that every player in the All Stars match strives for, and it serves as a reminder of the enduring legacy of Campbell's vision.

Beyond the All Stars match, Preston Campbell also played a key role in establishing the Indigenous Leadership Group, a collective of the game's elite Indigenous players. The Leadership Group is dedicated to promoting and preserving Indigenous culture within the NRL, and it organizes regular camps where Indigenous players come together to learn more about their heritage, share experiences, and support one another. These camps are vital for building a sense of community among Indigenous players and ensuring that they have the resources and support they need to succeed in their careers.

The work of the Indigenous Leadership Group extends beyond the players themselves. It also aims to educate the wider rugby league community about Indigenous culture and history, fostering greater understanding and respect for the contributions of Indigenous people to the sport. Through its efforts, the Leadership Group has helped to create a more inclusive and culturally aware environment within the NRL, benefiting players, fans, and the sport as a whole.

Preston Campbell's initiatives have had a profound impact on the NRL, and their influence continues to grow with each passing year. The All Stars match and the Indigenous Leadership Group have become integral parts of the rugby league landscape, promoting unity, respect, and cultural pride. They have also helped to raise the profile of Indigenous players within the sport, ensuring that their contributions are recognized and celebrated.

The success of these initiatives highlights the power of sport to bring people together and create positive change. Through the All Stars match and the Indigenous Leadership Group, Preston Campbell has shown that rugby league can be a force for good, promoting values of inclusivity, respect, and cultural pride. His vision has not only enriched the lives of Indigenous players but has also made the sport of rugby league stronger and more inclusive.

As the NRL continues to evolve, the legacy of Preston Campbell and his initiatives will remain a guiding force. The All Stars match and the Indigenous Leadership Group are shining examples of what can be achieved when players, clubs, and the league come together to promote unity and respect. These initiatives will continue to inspire future generations of players and fans, ensuring that the values of inclusivity and cultural pride remain at the heart of rugby league for years to come.

The initiatives pioneered by Preston Campbell have left an indelible mark on the NRL and the broader rugby league community. The All Stars match, with its unique focus on celebrating Indigenous culture, has become more than just an annual event; it is a powerful symbol of unity, respect, and pride. Through this game, Indigenous players are given a platform to honor their heritage, showcase their skills, and inspire others. The match also serves as a reminder of the significant contributions Indigenous athletes have made to the sport, helping to foster greater recognition and appreciation for their talents and cultural background.

The impact of the Indigenous Leadership Group, also founded by Campbell, extends far beyond the rugby field. This group has become a cornerstone of support and education for Indigenous players, providing them with opportunities to connect with their culture, learn from one another, and build a strong sense of community. The camps organized by the Leadership Group play a crucial role in preserving Indigenous traditions and ensuring that these players can navigate the challenges of professional sports while staying true to their roots.

Moreover, the Leadership Group's efforts to educate the wider rugby league community about Indigenous culture have had a profound effect on the sport. By promoting understanding and respect, the group has helped to create a more inclusive environment within the NRL, where players from all backgrounds can thrive. This cultural awareness not only benefits Indigenous players but also enriches the sport as a whole, making it more diverse and welcoming for everyone involved.

Preston Campbell's vision and dedication have shown that rugby league can be a powerful tool for positive change. The All Stars match and the Indigenous Leadership Group have not only highlighted the importance of cultural pride and inclusivity but have also set a standard for how the sport can continue to evolve in a way that honors its diverse player base. These initiatives have opened doors for Indigenous players and have ensured that their voices and contributions are recognized and celebrated.

As the NRL moves forward, the legacy of Preston Campbell will continue to influence the direction of the sport. His commitment to promoting Indigenous culture and supporting players through the Leadership Group has laid the groundwork for future generations to build upon. The values of unity, respect, and cultural pride that he championed will remain integral to the identity of rugby league, ensuring that the sport continues to grow in a way that reflects the diversity and richness of its players.

In the years to come, the impact of the All Stars match and the Indigenous Leadership Group will be felt not only within the NRL but across the entire rugby league community. These initiatives have set a powerful example of how sports can be a force for good, bringing people together and fostering a sense of belonging and mutual respect. Preston Campbell's legacy is a testament to the power of vision and leadership, and his contributions will be remembered as a turning point in the history of rugby league.

Chapter 43: The Evolution of the Salary Cap in the NRL

The introduction of the salary cap in 1990 to the New South Wales Rugby League (NSWRL) was a pivotal moment in the sport's history. Designed to level the playing field among teams in the Winfield Cup, the cap was a response to the growing financial disparity between clubs. Wealthier teams had begun to dominate the competition by attracting top-tier talent with lucrative contracts, leaving smaller clubs struggling to compete. The salary cap aimed to address this imbalance by setting a limit on the total amount each club could spend on player salaries, ensuring that success on the field was determined more by skill and strategy than by financial power.

Over the years, the salary cap has evolved to meet the changing needs of the league. By 2013, the club grant had risen to $7.1 million, covering the salary cap of $5.85 million and guaranteeing a minimum wage of $80,000 for the top twenty-five players at each club. This structure not only provided financial stability for the players but also ensured that clubs could retain their star athletes without exceeding their budgetary constraints. The gradual increase in the salary cap in subsequent years—$6.3 million in 2014, $6.55 million in 2015, $6.8 million by 2016, and $7 million in 2017—reflected the league's growth and the rising revenues generated by the sport.

The NRL has been diligent in policing the salary cap to maintain fairness across the competition. Penalties for clubs found breaching the cap include fines, with the amount being either half the value of the infraction or up to $500,000, depending on the severity of the breach. Additionally, clubs risk the deduction of premiership points, a penalty that can have significant implications for a team's chances in the competition. For instance, in 2003, six clubs were fined for minor infractions, which were often technical violations or resulted from unforeseen third-party factors like a sudden loss of sponsorship revenue that impacted salary allowances.

The salary cap regulations have continued to adapt to the complexities of modern rugby league. In 2007, the NRL introduced measures to create a more equitable and beneficial cap system for both players and clubs. These changes were designed to account for the diverse financial situations of clubs, allowing them to manage their rosters effectively while still adhering to the cap. The goal was to prevent any one team from gaining an unfair advantage while ensuring that all players received fair compensation for their contributions to the sport.

A significant development in the enforcement of the salary cap came in 2010, following the Melbourne Storm salary cap scandal. This incident, where the Storm was found to have systematically breached the cap over several years, led to the stripping of multiple premiership titles and a public outcry for stricter regulations. In response, the NRL introduced new requirements for players and their agents to sign statutory declarations, pledging that their contracts complied with the salary cap regulations. Previously, only club chairmen and chief executives were required to make such declarations during biannual salary cap audits. This change added another layer of accountability, ensuring that all parties involved in player contracts were responsible for maintaining the integrity of the cap.

The salary cap has played a crucial role in shaping the competitive landscape of the NRL. By limiting the financial power of wealthier clubs, it has allowed smaller teams to compete on a more equal footing, leading to a more unpredictable and exciting competition. The cap has also helped to prevent the kind of financial mismanagement that can lead to the collapse of a club, ensuring the long-term stability of the league as a whole.

Looking ahead, the NRL will likely continue to refine the salary cap to address new challenges and opportunities. As the league grows and revenues increase, the cap will need to strike a balance between rewarding players for their contributions and maintaining a level playing field for all clubs. The ongoing evolution of the salary cap reflects the dynamic nature of rugby league and the NRL's commitment to ensuring that the sport remains fair, competitive, and financially sustainable for all involved.

The salary cap is more than just a financial regulation; it is a cornerstone of the NRL's efforts to promote fairness, integrity, and sustainability within the sport. By controlling player salaries and enforcing strict penalties for breaches, the cap helps to ensure that the competition remains open and competitive, allowing every team, regardless of its financial resources, a chance to succeed. As the NRL continues to grow and evolve, the salary cap will remain a critical tool in maintaining the balance between financial success and competitive fairness, ensuring that rugby league remains one of Australia's most beloved and respected sports.

The salary cap has been a crucial element in maintaining the integrity and competitive balance of the NRL. By limiting the amount each club can spend on player salaries, it ensures that no single team can dominate the league simply by outspending others. This creates a more level playing field, where success is determined by strategy, teamwork, and talent rather than financial power. The introduction of the salary cap in 1990 marked a turning point in the league's history, setting the stage for a more equitable and competitive competition.

Over the years, the salary cap has been adjusted to reflect the changing financial landscape of the sport. The increases in the cap from 2013 to 2017, for instance, allowed clubs to offer more competitive salaries while still adhering to the league's financial regulations. These adjustments ensured that players were fairly compensated for their contributions, while clubs could build strong, competitive teams without risking financial instability. The cap has helped to prevent the kind of financial mismanagement that can lead to the collapse of a club, safeguarding the long-term sustainability of the league.

The enforcement of the salary cap has been another key aspect of its success. The NRL's commitment to policing the cap, including the imposition of fines and the deduction of premiership points for breaches, has sent a clear message that the league is serious about maintaining a level playing field. The introduction of statutory declarations for players and their agents, following the Melbourne Storm salary cap scandal, added an extra layer of accountability, ensuring that everyone involved in player contracts is responsible for upholding the rules.

The salary cap has also had a significant impact on the distribution of talent across the league. By preventing wealthier clubs from monopolizing the best players, the cap has encouraged a more even spread of talent, making the competition more unpredictable and exciting. This has been a key factor in the NRL's ability to attract and retain fans, as every team has a realistic chance of success, regardless of its financial resources.

The role of the salary cap in promoting fairness and integrity cannot be overstated. It has helped to create a more competitive and exciting league, where every club has an opportunity to succeed. By ensuring that all teams operate within the same financial constraints, the cap has fostered a sense of fairness and equality that is essential to the spirit of the sport. The cap has also played a vital role in maintaining the financial health of the league, ensuring that clubs do not overspend in their pursuit of success.

Looking forward, the salary cap will continue to be a key factor in the NRL's growth and development. As the league evolves and revenues increase, the cap will need to be adjusted to reflect these changes while maintaining the balance between financial sustainability and competitive fairness. The ongoing refinement of the salary cap will be essential to ensuring that the NRL remains one of the world's premier rugby leagues, attracting top talent while providing a fair and exciting competition for fans.

The impact of the salary cap extends beyond the financial and competitive aspects of the league. It is a symbol of the NRL's commitment to fairness, integrity, and sustainability. By limiting the financial power of wealthier clubs, the cap ensures that success is earned on the field, not bought. This has helped to preserve the essence of the sport, where teamwork, strategy, and determination are the keys to victory. As the NRL continues to grow, the salary cap will remain a cornerstone of the league's success, ensuring that rugby league remains a fair and competitive sport for all.

Chapter 44: The Bulldogs Salary Cap Scandal

In 2002, the National Rugby League (NRL) was rocked by one of the most significant scandals in its history. The Canterbury Bulldogs, one of the league's most successful and respected clubs, were found guilty of committing serious and systematic breaches of the salary cap. This was not just a minor infraction; the scale of the breaches was unprecedented, with a total of $2.13 million over a three-year period, including $750,000 in 2001 and a staggering $920,000 in 2002. The discovery of these breaches led to severe consequences for the club, its officials, and its fans.

The NRL's salary cap was designed to ensure fairness and parity among all clubs, preventing wealthier teams from dominating the competition by outspending others. However, the Bulldogs deliberately circumvented these rules to gain an unfair advantage. The NRL's chief executive at the time, David Gallop, described the breaches as "exceptional in both its size and its deliberate and ongoing nature." The extent of the deception was staggering, involving secret payments to players and complex arrangements to hide these from the league's auditors.

When the NRL uncovered the extent of the breaches, it took swift and decisive action. The Bulldogs were fined the maximum penalty of $500,000, a record amount at the time. However, the financial penalty was only part of the punishment. The club was also stripped of all 37 premiership points it had accumulated during the 2002 season. This penalty had a devastating impact, as the Bulldogs had been leading the competition table and were strong contenders for the premiership. The points deduction meant that the club plummeted to the bottom of the ladder, effectively handing them the wooden spoon, a humiliating outcome for a team that had been on top just days before.

The fallout from the scandal was not limited to the financial and competitive penalties. The club's reputation was severely damaged, and the trust between the Bulldogs and their fans was broken. The supporters, who had been riding high on the team's success, were left devastated and disillusioned. The scandal also sent shockwaves through the entire NRL, as other clubs and their fans watched in disbelief at the scale of the deception. It served as a stark reminder of the importance of integrity and the serious consequences of breaching the league's rules.

Further compounding the scandal, two senior club officials were found guilty of fraud and were jailed as a result. Their actions not only brought shame to the Bulldogs but also highlighted the lengths to which some individuals were willing to go to achieve success. The jailing of these officials was a clear indication that the breaches were not just a matter of bending the rules but involved criminal activity. This outcome further tarnished the club's image and underscored the severity of the situation.

The 2002 salary cap scandal had long-lasting effects on the Bulldogs and the NRL as a whole. For the Bulldogs, it marked a dark chapter in their history, one that took years to recover from. The club had to rebuild its reputation and regain the trust of its fans. The NRL, on the other hand, was forced to re-evaluate its enforcement of the salary cap rules. The league introduced stricter measures and more rigorous audits to prevent such breaches from occurring in the future. The scandal served as a catalyst for change, prompting the NRL to take a tougher stance on salary cap compliance.

In the years that followed, the Bulldogs worked hard to rebuild their image and return to the top of the NRL. They focused on restoring their integrity both on and off the field, emphasizing fair play and transparency in their operations. While the scars of the 2002 scandal would never fully heal, the club gradually regained its status as a competitive and respected team in the league. The lessons learned from this dark period served as a reminder to the entire NRL community of the importance of honesty, integrity, and playing by the rules.

The 2002 salary cap scandal remains one of the most significant events in the history of the NRL. It was a wake-up call for the league, the clubs, and the fans, highlighting the need for strict adherence to the rules and the severe consequences of failing to do so. The scandal also reinforced the role of the salary cap in maintaining a level playing field and ensuring that success in the NRL is achieved through hard work, skill, and fair competition, rather than financial manipulation and deceit.

The 2002 Bulldogs salary cap scandal stands as a pivotal moment in the history of the NRL, representing not just a breach of the league's financial regulations, but a profound violation of the spirit of the sport. The magnitude of the deception carried out by the Bulldogs, involving millions of dollars in hidden payments over several years, underscored the lengths to which some clubs were willing to go to gain a competitive edge. The punishment handed down by the NRL—stripping the Bulldogs of all their premiership points for the season and imposing a record fine—was unprecedented in its severity, reflecting the seriousness of the offense and the need to maintain the integrity of the competition.

For the Bulldogs, the consequences were devastating. What had been a season of triumph turned into one of disgrace, as the club went from leading the competition to finishing at the bottom of the ladder, a fall from grace that was as shocking as it was swift. The loss of all their premiership points not only dashed their hopes of winning the title but also plunged the club into a deep crisis, both financially and reputationally. The scandal left a lasting scar on the club, one that took years to heal, as the Bulldogs struggled to rebuild their image and restore the trust of their fans and the broader rugby league community.

The impact of the scandal extended far beyond the Bulldogs. It sent shockwaves throughout the NRL, prompting a widespread reassessment of the league's salary cap regulations and enforcement mechanisms. The scandal highlighted the vulnerabilities in the system, showing how easily it could be exploited by those willing to break the rules. In response, the NRL introduced stricter compliance measures and more rigorous audits, seeking to close the loopholes that had allowed the Bulldogs to carry out their scheme undetected for so long. These changes were essential in restoring confidence in the salary cap system and ensuring that all clubs played by the same rules.

The involvement of criminal activity, with two senior Bulldogs officials being jailed for fraud, further underscored the seriousness of the scandal. This aspect of the case revealed the darker side of the sport, where the pursuit of success at all costs led to illegal actions and the betrayal of the club's values. The criminal convictions served as a stark reminder of the consequences of crossing the line between aggressive competition and outright cheating, and they reinforced the importance of ethical leadership within sports organizations.

Despite the severity of the scandal, the Bulldogs eventually managed to recover, both on and off the field. The club's journey back to respectability was long and difficult, requiring significant changes in leadership, culture, and operations. The Bulldogs had to work hard to regain the trust of their supporters, who had been deeply hurt by the revelations of cheating and dishonesty. Over time, the club's commitment to transparency and fair play helped to rebuild its reputation, allowing it to once again become a competitive force in the NRL.

The lessons learned from the 2002 scandal have had a lasting impact on the NRL. The league's administrators, clubs, and players are now acutely aware of the importance of adhering to the salary cap and the severe penalties that await those who breach it. The scandal also highlighted the need for ongoing vigilance in monitoring compliance, ensuring that the rules are enforced consistently and fairly across the competition. In this way, the NRL has been able to maintain the integrity of the sport, ensuring that success is determined by talent, hard work, and fair competition, rather than financial manipulation.

As the NRL continues to evolve, the memory of the 2002 Bulldogs scandal remains a powerful reminder of the importance of integrity in sports. It serves as a cautionary tale for all clubs, demonstrating the potentially catastrophic consequences of cheating, not just in terms of lost titles and fines, but in the damage to a club's reputation and the trust of its fans. The scandal also reinforces the broader principle that sports should be played on a level playing field, where all participants have an equal opportunity to succeed based on their abilities and efforts.

In the end, the 2002 Bulldogs salary cap scandal is more than just a chapter in the history of the NRL; it is a defining moment that shaped the future of the league. It stands as a testament to the challenges of maintaining fairness and integrity in professional sports and the ongoing efforts of the NRL to uphold these values in the face of adversity.

Chapter 45: The 2005 New Zealand Warriors Salary Cap Scandal

The 2005 New Zealand Warriors salary cap scandal was another significant event in the NRL, highlighting the ongoing challenges of enforcing the league's financial rules. The scandal came to light when the Warriors' new management discovered that their predecessors had exceeded the salary cap by a staggering $1.1 million over the previous two seasons. This revelation shocked the rugby league community and led to severe consequences for the club.

The NRL responded quickly and decisively to the breach. The Warriors were fined $430,000, a substantial amount that put a significant strain on the club's finances. However, the financial penalty was not the only consequence. The NRL also imposed a four-premiership point deficit for the 2006 season, meaning the Warriors started the season at a disadvantage, effectively reducing their chances of making it to the finals.

The four-point penalty had a considerable impact on the Warriors' 2006 season. Starting with a deficit made it challenging for the team to climb up the ladder, and despite their efforts on the field, the Warriors ultimately missed out on a spot in the finals. This was a major disappointment for the club and its fans, as the team had shown promise and potential in the lead-up to the season.

The salary cap breach and the subsequent penalties also forced the Warriors to make significant changes to their payroll. The club was required to reduce its payroll by $450,000, a move that necessitated the release of some players and the restructuring of contracts. These changes were difficult for the club, as they had to balance the need to comply with the salary cap while maintaining a competitive team on the field.

The scandal served as a harsh lesson for the Warriors and the NRL as a whole. It underscored the importance of strict adherence to the salary cap and the potential consequences of failing to do so. For the Warriors, the scandal was a wake-up call, prompting the club to adopt more rigorous financial management practices and ensuring that such a breach would not happen again.

In the broader context of the NRL, the Warriors' scandal reinforced the league's commitment to enforcing the salary cap rules. The NRL made it clear that any club found to be in breach of the salary cap would face significant penalties, including fines, point deductions, and forced payroll reductions. This tough stance was essential in maintaining the integrity of the competition and ensuring that all clubs competed on a level playing field.

Despite the setbacks caused by the scandal, the Warriors eventually recovered. The club worked hard to rebuild its reputation and regain the trust of its fans and the rugby league community. Over time, the Warriors managed to stabilize their finances, restructure their team, and return to being a competitive force in the NRL.

The 2005 salary cap scandal remains a significant chapter in the history of the New Zealand Warriors. It was a challenging period for the club, but it also served as an important turning point. The lessons learned from the scandal helped to strengthen the club's resolve and commitment to fair play, ensuring that the Warriors would emerge from the experience as a more disciplined and focused team.

The New Zealand Warriors' salary cap breach in 2005 was a major event in the NRL that had lasting implications for the club and the league. The penalties imposed by the NRL were severe but necessary to uphold the integrity of the competition. The Warriors' journey to recover from the scandal was difficult, but it ultimately led to a stronger, more resilient club. The incident serves as a reminder of the importance of adhering to the rules and the consequences of failing to do so.

The 2005 salary cap scandal was a pivotal moment for the New Zealand Warriors and the NRL, marking a period of significant upheaval and reflection within the sport. The financial penalties and the four-premiership point deficit imposed on the Warriors not only impacted their immediate performance but also sent a clear message to all clubs about the serious consequences of breaching the salary cap. This incident underscored the importance of financial integrity within the NRL and highlighted the league's commitment to maintaining a level playing field for all teams.

For the Warriors, the fallout from the scandal was severe. Starting the 2006 season with a points deficit put the team at a considerable disadvantage, making it nearly impossible to secure a spot in the finals. This was a bitter pill to swallow for a club that had been striving to establish itself as a competitive force in the NRL. The financial strain imposed by the fine and the required payroll reduction further compounded the challenges faced by the club, forcing them to make difficult decisions regarding player contracts and team composition.

The scandal also had a broader impact on the NRL as a whole. It served as a reminder of the need for stringent oversight and enforcement of the salary cap rules. The league's response to the Warriors' breach was swift and decisive, reinforcing the idea that no club is above the rules. This tough stance was crucial in preserving the integrity of the competition and ensuring that all teams had an equal opportunity to succeed based on their on-field performance rather than financial advantages.

In the aftermath of the scandal, the Warriors were forced to undergo significant internal changes. The club's management had to adopt more rigorous financial practices and ensure that they were fully compliant with the salary cap regulations. These changes were necessary to restore the club's credibility and prevent a repeat of the mistakes that had led to the breach. The Warriors' journey to recovery was not easy, but it ultimately made the club stronger and more resilient.

The lessons learned from the 2005 scandal had a lasting impact on the Warriors and the NRL. The incident highlighted the importance of transparency and accountability within the sport, and it prompted the league to take a more proactive approach to monitoring and enforcing the salary cap. For the Warriors, the experience served as a catalyst for change, leading to a renewed focus on building a sustainable and competitive team within the confines of the salary cap.

Despite the challenges posed by the scandal, the Warriors eventually managed to rebuild their reputation and regain the trust of their fans. The club's efforts to comply with the salary cap and maintain a competitive team paid off, as they returned to the NRL with a renewed sense of purpose and determination. The experience also served as a valuable lesson for other clubs in the league, reinforcing the importance of adhering to the rules and maintaining financial discipline.

In the years that followed, the NRL continued to refine and strengthen its salary cap regulations, ensuring that the competition remained fair and equitable for all teams. The Warriors' experience in 2005 played a significant role in shaping the league's approach to financial management and set a precedent for how future breaches would be handled. The incident remains a key moment in the history of the NRL, serving as a reminder of the importance of integrity and fairness in professional sports.

Ultimately, the 2005 salary cap scandal was a turning point for the New Zealand Warriors and the NRL. While the consequences were severe, the experience helped to reinforce the values of the league and ensure that all clubs operate on a level playing field. The Warriors emerged from the scandal as a more disciplined and focused club, ready to face the challenges of the NRL with renewed determination and a commitment to fair play.

Chapter 46: The Melbourne Storm Salary Cap Scandal

The Melbourne Storm salary cap scandal of 2010 was one of the most significant events in the history of the National Rugby League (NRL). The scandal came to light on April 22, 2010, when an internal whistleblower revealed that the club had been systematically breaching salary cap regulations for several years. The club had been running a dual contract and bookkeeping system that allowed them to pay players a total of $3.78 million outside of the salary cap from 2006 to 2010. This deception allowed the Storm to build a team that was far stronger than what the salary cap would normally allow, giving them an unfair advantage over other clubs.

The details of the scandal were shocking. It was revealed that the club had hidden payments of $303,000 in 2006, $459,000 in 2007, $957,000 in 2008, $1.021 million in 2009, and $1.04 million in 2010. These payments were made in secret and were not reported to the NRL, allowing the club to sign and retain top players who otherwise might have been unaffordable under the salary cap. The systematic nature of the breaches and the amount of money involved made this one of the most serious violations of NRL rules in the league's history.

The NRL's response was swift and severe. The Melbourne Storm were stripped of their 2007 and 2009 premierships, as well as their 2006–2008 minor premierships. In addition, they were stripped of the 2010 World Club Challenge trophy. The club was also fined a record $1.689 million, which included $1.1 million in NRL prize money (which was redistributed to the remaining 15 clubs), $89,000 in World Club Challenge prize money (which was given to the Leeds Rhinos), and a maximum fine of $500,000 for breaching salary cap regulations. The club was also ordered to cut their payroll by $1.0125 million and was deducted all eight premiership points they had received during the 2010 season. They were further barred from earning any premiership points for the remainder of the 2010 season, which effectively meant they would finish the season with the wooden spoon, a dramatic fall from grace for a team that had been at the top of the league.

The fallout from the scandal was immense. The penalties imposed on the Melbourne Storm were unprecedented in their severity, and they sent a strong message to all clubs about the importance of adhering to the salary cap rules. The Storm were forced to restructure their entire organization, and the scandal damaged the club's reputation both within the NRL and in the wider sporting community. The club's former directors attempted to challenge the penalties in court, but their legal action was unsuccessful, and they were also ordered to pay the NRL's legal costs. The matter was referred to several authorities, including the Australian Securities and Investments Commission (ASIC), the Australian Tax Office, the Victorian State Revenue Office, and the Victoria

Police, to investigate possible fraud. However, by May 2011, these investigations were closed without any further action being taken.

Despite the severity of the penalties, the NRL determined that the players themselves were not at fault for the breaches. As a result, individual awards won by players during the period in question were still recognized, and the players remained eligible for selection for Test matches and the State of Origin series. This decision helped to preserve the integrity of the players who had been involved in the scandal, acknowledging that they were not responsible for the actions of the club's management.

The 2010 Melbourne Storm salary cap scandal had far-reaching consequences for the NRL. It led to a greater emphasis on transparency and accountability within the league, and the NRL implemented stricter measures to ensure compliance with the salary cap rules. The scandal also served as a cautionary tale for other clubs, highlighting the potential consequences of breaching the salary cap. The penalties imposed on the Storm were a clear demonstration of the NRL's commitment to maintaining a level playing field for all clubs, and the league's response to the scandal was widely praised for its decisiveness and fairness.

In the years that followed, the Melbourne Storm worked hard to rebuild their reputation and regain the trust of their fans and the wider rugby league community. The club implemented significant changes to its management and operations, and it took several years for the Storm to fully recover from the impact of the scandal. However, the lessons learned from the scandal ultimately made the club stronger, and the Storm went on to enjoy success in the years that followed, proving that they could compete at the highest level without resorting to underhanded tactics.

The 2010 salary cap scandal remains a defining moment in the history of the Melbourne Storm and the NRL. It was a stark reminder of the importance of integrity and fairness in professional sports, and it reinforced the need for strict enforcement of the rules governing the competition. While the scandal was a dark chapter in the club's history, it also provided an opportunity for the Storm to rebuild and refocus on the values that are essential to success in the NRL.

The Melbourne Storm salary cap scandal is a significant moment in the history of the NRL, serving as a cautionary tale for all clubs about the consequences of breaching the league's rules. The severity of the penalties, including the stripping of premiership titles, fines, and the deduction of points, demonstrated the NRL's commitment to maintaining fairness and integrity in the competition. The scandal was not just a financial and legal issue, but also a moral one, highlighting the importance of transparency and accountability in sports.

The impact of the scandal was felt far beyond the Melbourne Storm club. It shook the confidence of fans, players, and stakeholders in the fairness of the league. The stripping of premierships was particularly painful for the fans who had celebrated those victories, only to have them later erased from the record books. For the players, many of whom were unaware of the breaches, the scandal was a personal blow, as their achievements were overshadowed by the actions of the club's management. The integrity of the competition was called into question, and the NRL had to work hard to restore trust and credibility.

The NRL's response to the scandal set a precedent for how future breaches of the salary cap would be handled. The heavy fines, points deductions, and other sanctions were designed to deter other clubs from engaging in similar behavior. The introduction of stricter compliance measures and more rigorous auditing processes were direct results of the scandal, aimed at preventing such breaches from happening again. The league's actions reinforced the message that no club is above the rules and that any attempts to gain an unfair advantage would be met with severe consequences.

For the Melbourne Storm, the road to recovery was long and challenging. The club had to rebuild its reputation from the ground up, implementing new governance structures and ensuring that all financial dealings were transparent and above board. The scandal served as a turning point for the club, forcing it to reevaluate its values and priorities. Over time, the Storm managed to regain its standing in the league, but the shadow of the scandal lingered, a reminder of the high cost of dishonesty.

The scandal also had a lasting impact on the NRL as a whole. It prompted a broader discussion about the role of money in sports and the pressures that clubs face to remain competitive. The salary cap is designed to create a level playing field, but the Storm scandal showed how easy it can be to undermine that goal if the rules are not strictly enforced. The NRL's handling of the situation helped to reinforce the importance of the salary cap in ensuring that all clubs have a fair chance to succeed, regardless of their financial resources.

In the years following the scandal, the NRL has continued to emphasize the importance of integrity in the game. The league has introduced more stringent regulations and penalties for breaches, as well as initiatives to educate clubs and players about the importance of compliance. The lessons learned from the Melbourne Storm scandal have been integrated into the NRL's governance framework, helping to safeguard the future of the competition.

Ultimately, the Melbourne Storm salary cap scandal is a reminder of the dangers of prioritizing short-term success over long-term integrity. While the club may have enjoyed temporary gains from their breaches, the consequences were far-reaching and damaging.

The scandal serves as a warning to all clubs that the pursuit of victory must always be balanced with a commitment to fairness, honesty, and respect for the rules that govern the game.

Chapter 47: The Parramatta Eels Salary Cap Scandal

The Parramatta Eels entered the 2016 NRL season under a cloud of controversy, with the team facing potential sanctions due to salary cap breaches that occurred in 2015. Initially, the NRL threatened to deduct four competition points from the Eels before the season even began. However, after the club made governance changes and appeared to be taking steps to rectify the situation, the NRL decided not to impose the points deduction. This temporary reprieve allowed the Eels to start the season on equal footing with other teams, but the problems were far from over.

As the 2016 season progressed, more serious issues came to light. In March, it was revealed that several companies had made third-party payments to Eels players, a practice that is strictly prohibited under NRL regulations. These payments were not disclosed to the NRL, meaning they were not included in the club's salary cap calculations. The discovery of these payments indicated that the Eels had significantly exceeded the salary cap, raising concerns about the integrity of the club's operations.

On May 3, 2016, NRL CEO Todd Greenberg announced severe penalties against the Parramatta Eels. The club was stripped of the twelve competition points it had earned up to that point in the season, effectively ending any hope of reaching the finals. In addition, the Eels were fined $1 million, a substantial sum intended to reflect the seriousness of the breaches. The team was also stripped of the 2016 NRL Auckland Nines title, which they had won just a few months earlier. This decision sent a strong message to all clubs that salary cap breaches would not be tolerated, no matter how successful a team might be on the field.

The NRL did not stop there. The league also imposed a ban on the Eels from earning any further competition points until they could prove that their salary cap was compliant. At the time, the club was reported to be $500,000 over the cap, meaning they would need to shed players or renegotiate contracts to get under the limit. This placed the Eels in an extremely difficult position, as they were essentially playing for nothing until the issue was resolved. The penalties not only affected the club's standing in the competition but also demoralized the players and fans, who saw their season slipping away.

As part of the fallout from the scandal, five senior officials from the Parramatta Eels were sacked. These included chairman Steve Sharp, deputy chairman Tom Issa, director Peter Serrao, chief executive John Boulous, and football manager Daniel Anderson. The NRL held these individuals responsible for the breaches, believing that they had failed to uphold the standards of governance required to prevent such violations. Their removal was seen as a necessary step to restore trust in the club's management and to ensure that similar breaches would not occur in the future.

The penalties did not come into full effect immediately. For over two months, the club officials contested the preliminary sanctions, hoping to reduce the severity of the punishments. However, on July 9, 2016, the NRL finalized the penalties, adding an additional punishment by deducting the Eels' for-and-against points tally from rounds 1 to 9. This further damaged the club's standing and left the team with virtually no chance of making a comeback in the 2016 season. The Eels, once considered a strong contender, were left to face the harsh reality of their situation.

The Parramatta Eels salary cap scandal serves as a stark reminder of the importance of compliance and transparency in professional sports. The NRL's actions demonstrated its commitment to enforcing the salary cap rules and maintaining a level playing field for all clubs. The scandal also highlighted the significant consequences that can arise when clubs prioritize short-term gains over long-term integrity. For the Eels, the 2016 season became a symbol of lost opportunities and shattered dreams, with the club needing to rebuild both its reputation and its team in the years that followed.

The aftermath of the scandal left a lasting impact on the Parramatta Eels. The club had to make significant changes to its management structure and financial practices to ensure future compliance with the salary cap. The penalties also served as a cautionary tale for other NRL clubs, reinforcing the importance of adhering to the rules and the potential fallout of breaching them. While the Eels eventually began to recover from the scandal, the events of 2016 remain a defining chapter in the club's history, reminding everyone involved in the sport of the high stakes of financial mismanagement in the NRL.

The Parramatta Eels' 2016 salary cap scandal was a watershed moment for the club and the NRL as a whole. It was a stark reminder of the complexities and challenges inherent in managing a professional sports team within the confines of league regulations. The scandal underscored the delicate balance between pursuing success on the field and maintaining integrity off it. For the Eels, a team with a proud history and passionate fanbase, the fallout was particularly devastating. The penalties not only stripped the club of its hard-earned points and titles but also tarnished its reputation, casting a long shadow over its achievements that season.

The severity of the NRL's response was unprecedented, and rightly so. The league had to send a clear message that such breaches would not be tolerated, regardless of the club's standing or the impact on the competition. The fine, points deduction, and stripping of the Auckland Nines title were all designed to hit the Eels hard, both financially and competitively. The punishment was a reflection of the systematic and deliberate nature of the breaches, which had gone on for several years. It also highlighted the importance of transparency and accountability in the management of professional sports teams.

For the players and fans, the scandal was particularly painful. The players, many of whom had no involvement in the salary cap breaches, found themselves in the difficult position of competing in a season where their efforts on the field would not be rewarded with the chance of finals glory. The fans, who had supported the team through thick and thin, were left feeling betrayed by the actions of the club's management. The Eels' performances on the field, which had initially suggested a successful season, were overshadowed by the controversy, leaving a bitter taste for everyone associated with the club.

The removal of senior officials was a necessary step in the club's rebuilding process, but it also marked the end of an era. The individuals who were sacked had been responsible for the day-to-day running of the club and their departures signaled a significant shift in the club's direction. It was clear that a new approach was needed, one that prioritized compliance and ethical governance over short-term success. The Eels would have to rebuild not just their squad, but also their trust with the NRL, their fans, and the broader rugby league community.

In the wider context of the NRL, the Parramatta scandal served as a cautionary tale for other clubs.

The league's stringent enforcement of the salary cap was a reminder that no team, no matter how successful or influential, was above the rules. It reinforced the importance of proper financial management and the severe consequences of failing to adhere to the regulations. Other clubs would be wise to learn from the Eels' mistakes, ensuring that their own operations were above board to avoid similar penalties.

The 2016 season became a turning point for the Parramatta Eels, one that would shape the club's future for years to come. The impact of the scandal was felt long after the season ended, with the club needing to make significant changes to its management and operations to ensure it could compete fairly in the future. While the Eels eventually began to rebuild, the scars of 2016 remained, serving as a constant reminder of what can happen when the pursuit of success is not tempered by ethical considerations.

Ultimately, the Parramatta Eels' salary cap scandal highlighted the need for vigilance and integrity in professional sports. It was a lesson in the dangers of cutting corners and the importance of playing by the rules. For the Eels, the road to recovery would be long and challenging, but the club's resilience in the face of adversity would also become a defining feature of its identity. The events of 2016 would never be forgotten, but they would also serve as a catalyst for change, pushing the Eels to become a stronger, more accountable organization in the years that followed.

Chapter 48: The 2018 Manly-Warringah Sea Eagles Scandal

In 2018, the Manly-Warringah Sea Eagles became the center of attention for all the wrong reasons. The club was embroiled in a serious salary cap breach scandal that would have lasting repercussions on its reputation and future. The National Rugby League (NRL) launched an investigation into the club's financial dealings and discovered that third-party payments and deals had been made to lure players to the team, circumventing the league's strict salary cap rules.

The NRL took this matter very seriously, as it struck at the heart of the league's efforts to maintain a level playing field. The salary cap is designed to prevent wealthier clubs from hoarding talent and to ensure that all teams have a fair chance of competing for the premiership. When Manly's violations came to light, it was clear that the club had undermined this principle by engaging in unauthorized financial arrangements.

As a result of these breaches, the NRL handed down a hefty fine of $750,000 to the Sea Eagles. This fine was one of the largest in the league's history and was intended to serve as a stern warning to other clubs that might consider similar tactics. But the financial penalty was just the beginning. The NRL also imposed a $660,000 penalty on Manly's salary cap, spreading the reduction across the 2018 and 2019 seasons. This penalty significantly limited the club's ability to recruit and retain top talent, putting them at a competitive disadvantage.

The scandal did not end with financial penalties. Two key figures within the club, Neil Bare and Joe Kelly, were suspended from their roles. Their involvement in orchestrating the third-party payments was seen as a breach of trust and responsibility. The suspensions were a clear message from the NRL that individuals in leadership positions would be held accountable for their actions. For Manly, losing these officials was a significant blow, as they had played vital roles in the club's operations and decision-making processes.

The fallout from the scandal was felt throughout the entire organization. Fans were left disillusioned and disappointed, as their club's integrity was called into question. The team, already struggling on the field, now had to contend with the additional burden of public scrutiny and reduced resources. The morale within the club was low, and the players faced immense pressure to perform under difficult circumstances.

The impact of the penalties was immediately evident in the Sea Eagles' performance over the following seasons. The reduction in their salary cap meant that they could not compete financially with other clubs for top-tier players. This limitation affected the depth and quality of their squad, leading to inconsistent results on the field. For a club with a proud history of success, this period was particularly challenging.

Despite these setbacks, the Sea Eagles worked hard to rebuild their reputation and regain the trust of their supporters. The club implemented new governance measures to ensure compliance with NRL regulations and to prevent future breaches. These measures included increased transparency in financial dealings and stricter oversight of player contracts and third-party agreements.

Over time, Manly began to recover from the scandal, though the consequences lingered. The lessons learned from this episode were painful but necessary, and they underscored the importance of integrity in professional sports. The Sea Eagles' experience served as a cautionary tale for other clubs, highlighting the risks and repercussions of attempting to circumvent the rules.

In the years that followed, the NRL continued to monitor the Sea Eagles and other clubs closely, reinforcing the message that the salary cap is non-negotiable. The league's commitment to fairness and equality remained strong, ensuring that all teams had a fair chance to compete for the ultimate prize—the NRL premiership.

The 2018 scandal marked a dark chapter in the history of the Manly-Warringah Sea Eagles, but it also became a turning point. The club emerged from the ordeal with a renewed focus on ethics and compliance, determined to move forward with integrity and honor. The road to redemption was long, but the lessons learned during this period would shape the future of the Sea Eagles and the NRL for years to come.

The 2018 salary cap scandal involving the Manly-Warringah Sea Eagles serves as a significant moment in the club's history, encapsulating the broader challenges that professional sports organizations face in balancing competitiveness with compliance. The fallout from the scandal had far-reaching implications not only for the club but also for the NRL as a whole. The hefty fines, salary cap penalties, and suspensions of key officials highlighted the seriousness with which the NRL approached violations of its salary cap rules. These penalties were not merely punitive but were intended to reinforce the integrity of the competition and ensure that no club gained an unfair advantage through financial maneuvering.

For the Sea Eagles, the scandal was a harsh lesson in the importance of transparency and adherence to the rules. The club's actions, driven by a desire to maintain competitiveness, ultimately backfired, leading to significant financial and reputational damage. The loss of key officials further destabilized the club, leaving a void in leadership and creating uncertainty about the future direction of the team. The impact on the players and fans was profound, with the club's performance on the field suffering as a result of the penalties and the broader challenges associated with the scandal.

The repercussions of the 2018 scandal were felt for several years, as the Sea Eagles struggled to rebuild both on and off the field. The reduction in the salary cap limited the club's ability to attract and retain top talent, leading to a period of inconsistency and underperformance. However, the scandal also served as a catalyst for change within the organization. The Sea Eagles implemented new governance measures designed to prevent future breaches and to restore the trust of their supporters and the broader rugby league community.

This period of introspection and reform was crucial for the club's long-term recovery. The Sea Eagles recognized the need to operate with greater transparency and accountability, ensuring that all financial dealings were above board and fully compliant with NRL regulations. These changes were not easy to implement, but they were necessary to rebuild the club's reputation and to demonstrate a commitment to fairness and integrity.

The NRL, too, learned valuable lessons from the Manly-Warringah Sea Eagles scandal. The league's response to the breach was swift and decisive, setting a precedent for how future violations would be handled. The NRL reinforced its commitment to maintaining a level playing field, emphasizing that the salary cap was a non-negotiable aspect of the competition. This stance was essential to preserving the integrity of the league and ensuring that all clubs, regardless of their financial resources, had an equal opportunity to compete for the premiership.

In the years following the scandal, the Sea Eagles worked diligently to regain their standing within the NRL. While the road to recovery was long and fraught with challenges, the club's efforts to reform and rebuild were ultimately successful. The lessons learned from the 2018 scandal became a part of the Sea Eagles' identity, shaping their approach to governance and competition in the years that followed.

As the club moved forward, it did so with a renewed focus on ethical conduct and a commitment to doing things the right way. The Manly-Warringah Sea Eagles emerged from the scandal not just as a club that had been punished for its mistakes, but as an organization that had learned from its past and was determined to build a brighter future. The 2018 salary cap breach was a dark chapter in the club's history, but it also marked a turning point—a moment of reckoning that led to meaningful change and a stronger, more resilient organization.

In the end, the Sea Eagles' journey through the aftermath of the scandal was a testament to the power of accountability, reform, and perseverance. The club's experience served as a reminder to all NRL teams of the importance of upholding the values of fairness, transparency, and integrity—values that are essential to the success and sustainability of the league as a whole.

Chapter 49: The NRL Judiciary and Integrity Unit

The NRL Judiciary plays a crucial role in maintaining the integrity and discipline of the competition. Comprising former players, the judiciary is tasked with reviewing and ruling on incidents that occur during matches. This panel of experts ensures that the rules and regulations of the game are enforced consistently and fairly. The judiciary is currently chaired by Wollongong district court judge Paul Conlon. The panel includes experienced former players such as Mal Cochrane, Michael Buettner, Bradley Clyde, Sean Garlick, Don McKinnon, and Bob Lindner. Each member brings a deep understanding of the game, which is essential for making informed decisions on disciplinary matters.

The judiciary's role is to handle cases related to on-field incidents, such as foul play or misconduct. When a player is cited for a potential breach of the rules, the judiciary convenes to review evidence, hear testimonies, and determine the appropriate penalty. This process ensures that players are held accountable for their actions and that the game's standards are upheld. The decisions made by the judiciary can have significant impacts on players, teams, and the overall competition.

In addition to the judiciary, the NRL has established an Integrity Unit to oversee and manage issues related to the conduct and integrity of the game. The Integrity

Unit was formed on 7 February 2013 and was initially headed by former Federal Court judge Tony Whitlam. The unit was established to address concerns beyond on-field incidents, including matters related to player behavior, team management, and compliance with the league's rules and policies.

Under Tony Whitlam's leadership, the Integrity Unit focused on ensuring that the NRL maintained high standards of conduct and addressed any issues that could affect the league's reputation. The unit played a crucial role in investigating and resolving various matters, from player misconduct to compliance with regulations. The establishment of the Integrity Unit marked a significant step in the NRL's commitment to maintaining the game's integrity and upholding its values.

Since 2022, the NRL Integrity Unit has been led by Jason King, a former Manly Sea-Eagles front-row forward. King's appointment as head of the unit brings a fresh perspective and a wealth of experience from his time as a player. His role involves overseeing the unit's operations, ensuring that investigations are conducted thoroughly, and implementing measures to prevent and address issues related to player and team conduct.

The Integrity Unit, under King's leadership, continues to play a vital role in preserving the reputation of the NRL. The unit's responsibilities include investigating allegations of misconduct, managing issues related to player welfare, and ensuring compliance with the league's rules and policies. By addressing these matters proactively, the Integrity Unit helps to maintain the credibility of the competition and uphold the values of fairness and sportsmanship.

Together, the NRL Judiciary and the Integrity Unit work to ensure that the game is played with integrity and fairness. While the judiciary focuses on on-field incidents and disciplinary matters, the Integrity Unit addresses broader issues related to conduct and compliance. Both bodies are essential in maintaining the high standards of the NRL and ensuring that the competition remains a respected and reputable sporting event.

The NRL Judiciary and Integrity Unit are integral to the operation and governance of the league. Through their efforts, they uphold the rules of the game, address issues of misconduct, and ensure that the NRL remains a fair and credible competition. The collaboration between these two bodies reflects the league's commitment to maintaining the integrity of the game and promoting a culture of respect and professionalism within the sport.

The NRL Judiciary and Integrity Unit play essential roles in ensuring that the National Rugby League operates with integrity and fairness. The judiciary, comprised of former players and chaired by Judge Paul Conlon, is responsible for adjudicating on-field incidents and maintaining the standards of play within the competition. Their work involves not only reviewing evidence and hearing testimonies but also making decisions that uphold the rules and ensure that disciplinary actions are both appropriate and consistent. This role is crucial in managing the balance between competitive play and sportsmanship, reinforcing the values of the game while addressing breaches and ensuring fair outcomes.

The Integrity Unit, established in 2013 and currently led by Jason King, complements the judiciary's efforts by focusing on broader issues related to player and team conduct. Initially under the leadership of Tony Whitlam, the unit was tasked with overseeing the ethical and regulatory aspects of the league beyond immediate game-day incidents. This includes addressing player behavior, compliance with league rules, and managing any off-field matters that could impact the competition's integrity. The unit's proactive approach to investigating allegations and ensuring adherence to the NRL's policies reflects the league's commitment to upholding its reputation and ensuring a high standard of professionalism.

The work of both the Judiciary and the Integrity Unit is interconnected, as they address different aspects of maintaining the NRL's standards. While the judiciary focuses on direct disciplinary matters arising from games, the Integrity Unit tackles broader concerns that could affect the league's image and operations. Their combined efforts are vital in managing and mitigating risks, addressing misconduct, and promoting a culture of respect and fairness within the sport.

Over the years, both bodies have faced significant challenges, including high-profile cases of salary cap breaches and player misconduct. The judiciary's role in handling such cases, along with the Integrity Unit's oversight and investigation, ensures that these issues are addressed effectively and transparently. By imposing appropriate penalties and enforcing compliance, they contribute to maintaining the integrity of the competition and fostering a competitive yet fair environment for all participants.

The judiciary's decisions have a direct impact on teams and players, shaping the outcomes of matches and seasons while upholding the league's standards. Similarly, the Integrity Unit's work in managing broader issues helps to prevent and address problems before they escalate, ensuring that the league remains a respected and reputable organization. Both bodies, through their distinct but complementary roles, play a crucial part in the ongoing success and credibility of the NRL.

The NRL Judiciary and Integrity Unit are fundamental to the league's governance and operations. Their combined efforts ensure that the competition remains fair, transparent, and true to its values. By addressing on-field incidents and broader regulatory issues, they uphold the standards of the game and contribute to the league's integrity and reputation. The ongoing commitment to these roles reflects the NRL's dedication to maintaining a high standard of professionalism and ensuring that the sport continues to thrive as a leading and respected competition.

Part Seven: Crowning Achievements – The World of Rugby League Awards

Chapter 50: The Provan-Summons Trophy – A Symbol of Rugby League Glory

The Provan-Summons Trophy holds a special place in the hearts of rugby league fans and players alike. Awarded to the team that wins the NRL Premiership, it symbolizes the ultimate achievement in the sport. Its design is rooted in history, modeled after the iconic Winfield Cup trophy, which first appeared during the 1982 NSWRFL season. The trophy's centerpiece is a three-dimensional cast of a famous photograph known as *The Gladiators*. This image, taken after the 1963 NSWRFL Grand Final, captures a heartfelt moment between Norm Provan of St. George and Arthur Summons of Western Suburbs. Covered in mud, the two players embraced in a display of sportsmanship that transcended the fierce rivalry of the game.

For many years, the trophy was simply referred to as the NRL Premiership Trophy. It wasn't until 2013, the 50th anniversary of that memorable Grand Final, that it was officially named the Provan-Summons Trophy. This change was a tribute to the enduring legacy of the two men and the spirit of the game that they represented. The decision to name the trophy after them was met with widespread approval, as it acknowledged not just their individual contributions but also the values of respect and camaraderie that are central to rugby league.

The trophy is awarded to the captain of the winning team after the Grand Final, marking the culmination of a season's worth of hard work, determination, and teamwork. Lifting the Provan-Summons Trophy is a dream for every player who steps onto the field, and it represents the pinnacle of success in the NRL. The sight of the winning team hoisting the trophy aloft is one of the most iconic moments in Australian sport, often accompanied by the roar of thousands of fans and the flash of cameras capturing the celebration.

In addition to the trophy, each player from the premiership-winning team is awarded a Premiership Ring. These rings are a symbol of individual achievement, commemorating the player's contribution to their team's success. Crafted with intricate detail, the rings are highly prized by players, often becoming cherished keepsakes that are passed down through generations. They serve as a lasting reminder of the hard-fought battles on the field and the joy of ultimate victory.

In 2021, the Provan-Summons Trophy made headlines for an unexpected reason. During the post-match celebrations, the trophy was accidentally damaged, breaking apart in a way that surprised everyone. While the incident caused some initial concern, it was also seen as a testament to the passion and enthusiasm that surrounds the Grand Final. The trophy, like the game itself, is robust, but even it is not immune to the exuberance of victory. The incident sparked a flurry of media coverage, with fans and commentators alike sharing their thoughts on the significance of the trophy and what it means to the sport.

Despite the mishap, the Provan-Summons Trophy remains a symbol of rugby league's rich history and tradition. Each year, as the NRL season unfolds, teams battle not just for points on the ladder, but for the chance to etch their names into the annals of rugby league history. The trophy is a reminder of the glory that awaits the team that can rise above the rest and claim the title of NRL Premiers.

Looking ahead, the Provan-Summons Trophy will continue to be a central figure in the story of the NRL. Its legacy is intertwined with the memories of players and fans, and it will undoubtedly witness many more moments of triumph and celebration in the years to come. As new generations of players aspire to lift the trophy, they carry forward the values embodied by Norm Provan and Arthur Summons, ensuring that the spirit of *The Gladiators* lives on.

In the end, the Provan-Summons Trophy is more than just a piece of silverware. It is a symbol of the enduring appeal of rugby league, a sport that thrives on passion, skill, and the unbreakable bond between teammates. Each time the trophy is awarded, it marks the closing of one chapter and the beginning of another, as teams set their sights on the next season, eager to chase the dream of NRL glory once more.

The Provan-Summons Trophy stands as a beacon of excellence in the world of rugby league, embodying not just the triumphs of the winning teams but also the deep-seated traditions and values that have shaped the sport. As each season draws to a close, the presentation of this trophy marks the culmination of countless hours of training, the highs and lows of competition, and the relentless pursuit of victory that drives every team in the NRL. For the players, lifting the trophy is the ultimate reward, a tangible symbol of their success and a moment that will be etched in their memories forever.

Over the years, the Provan-Summons Trophy has seen its fair share of drama, from thrilling last-minute victories to moments of intense rivalry and passion. It has been at the center of some of the most unforgettable moments in the history of rugby league, and each season, it continues to inspire players and fans alike. The image of the winning captain holding the trophy aloft, surrounded by cheering teammates and fans, is a powerful reminder of what it takes to reach the pinnacle of the sport.

Beyond its physical presence, the Provan-Summons Trophy represents the spirit of rugby league – a spirit of camaraderie, sportsmanship, and respect that is at the heart of the game. The story of Norm Provan and Arthur Summons, immortalized in *The Gladiators* photograph, serves as a timeless example of these values. Their embrace after a hard-fought match is a reminder that, at its core, rugby league is about more than just winning; it's about the bonds forged on the field, the mutual respect between competitors, and the shared love of the game.

The incident in 2021, when the trophy was accidentally broken during celebrations, only added to its mystique. While the damage was quickly repaired, the event highlighted the deep emotional connection that players and fans have with the trophy. It is not just a piece of metal; it is a symbol of the dreams and aspirations of everyone involved in the NRL. The passion that led to the trophy's temporary damage is the same passion that fuels the players' drive to win it each year.

As the NRL continues to grow and evolve, the Provan-Summons Trophy remains a constant, a link between the sport's storied past and its exciting future. Each time a new team claims the trophy, they add their chapter to the ongoing narrative of rugby league, contributing to the rich tapestry of stories that define the sport. The trophy is a reminder of where the game has come from, the legends who have played it, and the heights that future players aspire to reach.

In the years to come, the Provan-Summons Trophy will continue to be the ultimate prize in rugby league, sought after by every team in the NRL. It will stand as a testament to the hard work, dedication, and talent required to succeed at the highest level of the sport. For the players who have the privilege of lifting it, the trophy represents the fulfillment of a lifelong dream, a moment of glory that will stay with them for the rest of their lives.

As the Provan-Summons Trophy is handed from one victorious team to the next, it carries with it the weight of history and the hopes of all those who compete for it. It is a symbol of excellence, a badge of honor, and a cherished piece of rugby league's legacy. With each passing season, the trophy's significance only grows, as new stories are written and new heroes are crowned. The Provan-Summons Trophy is more than just a prize; it is the heart and soul of rugby league, a symbol of everything the sport stands for, and a source of inspiration for generations to come.

Chapter 51: J. J. Giltinan Shield

The J.J. Giltinan Shield is one of the most prestigious awards in Australian rugby league, symbolizing excellence in performance throughout the regular season. Since its creation in 1951, the Shield has been awarded to the team that finishes the NRL premiership season at the top of the ladder, earning the title of minor premiers. Named in honor of James J. Giltinan, a key figure in the establishment of rugby league in Australia, the Shield represents the spirit and history of the sport. Giltinan's contribution to the game was so significant that, after his passing in 1950, the Shield was created to ensure his legacy lived on through the recognition of the best-performing team each season.

Winning the J.J. Giltinan Shield is no small feat. It requires consistency, determination, and a high level of skill over the course of the entire season. The minor premiers are often seen as the team to beat in the finals, having proven their dominance against all other teams. However, being crowned minor premiers does not guarantee a premiership victory. The finals series is a separate challenge, where the pressure intensifies, and every game becomes a do-or-die battle.

The J.J. Giltinan Shield holds a special place in the history of rugby league, not just because of its association with Giltinan, but also because of the prestige it brings to the winning club. The Shield has been awarded to some of the greatest teams in the history of the sport, and each winner is etched into the annals of rugby league history. For players, coaches, and fans alike, seeing their team lift the J.J. Giltinan Shield is a moment of immense pride and joy.

Over the years, the Shield has been awarded to a variety of clubs, reflecting the competitive nature of the NRL. While some teams have dominated certain eras, others have risen to the top unexpectedly, proving that in rugby league, anything can happen. This unpredictability is part of what makes the race for the J.J. Giltinan Shield so exciting each season. Clubs fight fiercely for the honor, knowing that finishing at the top of the ladder is a significant achievement, regardless of what happens in the finals.

In addition to the glory, the J.J. Giltinan Shield comes with tangible rewards. Minor premiers often gain a psychological advantage going into the finals, as well as the home-ground advantage in crucial matches. These benefits can make a significant difference in the high-stakes environment of finals football, where every little edge counts. The Shield not only recognizes the best team of the regular season but also sets the stage for their pursuit of the ultimate prize, the premiership.

The history of the J.J. Giltinan Shield is rich with memorable moments, from thrilling victories to heartbreaking near-misses. Each season, the competition to win the Shield is intense, with clubs leaving no stone unturned in their quest to be the best. Fans eagerly watch the ladder, calculating the chances of their team finishing first, while players push themselves to their limits, knowing that the Shield represents the culmination of their hard work throughout the year.

Since 1997, when the NRL was formed, the J.J. Giltinan Shield has continued to be awarded to the minor premiers, maintaining its status as one of the most coveted trophies in the sport. The tradition and honor associated with the Shield make it a symbol of rugby league's enduring legacy in Australia. Every year, new stories are written, and new heroes emerge as clubs vie for the chance to etch their name on this historic trophy.

For the teams that win the J.J. Giltinan Shield, the achievement is a testament to their skill, determination, and consistency. It is a reward for months of hard work, dedication, and sacrifice. And while the finals still lie ahead, winning the Shield is a moment to celebrate, a recognition of their status as the best team of the regular season. The J.J. Giltinan Shield is more than just a piece of silverware; it is a symbol of excellence in rugby league, a prize that every club aspires to claim, and a tribute to the legacy of James J. Giltinan, whose vision helped shape the sport we know and love today.

The J.J. Giltinan Shield stands as a symbol of excellence and a testament to the dedication, hard work, and consistency required to dominate an entire NRL season. It's more than just an award; it's a reflection of a team's ability to outperform all others over the long haul, showcasing resilience, skill, and the capacity to handle the intense demands of one of the world's toughest rugby leagues. Winning the Shield is a significant achievement that often sets the tone for a club's legacy, marking them as one of the elite in the sport.

For the players, lifting the J.J. Giltinan Shield is a moment of immense pride, recognizing the culmination of a season's worth of blood, sweat, and tears. It is a public acknowledgment of their superiority during the regular season, a moment that validates their efforts and cements their place in rugby league history. Coaches, too, see it as a validation of their strategies, leadership, and ability to inspire and manage their team through the highs and lows of a grueling campaign.

For the fans, the Shield represents bragging rights, a tangible reward for their unwavering support throughout the season. It's a moment of celebration, a time to revel in their team's success and dream of what might come in the finals. The Shield brings with it a sense of belonging and pride, uniting supporters as they cheer on their minor premiers in the crucial weeks that follow.

However, the journey to securing the J.J. Giltinan Shield is often fraught with challenges. Teams must navigate injuries, suspensions, and the ever-present threat of form slumps. The pressure of maintaining top position on the ladder can be immense, with every match carrying significant weight as rivals look to knock them off their perch. Yet, those who rise to the occasion and hold firm until the end are rewarded with a place in rugby league's rich tapestry.

The Shield's history is intertwined with the sport itself, and every club that has won it has contributed to the ongoing story of rugby league. It serves as a reminder of the legacy of James J. Giltinan and the vision he had for the game, a vision that has grown and evolved into the vibrant, competitive league we see today. As the years pass, the significance of the Shield only deepens, with each new winner adding another chapter to its storied past.

In recent years, the competition for the J.J. Giltinan Shield has been as fierce as ever, with clubs investing heavily in talent, training, and strategy to ensure they can secure the top spot. The increasing professionalism of the NRL means that winning the Shield is no longer just about talent; it's about preparation, mental toughness, and the ability to adapt to the ever-changing landscape of the sport. Clubs that succeed in this endeavor are those that can innovate and push the boundaries, setting new standards for others to follow.

Yet, while the Shield is a prestigious prize, it is also a reminder that the journey is not over. The finals loom large, and the true test of a club's mettle is often yet to come. The Shield winners enter the finals with a target on their backs, as other teams seek to dethrone them and claim the ultimate prize, the NRL Premiership. This duality – the joy of winning the Shield and the challenge of converting that success into a Premiership – is what makes rugby league so compelling and why the Shield remains one of the sport's most coveted awards.

The J.J. Giltinan Shield is more than just an accolade; it's a symbol of rugby league's enduring spirit and the pursuit of excellence that defines the NRL. It honors those who have achieved greatness over the course of a season, etching their names into the annals of history while reminding them of the challenges that still lie ahead. For players, coaches, and fans alike, it is a source of immense pride, a moment of triumph that is celebrated and remembered for years to come.

Chapter 52: The Clive Churchill Medal: Honoring Grand Final Greatness

The Clive Churchill Medal is one of the most prestigious individual honors in the National Rugby League (NRL), awarded to the player judged to be the standout performer in the annual Grand Final. This medal is named after Clive Churchill, who is widely regarded as one of the greatest rugby league players in Australian history. Introduced in 1986, the medal was created to honor Churchill following his passing in 1985, ensuring his legacy would continue in the sport he had so greatly influenced.

Winning the Clive Churchill Medal is a career-defining moment for any player. It signifies that they have not only performed at an exceptionally high level but have done so on the sport's biggest stage, the Grand Final. This medal represents excellence, skill, and the ability to shine under the immense pressure that comes with playing in a match that decides the season's champion.

The first recipient of the Clive Churchill Medal was Peter Sterling of the Parramatta Eels, who won the award in 1986. Since then, the medal has been awarded every year, with its recipients earning a special place in rugby league history. Players who receive this medal are often remembered for their extraordinary performances in the Grand Final, and their names are etched into the memories of fans and the annals of the sport.

The medal itself has undergone some changes over the years. Originally presented in a case, it was later updated in 2000 to include a ribbon, allowing the winner to wear it around their neck during the post-match celebrations. This change added to the ceremonial aspect of the award, making it even more symbolic and visible during the victory presentations.

Winning the Clive Churchill Medal more than once is an exceptional achievement, with only three players managing to do so: Bradley Clyde, Billy Slater, and Nathan Cleary. Clyde won the award in 1989 and 1991 while playing for the Canberra Raiders, showcasing his consistency and dominance in the biggest games. Slater, a legendary fullback for the Melbourne Storm, won the medal in 2009 and 2017, further cementing his status as one of the sport's all-time greats. Most recently, Nathan Cleary of the Penrith Panthers joined this elite group by winning the medal in both 2021 and 2023, highlighting his impact and leadership in crucial moments.

Interestingly, the Clive Churchill Medal has been awarded to players from the losing team on four occasions. This rare occurrence speaks volumes about the players' performances, as they were able to stand out even when their team did not win the Grand Final. Bradley Clyde was the first to achieve this in 1991, followed by Brad Mackay in 1993, Daly Cherry-Evans in 2013, and Jack Wighton in 2019. These instances underscore the impartiality and respect that the award commands, as it is given purely on merit, regardless of the final result.

The man after whom the medal is named, Clive Churchill, had a remarkable career that spanned both playing and coaching. He played for the South Sydney Rabbitohs and represented New South Wales, Queensland, and Australia at the highest levels. Churchill was known for his exceptional skills, leadership, and tactical acumen, which later saw him transition into a successful coaching role. His contributions to rugby league are immense, and the Clive Churchill Medal serves as a fitting tribute to his enduring legacy.

The awarding of the Clive Churchill Medal is one of the most anticipated moments of the Grand Final. As the game concludes and the celebrations begin, all eyes turn to the announcement of the winner. For the player who receives the medal, it is a moment of personal triumph and a validation of their hard work, dedication, and skill. The honor of being named the best player on the most important day of the rugby league calendar is something that stays with the recipient for life, earning them a place in the history books alongside the legends of the sport.

The Clive Churchill Medal is more than just an award; it is a symbol of excellence in the NRL. It represents the pinnacle of individual achievement in the sport, recognizing those who have risen to the occasion in the most critical moments. As the years pass and new players continue to emerge, the Clive Churchill Medal remains a coveted prize, inspiring future generations to strive for greatness on the Grand Final stage.

The Clive Churchill Medal represents much more than just an individual accolade; it symbolizes the pinnacle of rugby league excellence. It is awarded not just to recognize talent but to honor those rare moments when a player transcends the game itself, standing tall in the face of immense pressure and performing at a level that leaves a lasting impression on everyone who witnesses it. Winning the Clive Churchill Medal is about more than a single match; it is about etching one's name into the history of the sport, becoming a part of the rich legacy that has shaped rugby league in Australia.

The stories of those who have won the Clive Churchill Medal are stories of determination, resilience, and brilliance. Each winner has brought something unique to the game, whether it's the flair and creativity of Peter Sterling, the unyielding strength and consistency of Bradley Clyde, or the electrifying skill and tactical mastery of Billy Slater and Nathan Cleary. These players, and many others, have set a standard that future generations will aspire to reach, ensuring that the pursuit of this prestigious medal remains a driving force in the careers of NRL players.

The fact that the Clive Churchill Medal has been awarded to players from the losing side in the Grand Final speaks volumes about the integrity and respect that the award commands. It shows that even in defeat, individual brilliance can shine through, and the medal serves as a reminder that the game is not just about the final score but about the moments of brilliance that define the sport. For players like Brad Mackay, Daly Cherry-Evans, and Jack Wighton, winning the Clive Churchill Medal despite their team not winning the Grand Final is a testament to their exceptional abilities and their capacity to inspire even in challenging circumstances.

Clive Churchill's legacy as one of the greatest players in rugby league history is forever immortalized through this medal. His contributions to the game as a player and coach are legendary, and the medal serves as a constant reminder of the standards he set during his illustrious career. As the sport continues to evolve, the Clive Churchill Medal remains a beacon of excellence, reminding players of the level they must aspire to reach if they wish to be remembered as one of the greats.

Over the years, the Clive Churchill Medal has evolved in its presentation, but its significance has remained constant. From being awarded in a case to being worn proudly around the neck, the medal has become a symbol of personal triumph, a moment when a player's efforts are recognized and celebrated by the entire rugby league community. The moment when the Clive Churchill Medallist is announced is one of the most anticipated and celebrated events in the NRL calendar, a moment that every player dreams of experiencing.

As the game of rugby league moves forward, the Clive Churchill Medal will continue to inspire players to give their all on the biggest stage. It is a symbol of what is possible when talent, hard work, and opportunity come together, and it will remain one of the most coveted prizes in the sport. For every player who dreams of greatness, the Clive Churchill Medal represents the ultimate goal—a chance to be remembered as a player who rose to the occasion and delivered a performance that will be talked about for years to come.

In the end, the Clive Churchill Medal is not just a piece of metal; it is a symbol of everything that makes rugby league great. It is about the passion, the commitment, and the sheer love of the game. It is about the players who inspire us with their skill and determination, who give everything they have for the chance to be remembered as one of the best. The Clive Churchill Medal is a reminder that in rugby league, as in life, it is not just about winning but about how you play the game and the moments of brilliance that define your legacy.

Chapter 53: The Dally M Awards

The Dally M Awards are the pinnacle of individual recognition in Australian rugby league. Named after the legendary Herbert Henry "Dally" Messenger, who was a crucial figure in the early development of rugby league in Australia, these awards have become a symbol of excellence in the sport. Introduced in 1980 by News Limited, the Dally M Awards quickly became the most prestigious individual honors in the game. Since the unification of the NRL in 1998, the Dally M Medal has been recognized as the official Player of the Year award, overtaking the previously held Rothmans Medal as the highest individual accolade in the sport.

The Dally M Medal is awarded annually to the player deemed the best and fairest over the course of the NRL regular season. The significance of this award cannot be overstated, as it represents not just skill and performance but also sportsmanship and consistency throughout the season. The Dally M Awards night is one of the most anticipated events in the NRL calendar, where the top players, coaches, and rookies are celebrated for their outstanding contributions to the game.

The voting process for the Dally M Medal is meticulously organized. After each game, rugby league sports commentators assign points to the top three players on the field: three votes for the best player, two votes for the second-best, and one vote for the third. This method ensures that the award truly reflects a player's performance across the entire season. However, if a player is suspended during the season, they lose three votes for each week of suspension. This rule emphasizes the importance of discipline and fair play, ensuring that only the most deserving players are in contention for the award.

Up until Round 12 of the 26-round season, the votes are made public, creating excitement and speculation among fans and players alike. After this point, the votes are kept secret, building suspense leading up to the Dally M Awards ceremony. This secrecy adds to the drama and prestige of the event, as no one knows who will take home the coveted medal until the moment it is announced.

The Dally M Awards are not just about the Player of the Year, though. They also recognize the best players in each position, the most outstanding rookie, and the top coach of the season. This comprehensive approach ensures that all aspects of the game are celebrated, from the individual brilliance of players to the strategic genius of coaches. The awards provide a platform for recognizing the diverse talents and contributions that make rugby league such an exciting and dynamic sport.

Over the years, the Dally M Medal has been awarded to some of the greatest players in the history of rugby league. These players have not only excelled on the field but have also embodied the values of the sport: determination, integrity, and a commitment to excellence. Winning the Dally M Medal is a career-defining achievement, placing a player in the company of legends and ensuring their place in the annals of rugby league history.

The Dally M Awards also serve as a reflection of the season that was. They highlight the key moments, the standout performances, and the players who have left an indelible mark on the game. For fans, the awards night is a chance to relive the highs and lows of the season, to celebrate the best of the best, and to look forward to what the next season might bring.

The Dally M Awards are more than just a series of accolades; they are a celebration of the very best in rugby league. From the voting process to the suspenseful awards night, every aspect of the Dally M Awards is designed to honor the players, coaches, and teams that make rugby league one of the most exciting sports in the world. As the NRL continues to grow and evolve, the Dally M Awards will remain a cornerstone of the game, a symbol of the excellence that every player strives to achieve.

The Dally M Awards stand as a significant milestone in the rugby league season, marking the culmination of months of hard work, dedication, and outstanding performances by the players. The prestige associated with the Dally M Medal, in particular, reflects the respect and admiration that the rugby league community holds for individual excellence within the team-oriented sport. As the ultimate recognition of a player's contributions throughout the year, this award encapsulates both the player's skill on the field and their consistency over the grueling NRL season.

Throughout its history, the Dally M Awards have celebrated the extraordinary talents that have shaped the game. These accolades are not just about winning; they represent the journey, the perseverance, and the ability to rise to the occasion week after week. The names etched into the history of the Dally M Medal are those of players who have become icons of the sport, whose performances have captivated fans and inspired future generations of rugby league players.

The meticulous voting process ensures that the award is truly reflective of a player's influence over the season. The transparency of the votes up until a certain point keeps fans engaged, while the secrecy in the latter part of the season adds an element of suspense that culminates in the excitement of the awards night. This blend of transparency and mystery enhances the prestige of the Dally M Medal, making it not just a recognition of past achievements but a symbol of the ongoing drama and passion that define rugby league.

The Dally M Awards also serve a broader purpose within the sport. By recognizing the best players in each position, the top rookie, and the leading coach, the awards highlight the diversity of talent required to succeed in rugby league. They acknowledge that rugby league is not just about individual brilliance but about the collective effort of teams and the strategic vision of coaches. This holistic approach to the awards ensures that every aspect of the game is celebrated, from the explosive plays of the backs to the hard graft of the forwards and the tactical acumen of the coaching staff.

For the players, receiving a Dally M Award is not just a career highlight but a testament to their impact on the game. It is an acknowledgment from their peers, the media, and the fans that they are among the elite in rugby league. This recognition can be a defining moment in a player's career, often elevating them to legendary status within the sport. The Dally M Medal, in particular, places the recipient in an exclusive club of players who have reached the pinnacle of individual achievement in rugby league.

The legacy of the Dally M Awards is one of celebrating excellence while maintaining the integrity of the game. The inclusion of penalties for suspensions in the voting process underscores the importance of fair play and sportsmanship, ensuring that the award remains a true reflection of the values that rugby league holds dear. This commitment to integrity is a cornerstone of the Dally M Awards, reinforcing their status as the most respected individual honors in the sport.

As the NRL continues to evolve, the Dally M Awards will remain a constant, a touchstone of excellence that players aspire to throughout their careers. The awards night, with its mix of glamour and gravitas, is a fitting tribute to the season's best, bringing together the rugby league community to celebrate the sport they love. It is a moment of reflection on the achievements of the past year and a moment of anticipation for the seasons to come.

In the grand narrative of rugby league, the Dally M Awards occupy a special place. They are not just awards; they are a celebration of what makes rugby league great—the skill, the passion, the dedication, and the enduring spirit of competition. As each season draws to a close, the Dally M Awards ensure that the players who have given their all on the field receive the recognition they deserve, immortalizing their contributions in the annals of rugby league history.

Chapter 54: The Immortals

The Immortals represent the pinnacle of recognition in Australian rugby league, reserved for players who have left an indelible mark on the sport. The concept was born in 1981 when Rugby League Week, a popular sports magazine, decided to honor the game's greatest players by naming four former Test captains—Clive Churchill, Bob Fulton, Reg Gasnier, and Johnny Raper—as the inaugural Immortals. This recognition was not just a celebration of their on-field achievements but also a tribute to their lasting influence on the game and its history.

Initially, the Immortals list was met with widespread respect, as these players were already regarded as legends in the rugby league community. Their inclusion in this elite group cemented their status as the very best in the sport. The decision to name only post-war players, however, did stir some debate. Critics argued that the award should also recognize the achievements of pre-war players who had laid the foundation for the modern game. Despite this, the decision to focus on players the judges had personally witnessed playing ensured that the selections were based on firsthand knowledge and appreciation of their talents.

For many years, the Immortals list remained exclusive, with new members added only occasionally. In 1999, two more players, Graeme Langlands and Wally Lewis, were inducted, followed by Arthur

Beetson in 2003. These additions were carefully considered and reflected the evolving recognition of players who had significantly shaped the game's history. The process of selecting new Immortals was rigorous, involving a panel of experts who were well-versed in the game's history and nuances.

The induction of Andrew Johns in 2012 marked a significant moment in the evolution of the Immortals. His selection was notable not just for his exceptional skill and influence on the game but also for the controversy surrounding his off-field issues, including admitted drug use. To address this, the criteria for selection were clarified, emphasizing that the Immortals were to be judged solely on their playing ability and contribution to the game, rather than their personal lives. This move ensured that the focus remained on celebrating the sport's greatest talents without the distraction of off-field matters.

The closure of Rugby League Week in 2017 could have spelled the end for the Immortals concept, but instead, it was taken over by the Australian Rugby League Commission. This transition allowed the tradition to continue and even expand. In 2018, the Commission made a bold move by inducting five new members at once: Dave Brown, Frank Burge, Mal Meninga, Dally Messenger, and Norm Provan. This expansion was significant for several reasons. First, it addressed the long-standing criticism that pre-war players had been overlooked, finally recognizing their contributions to the sport. Second, it brought the total number of Immortals to thirteen, making the group more inclusive while maintaining its exclusivity.

The inclusion of players like Dally Messenger, who was instrumental in the early development of rugby league in Australia, highlighted the importance of honoring the game's entire history, not just its modern era. By expanding the Immortals to include these earlier players, the Australian Rugby League Commission demonstrated a commitment to preserving the rich heritage of rugby league and ensuring that the pioneers of the game received the recognition they deserved.

To be considered for the Immortals, a player must first be a member of the National Rugby League Hall of Fame, ensuring that only those with a proven record of excellence are eligible. This strict eligibility criterion maintains the integrity of the Immortals and ensures that the title remains one of the highest honors in the sport. It also means that players who are inducted as Immortals have already been recognized for their outstanding contributions to rugby league, adding another layer of prestige to their selection.

The Immortals are more than just a list of great players; they represent the essence of rugby league. Each Immortal embodies the spirit of the game, from the early days of the sport to the modern era. Their stories, achievements, and impact on rugby league are celebrated not just by fans and historians but by the sport itself. The Immortals remind us of the legacy of those who have shaped rugby league into what it is today and inspire future generations to strive for greatness.

As the game continues to evolve, the Immortals will remain a cornerstone of rugby league's identity, ensuring that the contributions of its greatest players are never forgotten. The Immortals are a testament to the enduring appeal of rugby league and the extraordinary individuals who have made it one of Australia's most beloved sports. Through this recognition, the game honors its past while looking forward to the future, where new legends will emerge to continue the legacy of the Immortals.

The Immortals represent the ultimate accolade in Australian rugby league, encapsulating the highest level of excellence that players can achieve. This chapter underscores the significance of their contributions, not only as exceptional athletes but also as figures who have defined and shaped the very fabric of the sport. Their recognition as Immortals is not just about their individual achievements; it is about their lasting impact on rugby league, an impact that transcends generations and continues to inspire both players and fans alike.

Each Immortal, from the original four to the most recent inductees, has left an indelible mark on the game. Their names are synonymous with greatness, their careers studied and admired by those who aspire to reach similar heights. The Immortals serve as a bridge between the past and the present, connecting the history of rugby league with its current state and its future. By honoring these players, the sport acknowledges its roots, celebrates its present, and sets a standard for those who follow.

The expansion of the Immortals list in 2018 was a pivotal moment in the history of this prestigious group. By including pre-war players, the Australian Rugby League Commission made a bold statement about the importance of recognizing the pioneers of the game. This decision broadened the scope of the Immortals, ensuring that the honor is inclusive of all eras of rugby league, not just the post-war period. It was a move that added depth to the concept, highlighting the rich heritage of the sport and ensuring that the contributions of early players are remembered alongside those of more recent legends.

The criteria for selection as an Immortal, which requires prior induction into the National Rugby League Hall of Fame, ensures that only the most deserving players are considered for this honor. This strict standard maintains the integrity of the Immortals, making it a title that is revered and respected across the rugby league community. It is a recognition that comes with the understanding that these players have not only excelled on the field but have also contributed to the sport in ways that have had a lasting impact.

The Immortals concept has evolved over time, adapting to changes in the sport and responding to the need to recognize a broader range of players. Despite the initial criticism of its exclusivity and the focus on post-war players, the concept has grown to become a more comprehensive celebration of rugby league's history. The expansion of the Immortals in 2018 was a testament to this evolution, ensuring that the honor remains relevant and reflective of the entire history of the game.

As rugby league continues to grow and evolve, the Immortals will remain a symbol of the highest standard of excellence in the sport. They are a source of inspiration for players, reminding them of the level of greatness that is possible through dedication, skill, and a deep love for the game. For fans, the Immortals are a reminder of the incredible talents that have graced the rugby league field, providing memories that are cherished and passed down through generations.

The Immortals also play a crucial role in preserving the legacy of rugby league. By celebrating the greatest players in the sport's history, the Immortals ensure that the stories of these athletes are not lost to time. They keep the history of rugby league alive, allowing future generations to learn about and appreciate the contributions of those who have shaped the game. This preservation of history is vital for maintaining the sport's cultural significance and for continuing the traditions that make rugby league such an integral part of Australian life.

The Immortals represent the pinnacle of achievement in rugby league, embodying the best of what the sport has to offer. Their stories are a testament to the power of skill, dedication, and passion for the game. As the sport continues to evolve, the Immortals will remain a beacon of excellence, inspiring new generations of players to strive for greatness and reminding fans of the rich history that makes rugby league one of Australia's most beloved sports. The Immortals are not just a list of names; they are a living legacy that continues to shape the future of rugby league.

Chapter 55: Queensland Rugby League's Team of the Century

The Queensland Rugby League's Team of the Century is one of the most prestigious honors in Australian rugby league history. It celebrates the best players who represented Queensland from 1909 to 2008, covering almost a century of the sport's evolution. The team was carefully selected by a panel of six expert judges, who had the difficult task of choosing from a list of 100 nominated players. The final team was announced on June 10, 2008, at the Brisbane Convention and Exhibition Centre, just before the second State of Origin game that year.

This team is not just a collection of talented players but a tribute to the rich history and development of rugby league in Queensland. The sport began in the state in 1909 with the formation of the Queensland Rugby Football League competition. Over the years, this competition evolved into the Brisbane Rugby Football League in 1922, showcasing the best rugby talent in Queensland. By 1988, the national competition had expanded to include all Australian states, and Queensland clubs became a vital part of this national league. The Queensland Rugby League Team of the Century honors the players who have significantly contributed to the state's rugby legacy.

The selection process for the team was rigorous, ensuring that only the best of the best were included. The judges responsible for picking the team were former administrator Kevin Brasch, ex-Queensland halfback Cyril Connell, renowned writer Ian Heads, historian Professor Max Howell, commentator John McCoy, and historian Greg Shannon. These experts brought a wealth of knowledge and experience to the table, making sure the team reflected the highest standards of excellence in Queensland rugby league.

One of the unique aspects of this team is that it included players who, despite playing for New South Wales under residential selection rules, were originally from Queensland. This allowed the judges to consider a broader range of talent and acknowledge the contributions of players who may have left the state but were still deeply connected to Queensland's rugby league heritage. The inclusion of these players highlights the impact of Queensland-born talent on the national rugby league scene.

The announcement of the team was a momentous occasion, filled with pride and celebration. It brought together past and present players, fans, and officials, all of whom were eager to see which legends of the game would be honored. The Brisbane Convention and Exhibition Centre was buzzing with excitement as the names of the chosen players were revealed. Each player selected was celebrated not just for their individual skills and achievements but also for their role in building and sustaining the rich tradition of rugby league in Queensland.

The Queensland Rugby League Team of the Century serves as a powerful reminder of the state's long and successful history in the sport. It honors players from different eras, reflecting the changing nature of the game and the consistent production of high-caliber talent in Queensland. From the early days of the Queensland Rugby Football League to the modern era of the National Rugby League, the team represents the very best of what Queensland rugby league has to offer.

This team is more than just a list of great players; it is a testament to the passion, dedication, and skill that have defined rugby league in Queensland for nearly a century. The players selected for the Team of the Century have left a lasting legacy, inspiring future generations of rugby league players and fans. Their achievements on the field are a source of pride for all Queenslanders and a benchmark for excellence in the sport.

The Queensland Rugby League's Team of the Century is a fitting tribute to the history and tradition of rugby league in the state. It celebrates the players who have shaped the game, acknowledging their contributions and ensuring that their legacies are remembered for years to come. The team is a symbol of Queensland's enduring love for rugby league and a reminder of the state's significant role in the sport's development in Australia.

The Queensland Rugby League's Team of the Century stands as a monumental achievement in the history of the sport, encapsulating the essence of Queensland rugby league across nearly a hundred years. The selection of this team was not just about recognizing individual talent but about celebrating the collective history and identity of Queensland rugby league. Each player who was chosen represents a chapter in the state's rich sporting narrative, symbolizing the spirit, dedication, and excellence that have come to define rugby league in Queensland.

This team is more than a simple acknowledgment of past glories; it is a bridge connecting generations of rugby league players and fans. By looking back at the origins of the sport in Queensland and honoring those who have contributed to its growth, the team helps to preserve the legacy of rugby league for future generations. The inclusion of players who made their mark in different eras reminds us of the enduring quality and talent that have been a hallmark of Queensland rugby league. It shows that while the game has evolved, the passion and commitment to excellence have remained constant.

The announcement of the team in 2008 was a moment of great pride for Queenslanders. It was an opportunity to reflect on the state's achievements in the sport and to celebrate the individuals who have made those achievements possible. The event was a gathering of rugby league royalty, with past players, coaches, and officials coming together to honor the selected team. The atmosphere was electric, as fans and players alike shared in the joy of seeing their heroes recognized for their contributions to the game.

The Queensland Rugby League's Team of the Century is also a reminder of the strong tradition of rugby league in the state. From its humble beginnings in 1909 to the present day, the sport has grown and flourished in Queensland, becoming an integral part of the state's culture. The players who were selected for the team have not only excelled on the field but have also become symbols of the state's sporting identity. They have inspired countless young players to pursue their dreams and have helped to foster a deep love for the game among Queenslanders.

The selection process for the team was meticulous, ensuring that only the most deserving players were included. The judges faced a difficult task, as they had to choose from a long list of outstanding players who had all made significant contributions to Queensland rugby league. The final team is a reflection of the highest standards of excellence, showcasing the very best that the state has produced. It is a testament to the depth of talent that has come out of Queensland and the impact that these players have had on the game at both the state and national levels.

The Queensland Rugby League's Team of the Century also highlights the importance of remembering and honoring the past. In a sport that is constantly evolving, it is easy to forget the contributions of those who came before. This team serves as a reminder that the history of rugby league in Queensland is rich and full of remarkable achievements. By recognizing the players who have shaped the game, the team helps to keep their legacies alive and ensures that their stories continue to inspire future generations.

As we look to the future of rugby league in Queensland, the Team of the Century serves as a benchmark for excellence. It challenges current and future players to strive for greatness and to continue the tradition of success that has been established over the past century. The players who were selected for the team have set a high standard, and their achievements will continue to be a source of motivation for those who follow in their footsteps.

The Queensland Rugby League's Team of the Century is a fitting tribute to the players who have made a lasting impact on the sport. It is a celebration of the rich history and tradition of rugby league in Queensland, and a reminder of the state's significant contributions to the game. The team not only honors the past but also inspires the future, ensuring that the legacy of Queensland rugby league will continue for many years to come.

Chapter 56: New South Wales Rugby League's Team of the Century

The New South Wales Rugby League's Team of the Century is a prestigious honor that celebrates the greatest rugby league players from 1908 to 2007. This team is a hypothetical lineup, meaning it was created to represent the best players in each position over almost a century of rugby league history in New South Wales. Rugby league in New South Wales began in 1908 with the New South Wales Rugby Football League, which later evolved into the New South Wales Rugby League in 1984. This rich history has seen many talented players emerge, and this team represents the best of the best.

The team was officially announced on 19 May 2008, just before the first State of Origin game in Sydney. The timing was significant, as the State of Origin series is one of the most anticipated events in rugby league, where New South Wales and Queensland compete fiercely. The announcement of the Team of the Century added even more excitement to the occasion, as it allowed fans and players alike to reflect on the incredible talent that has come from New South Wales over the years.

Clive Churchill, often referred to as "The Little Master," was named the fullback and captain of the team. Churchill was known for his incredible skill, leadership, and vision on the field. He played for South Sydney and is remembered as one of the greatest players in rugby league history. His inclusion as captain of the Team of the Century highlights his importance to the game and his lasting legacy.

Ken Irvine, who was named on the wing, was famous for his speed and try-scoring ability. Irvine played for North Sydney and Manly Warringah, and he still holds the record for the most tries scored in Australian rugby league history. His inclusion in the Team of the Century is a testament to his incredible athleticism and his ability to change the course of a game with his brilliance.

Reg Gasnier and Graeme Langlands were named as the centers. Both players were key figures for the St. George Dragons, one of the most successful clubs in New South Wales rugby league history. Gasnier, known as "The Prince of Centres," was admired for his graceful playing style and his ability to read the game. Langlands, who was also known as "Changa," was a versatile player who excelled in multiple positions, including fullback and center. Together, they formed a formidable pairing that struck fear into the hearts of their opponents.

The halfback position was awarded to Andrew Johns, one of the most talented and influential players in the history of rugby league. Johns, who played for the Newcastle Knights, was known for his incredible game sense, kicking ability, and leadership. He played a crucial role in many of New South Wales' victories in the State of Origin series and is widely regarded as one of the greatest halfbacks of all time. His inclusion in the Team of the Century is a recognition of his outstanding contributions to the sport.

The forward pack of the Team of the Century is equally impressive, with legends like Frank Burge, Glenn Lazarus, and Ron Coote taking their places. Burge, who played in the early 20th century, was known for his toughness and try-scoring ability as a forward. Lazarus, who played in the 1980s and 1990s, was a key figure in the success of multiple clubs, including Canberra, Brisbane, and Melbourne. Coote, who was known for his tireless work rate and leadership, played for both South Sydney and Eastern Suburbs and was a dominant force in the forward pack.

The selection of Jack Gibson as the coach of the Team of the Century was a fitting tribute to one of the most successful and respected coaches in rugby league history. Gibson, who coached teams like Eastern Suburbs and Parramatta, was known for his innovative coaching methods and his ability to get the best out of his players. He won multiple premierships during his coaching career and is often referred to as the "Super Coach" of rugby league.

The New South Wales Rugby League's Team of the Century is a celebration of the state's rich rugby league history and the incredible players who have contributed to the sport's success. This team represents the pinnacle of achievement in New South Wales rugby league, with each player chosen for their outstanding skills, leadership, and impact on the game. The announcement of the team was a moment of great pride for New South Wales and provided an opportunity for fans to reflect on the remarkable talent that has graced the rugby league fields over the past century.

The New South Wales Rugby League's Team of the Century serves as a powerful reminder of the rich history and tradition of rugby league in New South Wales. The players selected for this team are more than just exceptional athletes; they are icons of the game who have left an indelible mark on the sport. Their contributions have shaped the course of rugby league, not only in New South Wales but across Australia and the world.

Each player chosen for this prestigious team represents the pinnacle of rugby league talent in their respective eras. From the early days of the sport, where players like Dally Messenger and Frank Burge laid the foundation, to the modern era, where legends like Andrew Johns and Glenn Lazarus took the game to new heights, these athletes have all played a vital role in the evolution of rugby league. The team is a testament to the enduring legacy of these players, whose names are etched in the annals of rugby league history.

The selection process for the Team of the Century was rigorous and carefully considered, reflecting the deep respect and admiration that the rugby league community holds for its greatest players. The panel of judges, comprising former players, historians, and commentators, had the daunting task of narrowing down a list of 100 nominees to just 17 players. The final team is a perfect blend of skill, determination, and leadership, showcasing the very best that New South Wales rugby league has to offer.

The announcement of the team ahead of the State of Origin series added an extra layer of significance to the event. State of Origin is a fierce rivalry between New South Wales and Queensland, and the Team of the Century highlighted the incredible talent that has come out of New South Wales over the years. It served as a reminder of the state's dominance in the sport and its proud tradition of producing world-class players.

The impact of these players extends beyond the field. They have inspired generations of young athletes to take up the sport and have set a standard of excellence that continues to influence the game today. Their achievements have been celebrated by fans, coaches, and fellow players alike, and their legacies continue to be honored through various awards and recognitions.

As time goes on, new players will emerge, and the game will continue to evolve. However, the legacy of the New South Wales Rugby League's Team of the

Century will remain intact. These players have set the benchmark for greatness, and their contributions will never be forgotten. The team not only represents the best of the past but also serves as a source of inspiration for the future.

The New South Wales Rugby League's Team of the Century is more than just a collection of names; it is a symbol of the spirit, passion, and dedication that define rugby league. It is a celebration of the players who have given their all for the sport and have left a lasting impact on the game. This team will forever be remembered as a testament to the greatness of New South Wales rugby league and the incredible players who have made it what it is today.

Part Eight: The Fans and the Media

Chapter 57: The 2022 Season Viewership and Attendance

The 2022 NRL season was a remarkable year for rugby league in Australia, not just for the intense competition on the field, but also for the audience engagement off the field. This chapter dives into the viewership statistics and attendance records that highlight the sport's popularity and the challenges it faced.

In 2022, the NRL season reached a staggering 134.447 million viewers across Australia. On average, each game was watched by about 620,000 people. This impressive number reflects the sport's deep roots in Australian culture and its ability to attract a broad audience. The viewership was split between free-to-air broadcasts on Nine Network and subscription services like Fox League and Kayo Sports, with a 60/40 distribution. This split shows the growing trend towards paid television and streaming services, although traditional free-to-air broadcasts still play a vital role in reaching the masses.

Attendance at the games has always been a key indicator of the sport's popularity. Over the years, the numbers have seen fluctuations, influenced by various factors, including the performance of teams, economic conditions, and external events like the COVID-19 pandemic. In 1998, the total season attendance was 2,937,741, with an average of 11,612 per game. By 2022, the attendance had grown to 3,265,911, with an average of 16,248 per game, showcasing the steady growth of the sport's fanbase.

One of the most striking attendance records was set in 1999 when the season's total attendance reached 3,273,372, with an astonishing Grand Final attendance of 107,999. This was a record high for the NRL, highlighting the peak interest in the sport during that period. The Grand Final has always been a major draw, with crowds often exceeding 80,000 spectators, making it one of the most significant sporting events in Australia each year.

However, the NRL also faced challenges, particularly during the COVID-19 pandemic. The 2020 season saw a dramatic drop in attendance, with only 671,412 spectators recorded for the entire season. The average attendance plummeted to 5,245 per game, a record low, as games were played in empty venues or with severely restricted crowds due to biosecurity protocols. The pandemic's impact was also felt in the 2021 season, with some games played without spectators and an overall average attendance of just 10,364 per game.

Despite these challenges, the 2022 season marked a significant recovery, with attendance figures bouncing back to near pre-pandemic levels. The Grand Final that year attracted 82,415 fans, a clear sign that the passion for rugby league remained strong even after the disruptions caused by the pandemic. The resilience of the sport and its fans was evident, as they returned in large numbers to support their teams.

The 2023 season further solidified the sport's recovery, with a total attendance of 4,086,547, averaging 19,186 spectators per game. Although the Grand Final attendance slightly dipped to 81,947, the overall increase in season attendance was a positive indicator of the sport's enduring appeal.

The 2022 NRL season was a testament to the sport's ability to captivate a large audience, both through television broadcasts and live game attendance. The viewership numbers highlighted the balance between traditional and modern broadcasting methods, while the attendance figures reflected the sport's recovery from the challenges posed by the COVID-19 pandemic. As the NRL continues to grow and adapt, the 2022 season will be remembered as a pivotal year that demonstrated the unwavering support of rugby league fans across Australia.

The 2022 NRL season, with its impressive viewership and resilient attendance figures, underscores the enduring passion for rugby league in Australia. The year was marked by a strong recovery from the disruptions of the previous two seasons, where the COVID-19 pandemic had significantly impacted how the sport was consumed by fans. Despite these challenges, the sport bounced back, drawing in millions of viewers and filling stadiums once again, highlighting the deep connection between the game and its supporters.

The viewership statistics, with over 134 million tuning in, demonstrate the wide-reaching appeal of the NRL. The balance between free-to-air broadcasts and subscription services shows that while new media platforms are gaining traction, traditional broadcasting still holds a crucial place in reaching large audiences. The 60/40 split between viewers on free-to-air and subscription services reflects changing habits in how people watch sports, but also confirms that the NRL has successfully adapted to these shifts.

Attendance figures over the years have mirrored the sport's fluctuating fortunes, but the steady increase in numbers leading up to 2022 tells a story of growth and resilience. The return of fans to the stadiums in large numbers, particularly after the pandemic, highlights the importance of live sports experiences. For many, attending games is more than just watching a match; it's about being part of a community, sharing the highs and lows with fellow supporters, and feeling the collective energy that only live events can provide.

The record highs and lows in attendance across different seasons offer a snapshot of the sport's history, reflecting moments of triumph and challenge. The all-time high in 1999 with over 107,000 attending the Grand Final remains a benchmark for the sport, a testament to the peak interest in rugby league during that era. Conversely, the record lows in 2020 serve as a reminder of the unprecedented impact of global events on sports, yet also of the sport's capacity to overcome such obstacles.

The gradual recovery in attendance in 2021 and the substantial rebound in 2022 indicate the strength of the sport's fanbase. Even with the lingering effects of the pandemic, fans showed their dedication by returning to the stadiums as soon as it was safe to do so. The consistent high numbers, particularly for the Grand Finals, underscore the event's status as a pinnacle of Australian sports culture, an occasion that draws fans from across the country to witness the crowning of the season's champions.

As the sport moves forward, the lessons from the 2022 season will be essential for future growth. The ability to attract and retain viewers, both on television and in stadiums, will be key to sustaining the sport's popularity. Continued adaptation to changing viewing habits, such as the rise of streaming services, and maintaining the appeal of live events will ensure that rugby league remains a cornerstone of Australian sports.

The 2022 season, therefore, stands as a significant chapter in the NRL's history, not just for the numbers it produced, but for what those numbers represent. They tell a story of recovery, resilience, and the unbreakable bond between the sport and its fans. Looking ahead, the NRL can build on this momentum, striving to reach new heights in viewership and attendance, while continuing to deliver the thrilling, high-energy competition that has made rugby league one of Australia's most beloved sports.

Chapter 58: ANZ and Pacific

Rugby league has become a significant part of the sports culture in Australia, New Zealand, and across the Pacific. The broadcast agreements in these regions reflect the sport's popularity and the demand for high-quality coverage. Within Australia, all NRL matches are broadcast on both the Nine Network and Fox Sports, ensuring that fans can watch every game, regardless of where they are. This comprehensive coverage is a testament to the sport's wide-reaching appeal, with both free-to-air and subscription options available to cater to different viewing preferences.

The partnership with Fox Sports, which was solidified in May 2020, guarantees that rugby league fans will continue to enjoy uninterrupted access to their favorite sport through 2027. This deal was a significant step in maintaining the sport's visibility and accessibility, ensuring that fans can watch all the action live, whether at home or on the go. The extension of Nine's contract in December 2021 to match the length of Fox Sports' deal further strengthens the sport's media presence, giving viewers multiple platforms to enjoy the games.

In New Zealand, rugby league also enjoys extensive coverage, with Sky Sport broadcasting all matches live, including key representative fixtures like the All Stars Match and the State of Origin series. This arrangement ensures that New Zealand fans have access to the same high-quality broadcasts as their

Australian counterparts, fostering a strong rugby league following across the Tasman. The commitment to live coverage of every match underscores the importance of rugby league in New Zealand's sports landscape, where it continues to grow in popularity.

Additionally, Prime, a free-to-air channel in New Zealand, began broadcasting select NRL games live starting from the 2022 season. This move was particularly significant for fans of the New Zealand Warriors, as Prime committed to broadcasting every Warriors match on delay. This ensures that fans who may not have access to pay-TV services can still watch their favorite team play, keeping the Warriors' passionate fanbase engaged and connected to the sport.

The reach of rugby league extends beyond Australia and New Zealand, with growing interest in the Pacific Islands. The sport has a strong following in countries like Papua New Guinea, Fiji, and Samoa, where rugby league is not just a sport but a significant part of the cultural identity. Broadcasts of NRL matches and representative fixtures in these regions help to maintain and grow this connection, allowing Pacific Islanders to follow their favorite teams and players, many of whom hail from the Pacific themselves.

The NRL's commitment to broadcasting in these regions reflects a broader strategy to expand the game's reach and tap into new markets. The popularity of rugby league in the Pacific Islands also means that there is a growing talent pool from these regions, with many Pacific Islanders becoming key players in the NRL. The visibility of these players on the global stage not only boosts the sport's popularity but also inspires the next generation of rugby league stars in the Pacific.

The contracts with broadcasters in Australia and New Zealand are crucial for the continued growth and success of rugby league in these regions. By securing long-term deals, the NRL has ensured that the sport will remain a staple of the sports viewing landscape, reaching millions of fans across multiple platforms. This accessibility is key to maintaining the sport's popularity and attracting new fans, as well as providing stability for the NRL as it looks to the future.

Looking ahead, the NRL will likely continue to explore ways to expand its reach, both within the ANZ region and into new territories. The sport's growing popularity in the Pacific Islands presents opportunities for further engagement, whether through grassroots development, more targeted broadcasts, or even the possibility of hosting NRL games in these regions. The goal will be to build on the strong foundation that has been established, ensuring that rugby league continues to thrive and inspire fans across Australia, New Zealand, and the Pacific.

The coverage of rugby league in Australia, New Zealand, and the broader Pacific region underscores the sport's importance and the significant role it plays in the lives of millions. The comprehensive broadcast agreements, particularly those secured with the Nine Network and Fox Sports, demonstrate the commitment to ensuring that fans have consistent access to every match, no matter where they are. These long-term deals reflect the enduring popularity of rugby league and its place as a central pillar of sporting culture in these regions.

In Australia, the dual-platform coverage provided by Nine and Fox Sports allows for a broad reach, catering to both free-to-air viewers and those who prefer subscription services. This approach ensures that the sport is accessible to a wide audience, fostering a strong connection between the game and its fans. The partnership with Fox Sports, in particular, highlights the importance of high-quality, uninterrupted coverage, while the extension of Nine's contract shows a unified effort to maintain rugby league's visibility.

New Zealand's commitment to broadcasting all NRL matches live on Sky Sport, along with Prime's decision to air select games and every Warriors match on delay, illustrates the growing significance of rugby league across the Tasman. These broadcasting decisions ensure that the sport continues to grow in popularity, with fans in New Zealand enjoying the same level of access and coverage as those in Australia. The focus on live coverage also enhances the viewing experience, keeping fans engaged and invested in the sport.

The inclusion of the Pacific Islands in the broadcast strategy acknowledges the deep connection between these regions and rugby league. For many in the Pacific, rugby league is more than just a sport—it is a source of pride and cultural identity. The visibility of NRL matches in these areas not only strengthens this connection but also provides inspiration to young athletes who aspire to play at the highest levels. The presence of Pacific Island players in the NRL further reinforces this bond, as these players serve as role models for the next generation.

The NRL's broadcast agreements are more than just business deals; they are a reflection of the sport's impact on communities across Australia, New Zealand, and the Pacific. By securing long-term coverage, the NRL has ensured that rugby league will continue to be a part of daily life for millions of fans. This stability is crucial for the sport's growth, as it allows for the development of new initiatives, the nurturing of talent, and the exploration of new markets.

The reach and accessibility provided by these broadcasting agreements are key to maintaining rugby league's position as a premier sport in the ANZ region. As the sport continues to evolve, these partnerships will play a vital role in its future success. They provide the platform for the NRL to not only retain its current fanbase but also to attract new fans, both in established markets and in emerging ones.

Looking forward, the NRL's ability to adapt and expand its broadcast strategy will be essential in meeting the challenges and opportunities that lie ahead. The continued engagement with fans in Australia, New Zealand, and the Pacific will ensure that rugby league remains a vibrant and thriving sport. The foundations laid by these broadcast agreements provide a solid base upon which the NRL can build, ensuring that the sport continues to captivate audiences and inspire future generations across the region.

Chapter 59: Detailed Australian Coverage

The way rugby league is broadcast in Australia is carefully planned to give fans the best viewing experience. Each matchday has its own special time slots, and different networks share the responsibility of bringing the games to the audience. This chapter breaks down how each day of the week is covered, the role of each network, and the major events that receive special attention.

Thursday Night Footy is the first game of the round and is broadcast live on the Nine Network. For fans who prefer watching on pay TV, it is also simulcast on Fox League and Kayo. The match kicks off at 7:50 pm, making it a prime time event that sets the tone for the weekend. This game often features top teams, making it a must-watch for rugby league enthusiasts.

Friday Night Football is a doubleheader, meaning there are two games back-to-back. The first match starts at 6:00 pm and is exclusively on Fox League. This game is perfect for fans who like to start their weekend with some early evening rugby league action. The second match kicks off at 8:00 pm and is broadcast live on the Nine Network, with simulcast options available on Fox League and Kayo. This later game is usually the main event of the night, often featuring highly anticipated matchups.

Super Saturday is a fan-favorite, featuring three games in a row. The action starts at 3:00 pm with the first match, followed by a 5:30 pm kickoff for the second game. The day wraps up with a 7:35 pm match. All three games are broadcast live on Fox League and simulcast on Kayo, ensuring fans can watch the entire day's action without interruption. During the last five rounds of the season, the 7:35 pm match is also simulcast on the Nine Network, giving even more viewers access to this prime-time game.

NRL Sunday Ticket wraps up the round with two games. The first game kicks off at 2:00 pm and is available on Fox League and Kayo. The second match is the highlight of the day, starting at 4:10 pm and being broadcast live on the Nine Network, with simulcasts on Fox League and Kayo. During daylight savings time, the first game is moved to a 6:15 pm kickoff, adjusting the schedule to fit the later sunset. This ensures that fans can enjoy rugby league well into the evening.

When it comes to network coverage, **Fox League and Kayo** are the go-to platforms for fans who want to watch every game live and without commercials. They broadcast all matches, except for the grand final, which is exclusively on free-to-air TV. This makes Fox League and Kayo essential for die-hard fans who don't want to miss a single moment of the season.

The **Nine Network** focuses on the most popular games, including the Thursday night game, the second

Friday night game, and the second Sunday afternoon game, which becomes the first game during daylight savings. Nine also broadcasts the final five Saturday night games of the year at 7:30 pm. In addition to these regular matches, Nine covers special events like the NRL Good Friday Game and the Anzac Day Cup, which are key fixtures in the rugby league calendar. During the finals series, Nine takes on the responsibility of broadcasting all games, including the highly anticipated NRL Grand Final, which has become a tradition in Australian sports.

The **State of Origin series**, one of the most watched and celebrated events in rugby league, is exclusively broadcast live on the Nine Network. This series between New South Wales and Queensland captivates millions of viewers, with extensive pre-game and post-game coverage providing in-depth analysis and fan engagement. The games start at 7:00 pm, ensuring prime-time viewership across the nation.

Finally, the **NRL Grand Final** is the pinnacle of the season, drawing in a massive audience. It is broadcast exclusively live on the Nine Network, with a kickoff time of 7:30 pm. Since 2013, this time slot has become a staple, allowing families and fans across the country to gather for the most important game of the year.

The detailed broadcast schedule for rugby league in Australia ensures that fans have multiple options to watch their favorite teams in action. The careful planning by the networks, with specific time slots for each matchday and exclusive coverage of major events, highlights the importance of rugby league in Australian sports culture. This structured approach not only maximizes viewership but also strengthens the connection between the game and its passionate fanbase. As the sport continues to grow, these broadcasting strategies will play a crucial role in maintaining rugby league's popularity across the nation.

The comprehensive broadcast strategy outlined in this chapter underscores the immense popularity of rugby league in Australia and the careful planning that goes into ensuring fans can access the games they love. With the sport being a cornerstone of Australian culture, the collaboration between networks like Fox League, Kayo, and the Nine Network plays a pivotal role in maintaining its widespread appeal. Each day of the week is meticulously scheduled to cater to different segments of the audience, providing them with multiple opportunities to engage with the sport, whether they prefer to watch on free-to-air TV or through subscription services.

The division of matches across different networks also speaks to the strategic partnerships that help maximize reach and viewership. Fox League and Kayo's commercial-free, live broadcasts ensure that dedicated fans can immerse themselves in every match without interruptions. On the other hand, the Nine Network's focus on prime-time games and special events like the State of Origin series and the

NRL Grand Final helps bring the excitement of rugby league to the broader public. This dual approach caters to both the hardcore fanbase and the casual viewers, ensuring that the sport remains accessible and engaging for all.

The inclusion of special fixtures like the Good Friday Game and the Anzac Day Cup in Nine's broadcast schedule further highlights the cultural significance of rugby league in Australia. These games are more than just sporting events; they are moments that bring communities together, often carrying symbolic meaning that resonates beyond the field. By broadcasting these games, Nine not only showcases high-quality rugby league but also contributes to the social fabric by reinforcing shared values and traditions.

Furthermore, the scheduling adjustments during daylight savings and the final rounds of the season demonstrate the networks' responsiveness to viewer needs. By moving game times and offering simulcasts, they ensure that fans can continue to enjoy rugby league without disruption. This flexibility is key to maintaining viewer engagement throughout the entire season, especially as the competition heats up towards the finals.

The exclusivity of the State of Origin series on the Nine Network highlights the event's status as a premier sporting spectacle in Australia. The extensive coverage surrounding these matches ensures that fans are not only entertained by the on-field action but are also immersed in the narratives, rivalries, and traditions that make the series so special. It's a testament to the enduring appeal of State of Origin, which has become a cultural institution in its own right.

Finally, the NRL Grand Final's prime-time slot on the Nine Network solidifies its place as the most important event in the rugby league calendar. The build-up to the Grand Final, coupled with the extensive live coverage, ensures that it remains a unifying event for fans across the country. The consistent 7:30 pm kickoff time since 2013 has established a tradition that millions of Australians look forward to each year, creating lasting memories and moments of celebration.

The detailed broadcast arrangements for rugby league in Australia reflect the sport's deep-rooted connection with its audience. The collaboration between networks, the careful scheduling of matches, and the emphasis on special events all contribute to a comprehensive viewing experience that caters to a diverse and passionate fanbase. As rugby league continues to evolve, these broadcast strategies will be essential in sustaining its popularity and ensuring that the sport remains a central part of Australian life for years to come.

Chapter 60: NRL-Related Television Programmes

Rugby league has a special place in Australian culture, and its popularity extends beyond the live matches. There are several television shows dedicated to discussing, analyzing, and celebrating the NRL. These programs offer fans in-depth coverage, insights, and entertainment, creating a comprehensive rugby league experience that goes beyond the game itself. In this chapter, we will explore some of the most popular NRL-related television programs, highlighting how they contribute to the sport's vibrant media landscape.

The Sunday Footy Show kicks off the week's NRL coverage with an engaging mix of game recaps and previews. Airing at 11:00 am on Channel Nine, this show is the perfect way for fans to catch up on the action from Thursday, Friday, and Saturday, while also getting a sneak peek at the upcoming Sunday games. Hosted by Danika Mason, the show brings together a panel of experts who share their thoughts on the performances, key moments, and strategies of the teams. The Sunday Footy Show has become a staple for many NRL fans, offering a blend of analysis and light-hearted banter that keeps viewers coming back each week.

Sunday Night with Matty Johns, airing after Sunday Football on Fox League, continues the weekend's rugby league conversation. Hosted by the charismatic Matthew Johns, this show adds a dose of humor and personality to the game analysis. With a mix of guests, including former players and current stars, the show offers unique insights and stories from within the rugby league world. The relaxed atmosphere and entertaining segments make it a favorite among fans who enjoy a more casual, yet informative, look at the sport.

NRL 360 is one of the most influential NRL programs, airing on Fox League from Monday to Wednesday at 6:30 pm. Hosted by Braith Anasta and Paul Kent, the show delves into the latest news, controversies, and developments in the NRL. NRL 360 is known for its robust discussions and debates, often tackling the most pressing issues in the game. The hosts are joined by a rotating panel of experts, including journalists, former players, and coaches, who provide a variety of perspectives on the topics at hand. For fans who want to stay up-to-date with everything happening in the rugby league world, NRL 360 is a must-watch.

100% Footy offers a late-night take on the weekend's results, airing on Channel 9 at 10:30 pm on Mondays. Hosted by James Bracey, this show combines match analysis with broader discussions about the major issues facing the NRL. The show often features interviews with key figures in the game, providing viewers with deeper insights into the decisions and dynamics that shape the league. The relaxed, yet informative, style of 100% Footy makes it a great option for fans who want a more in-depth understanding of the sport.

The Fan, hosted by Andrew Voss with Lara Pitt, airs on Fox League at 7:30 pm on Tuesdays. This show takes a different approach by focusing on the stories and personalities that make rugby league special. The Fan explores the history of the sport, profiles of legendary players, and the unique culture surrounding the NRL. It's a show that celebrates the passion of rugby league fans and provides a platform for the more quirky and interesting aspects of the game. For viewers who enjoy the storytelling side of sports, The Fan is an engaging and enjoyable watch.

Over The Black Dot, airing on NITV at 8:30 pm on Wednesdays, offers an Indigenous Australian perspective on the NRL. This show is important not only for its rugby league content but also for its focus on Indigenous culture and the contributions of Indigenous players to the sport. The show features highlights, discussions, and interviews, providing a unique and valuable perspective on the game. Over The Black Dot helps to broaden the rugby league conversation and ensures that Indigenous voices are heard within the sport.

The Late Show with Matty Johns adds a touch of humor and entertainment to Thursday nights, airing at 10:00 pm on Fox League. Hosted by Matthew Johns, this show is a mix of comedy, interviews, and game previews. The Late Show with Matty Johns is known for its light-hearted and fun approach, making it a great way to wind down after a day of rugby league action. The show's comedic segments and entertaining interviews make it a hit with fans who enjoy a good laugh along with their rugby league content.

League Legends, which airs during the off-season on Sundays at 6:30 pm on Fox League, offers fans a chance to look back at the careers of some of the greatest players in NRL history. Hosted by Tim Sheridan, the show features interviews with rugby league legends, exploring their journeys, achievements, and the impact they have had on the sport. League Legends provides an important connection between the past and present of rugby league, allowing fans to appreciate the history and evolution of the game.

Finally, **Bloke in a Bar** offers a different kind of rugby league content, available on YouTube on Mondays, Wednesdays, and Fridays at 3:00 pm. Hosted by former NRL player Denan Kemp, this show is a mix of match analysis, player interviews, and fan interaction. Bloke in a Bar has a casual, conversational style that appeals to a broad audience, and its presence on YouTube makes it easily accessible to fans. The show's focus on fan engagement and its relaxed format make it a popular choice for those looking for rugby league content outside of traditional television.

The wide variety of NRL-related television programs in Australia reflects the sport's massive popularity and the diverse interests of its fanbase. Whether it's in-depth analysis, light-hearted entertainment, or a focus on the history and culture of rugby league, there's a show for every type of fan. These programs play a crucial role in keeping the rugby league community informed, entertained, and connected, ensuring that the sport continues to thrive both on and off the field.

The array of NRL-related television programs in Australia highlights the depth and breadth of rugby league's influence on the nation's culture. These shows do more than just report on the games—they offer a comprehensive view of the sport, delving into the history, personalities, and stories that make rugby league so compelling. Each program serves a unique purpose, whether it's providing detailed analysis, showcasing the lighter side of the sport, or giving a platform to voices that may otherwise be overlooked. Collectively, they ensure that the NRL is more than just a weekend event; it's a continuous narrative that keeps fans engaged throughout the week and the year.

One of the key roles these shows play is in connecting the fans with the players and the game on a more personal level. Shows like "The Fan" and "League Legends" bring to life the stories behind the statistics, allowing viewers to see the human side of their favorite athletes. This connection helps build loyalty and a deeper emotional investment in the sport, making every try, tackle, and victory more meaningful for the fans. The focus on history and the legends of the game also fosters a sense of continuity and tradition, which is vital in a sport with such a rich heritage.

The variety of perspectives offered by these programs also enriches the rugby league conversation. Whether it's the Indigenous perspective provided by "Over The Black Dot" or the fan-driven content of "Bloke in a Bar," these shows ensure that the discourse around rugby league is inclusive and diverse. This is particularly important in a sport that plays such a significant role in the cultural identity of many Australians. By giving a voice to different communities and viewpoints, these programs contribute to a more nuanced and well-rounded understanding of the NRL.

Moreover, the accessibility of these shows across different platforms—from traditional television to digital streaming—ensures that the NRL can reach a wide and varied audience. This accessibility is crucial in maintaining and growing the sport's fanbase. Whether fans are watching live on Fox League, catching up on highlights on YouTube, or enjoying a late-night recap on Channel 9, there's always a way to stay connected to the game. The integration of new media platforms, like YouTube for "Bloke in a Bar," shows how rugby league is evolving with the times, ensuring that it remains relevant and engaging in the digital age.

The blend of entertainment and analysis in these programs also adds to the appeal of the NRL. Shows like "Sunday Night with Matty Johns" and "The Late Show with Matty Johns" inject humor and personality into the rugby league coverage, making it enjoyable even for casual viewers. This approach helps to broaden the sport's appeal, attracting new fans who might not be as interested in the technical aspects of the game but enjoy the entertainment value. These shows demonstrate that rugby league is not just a sport but a form of entertainment that can be enjoyed in many different ways.

Finally, the continuous coverage provided by these programs helps to keep rugby league at the forefront of the public's consciousness. Even during the off-season, shows like "League Legends" keep the conversation going, ensuring that the sport remains a constant presence in the lives of its fans. This year-round engagement is critical in maintaining the sport's popularity and ensuring that when the new season starts, the fans are just as excited and invested as ever. It also helps to build anticipation for upcoming matches and events, keeping the excitement levels high.

NRL-related television programs play a pivotal role in the success and popularity of rugby league in Australia. They provide a platform for analysis, storytelling, and entertainment, ensuring that the sport remains a vital part of the national conversation. Through these shows, fans are able to connect with the game in deeper and more meaningful ways, ensuring that their passion for rugby league continues to grow. Whether through in-depth discussions, light-hearted banter, or historical retrospectives, these programs enrich the rugby league experience and help to sustain the sport's vibrant culture.

Chapter 61: Former Shows

The history of rugby league coverage in Australia is rich with television programs that have come and gone. These shows were integral in shaping how fans engaged with the sport, offering a variety of perspectives and styles of content. Some of these shows focused on deep analysis, while others provided entertainment and humor. Though they are no longer on the air, their impact on rugby league culture remains significant.

One of the well-known former shows was "Barefoot Sports," which aired on NITV every Thursday at 8:30 pm. Hosted by Brad Cooke, it was previously known as "The Barefoot Rugby League Show." This program was unique in its approach, offering an Indigenous perspective on the game and celebrating the contributions of Aboriginal and Torres Strait Islander players. It wasn't just about the game itself but also about the communities and cultures that are deeply connected to rugby league. The show's focus on inclusivity and diversity helped broaden the conversation around the sport, making it more accessible to all Australians.

"One Week at a Time" was another popular show that aired on Mondays at 9:30 pm on One. This program provided a recap of the weekend's games, offering fans a chance to catch up on all the action they might have missed. With its straightforward format, the show focused on delivering highlights and key moments from each match, making it a go-to for fans who wanted to stay informed without the need for in-depth analysis. Its simplicity and focus on the game itself made it a staple for many rugby league enthusiasts during its run.

"The Game Plan," which aired on Channel Ten every Thursday at 8:30 pm, was a more analytical program. Hosted by Steve Roach, Joel Caine, and Andrew Moore, it delved into the strategies and tactics of the game. The show's hosts brought a wealth of experience and knowledge, making it an essential watch for fans who wanted to understand the intricacies of rugby league. "The Game Plan" catered to a more serious audience, those who were keen on understanding the sport beyond just the scores and highlights.

"The Matty Johns Show," airing on Channel Seven on Thursdays at 7:30 pm, took a different approach. Unlike its more serious counterparts, this show was oriented towards sketches and regular segments, adding a touch of humor to rugby league coverage. Hosted by the charismatic Matty Johns, it wasn't related to "Monday Night with Matty Johns" but shared a similar tone of lightheartedness. The show's blend of comedy and rugby league content made it a refreshing change from the typical sports analysis shows, attracting a broad audience who enjoyed a good laugh along with their sports news.

Another memorable show was "The Sunday Roast," which aired on Channel Nine at midday every Sunday. This program was later incorporated into the "Sunday Footy Show." "The Sunday Roast" was known for its casual and relaxed approach to discussing the game, making it feel like a group of friends chatting about rugby league over a barbecue. Its easy-going style made it a favorite among viewers who appreciated a more laid-back discussion of the weekend's events.

"NRL Full-time" was a weekly half-hour highlights show specifically designed for the UK audience. It provided an essential service for rugby league fans overseas, giving them a way to stay connected with the sport from afar. The show's focus on delivering the best moments from each week ensured that even those not in Australia could enjoy the thrill of the NRL, helping to spread the sport's popularity beyond Australian borders.

"On the Couch with Sterlo" was another show that left its mark on rugby league broadcasting. Hosted by Peter Sterling, it provided in-depth analysis and interviews with key figures in the sport. The show's intimate and insightful format allowed for deep dives into the game, offering viewers a chance to hear from players, coaches, and experts. It was a show for the true rugby league aficionado, providing content that went beyond the usual match-day coverage.

Other notable former shows include "League Life," "Queenslanders Only," and "Narrow World of Sports," all of which aired on Fox League 502. "League Life," hosted by Yvonne Sampson, focused on the stories behind the game, featuring interviews and discussions with players and figures within the sport. "Queenslanders Only," hosted by Hannah Hollis, catered specifically to the Queensland audience, celebrating the state's rich rugby league culture. "Narrow World of Sports," hosted by James 'The Professor' Rochford, brought a humorous and satirical take on the sport, adding another layer of entertainment for fans.

These former rugby league television programs played a significant role in shaping how the sport was consumed and discussed in Australia. Each show brought something unique to the table, whether it was in-depth analysis, humor, or a focus on community and culture. Although they are no longer on the air, their legacy continues to influence how rugby league is covered and appreciated today. The variety of shows ensured that there was something for every type of fan, helping to grow and sustain the sport's popularity across the nation.

The legacy of former rugby league television programs is a testament to the sport's deep connection with its audience. These shows were more than just entertainment; they were a crucial part of the fabric that wove rugby league into the everyday lives of fans. Each program offered a unique lens through which the game could be viewed, whether through humor, in-depth analysis, or cultural perspectives. They catered to different tastes, ensuring that every fan could find something that resonated with them. The diversity in programming reflected the diversity of the rugby league community itself, with each show contributing to the broader understanding and appreciation of the sport.

Shows like "Barefoot Sports" brought an important cultural perspective to the fore, emphasizing the contributions of Indigenous players and communities to rugby league. This was more than just a sports show; it was a platform for voices that are often underrepresented in mainstream media. By highlighting the intersection of sport and culture, "Barefoot Sports" played a significant role in fostering inclusivity within the rugby league community, making the sport more accessible to all Australians.

On the other hand, programs like "One Week at a Time" and "The Game Plan" focused more on the technical and strategic aspects of the game. These shows were essential for fans who wanted to deepen their understanding of rugby league, going beyond the surface-level excitement of the matches to explore the tactics and strategies that define the sport. They provided viewers with insights that enhanced their appreciation of the game, making each match more engaging and meaningful.

"The Matty Johns Show" and "The Sunday Roast" brought a lighter touch to rugby league coverage, infusing humor and entertainment into the sports discussion. These programs reminded viewers that rugby league is not just a serious competition but also a source of joy and camaraderie. By incorporating comedy and relatable segments, these shows created a more relaxed and enjoyable viewing experience, attracting a broader audience that included not just die-hard fans but also casual viewers who appreciated the entertainment value.

Internationally, "NRL Full-time" played a crucial role in connecting overseas fans with the NRL. By providing highlights and key moments from the week's games, it allowed rugby league enthusiasts in the UK to stay connected with the sport, despite the geographical distance. This program was a vital link for the global rugby league community, ensuring that the passion for the sport extended beyond Australia's borders.

"On the Couch with Sterlo" and other analysis-driven programs like "League Life" provided viewers with a deeper understanding of the sport by offering expert opinions and interviews with key figures. These shows were instrumental in shaping the narrative around rugby league, providing context and analysis that enriched the viewing experience. They allowed fans to engage with the sport on a more intellectual level, making each game not just a spectacle but a topic for thoughtful discussion.

Programs like "Queenslanders Only" and "Narrow World of Sports" catered to specific segments of the rugby league audience, reflecting the regional and cultural diversity within the fanbase. By focusing on the unique aspects of Queensland's rugby league culture or providing a satirical take on the sport, these shows added layers of richness to the overall coverage of rugby league. They ensured that every fan, regardless of where they were from or how they engaged with the sport, had content that spoke to their interests.

The former rugby league television programs discussed in this chapter played a vital role in the sport's evolution and its relationship with its audience. They were not just shows; they were cultural touchstones that helped shape the identity of rugby league in Australia. Each program, in its way, contributed to the sport's growth and popularity, ensuring that rugby league remained a central part of Australian life. Although these shows are no longer on the air, their impact continues to be felt, as they laid the foundation for the current landscape of rugby league coverage. The legacy of these programs is a reminder of the enduring power of sports media to connect, entertain, and educate, bringing fans closer to the game they love.

Chapter 62: New Zealand Coverage

Rugby league is a beloved sport in New Zealand, with a dedicated fan base that eagerly follows both local and international games. The television coverage in New Zealand ensures that fans have access to all the action, whether it's the regular NRL season, the high-stakes State of Origin series, or the thrilling grand final. This chapter will explore the various ways rugby league is broadcasted in New Zealand, focusing on the channels that bring the game to the people.

Sky Sport is the primary broadcaster for rugby league in New Zealand. Sky Sport 4 is the dedicated channel where fans can watch all NRL games live. This includes not only the regular season matches but also special events like the State of Origin series and the grand final. The ability to watch these games live is crucial for fans who want to keep up with the latest developments and support their favorite teams as the action unfolds.

The State of Origin series is one of the most anticipated events in the rugby league calendar. It's a fierce rivalry between New South Wales and Queensland that draws massive audiences. In New Zealand, Sky Sport ensures that every match of the State of Origin series is broadcast live, allowing fans to experience the intensity and excitement of these games in real-time. The live coverage of the grand final, the climax of the NRL season, is another highlight, bringing the drama and spectacle of the sport to New Zealand screens.

In addition to Sky Sport 4, Sky Open plays an important role in the coverage of rugby league in New Zealand. While Sky Sport 4 offers comprehensive live coverage, Sky Open provides access to Warriors games on delay. The Warriors, New Zealand's very own NRL team, have a strong following, and Sky Open's delayed broadcasts ensure that fans who may not have access to Sky Sport 4 can still watch their team in action. This delayed coverage helps to keep the Warriors' fan base engaged and connected to the team throughout the season.

Sky Open also broadcasts some select matches live. These are typically high-interest games that attract a broader audience. By offering these live broadcasts, Sky Open expands the reach of rugby league in New Zealand, allowing more people to enjoy the sport. This is particularly important for maintaining the sport's popularity and ensuring that key games are accessible to as many fans as possible.

Another important broadcaster in New Zealand is Three. This channel focuses on select State of Origin games, broadcasting them live. The State of Origin series is a major event in the rugby league world, and having it broadcast on a free-to-air channel like Three means that even those without access to Sky Sport can still enjoy some of the biggest matches of the season. This helps to bring rugby league to a wider audience, increasing the sport's visibility and popularity in New Zealand.

The coverage provided by these channels ensures that rugby league remains a prominent sport in New Zealand. With live broadcasts, delayed games, and select matches available on different platforms, fans have multiple ways to engage with the sport. This comprehensive coverage helps to sustain the passion for rugby league in New Zealand, keeping fans connected to the game and their favorite teams.

The television coverage of rugby league in New Zealand is extensive and well-rounded, catering to the needs of the sport's passionate fan base. Whether through live broadcasts on Sky Sport 4, delayed games on Sky Open, or select matches on Three, fans have plenty of opportunities to watch and enjoy rugby league. This level of coverage plays a crucial role in maintaining the sport's popularity and ensuring that it continues to thrive in New Zealand.

The television coverage of rugby league in New Zealand plays a crucial role in the sport's enduring popularity and connection with fans. With Sky Sport providing live broadcasts of all NRL games, including the much-anticipated State of Origin series and the grand final, fans have unprecedented access to their favorite teams and players. This live coverage is vital for keeping the excitement and engagement levels high among rugby league enthusiasts, ensuring they never miss a moment of the action.

Sky Open complements this by offering delayed broadcasts of Warriors games, catering to fans who may not have access to Sky Sport. This delayed coverage allows the Warriors' passionate supporters to stay connected with the team, even if they can't watch the games live. Sky Open's role in broadcasting select matches live further extends the reach of rugby league in New Zealand, bringing more fans into the fold and expanding the sport's audience.

The inclusion of rugby league on a free-to-air channel like Three, particularly with select State of Origin games broadcast live, broadens the sport's accessibility. This ensures that even those without a Sky Sport subscription can enjoy some of the biggest and most exciting matches of the season. By making these high-profile games available to a wider audience, Three helps to sustain and grow rugby league's popularity in New Zealand, ensuring that the sport remains a significant part of the country's cultural and sporting landscape.

The comprehensive coverage provided by these broadcasters is not just about showing games; it's about fostering a deep connection between the sport and its fans. The ability to watch every game live, follow the Warriors' journey, and witness the drama of the State of Origin series keeps fans engaged and invested in rugby league. This level of access helps to maintain the sport's strong presence in New Zealand, ensuring that it continues to thrive and evolve.

Moreover, this coverage also plays a critical role in the development of rugby league at the grassroots level. By providing young fans and aspiring players with regular access to professional games, these broadcasts inspire the next generation of rugby league talent. Watching their heroes compete on the big stage motivates young players to pursue their dreams and contribute to the future of the sport in New Zealand.

In addition to its role in fan engagement and player development, the television coverage of rugby league in New Zealand also has a broader cultural impact. Rugby league is more than just a sport; it's a key part of New Zealand's identity. The stories, rivalries, and moments of brilliance that unfold on the screen resonate deeply with fans, creating shared experiences and memories that strengthen the sense of community around the sport.

The combination of live and delayed broadcasts, along with the accessibility provided by channels like Sky Sport, Sky Open, and Three, ensures that rugby league remains an integral part of New Zealand's sporting landscape. This coverage not only satisfies the current demand for rugby league content but also lays the groundwork for the sport's future growth and success in the country.

In the end, the television coverage of rugby league in New Zealand is more than just a service to fans; it's a lifeline that keeps the sport thriving. By making the game accessible to a wide audience, these broadcasters help to sustain the passion for rugby league, ensuring that it continues to be a beloved and celebrated sport in New Zealand for generations to come.

Chapter 63: Pacific Broadcasting Reach

Rugby league's influence in the Pacific is significant, and the role of television broadcasting in these nations is crucial for maintaining and growing the sport's fan base. In countries like Tonga, Samoa, Papua New Guinea, and Fiji, rugby league is more than just a sport; it's a cultural phenomenon. The way the games are broadcast in these regions reflects the deep-rooted passion and enthusiasm for rugby league, ensuring that fans have consistent and widespread access to every match.

In Tonga, Digicel and Tonfon TV bring the excitement of rugby league into the homes of fans across the nation. These broadcasters ensure that every tackle, try, and triumph is captured and shared with the Tongan audience, who are known for their fervent support of the sport. The availability of rugby league on these networks means that fans can follow the progress of their favorite teams and players, keeping them connected to the game regardless of where they are in the country.

Samoa also enjoys comprehensive coverage of rugby league, with Digicel and TV3 providing live broadcasts of all matches. This access is vital for maintaining the sport's popularity in Samoa, where rugby league holds a special place in the hearts of many. The broadcasts allow fans to experience the highs and lows of the season, ensuring that the sport continues to thrive in this rugby-loving nation.

Papua New Guinea, often referred to as the spiritual home of rugby league, has one of the most passionate fan bases in the world. Here, Digicel and TVWan play a critical role in bringing the game to the masses. Rugby league is almost like a religion in PNG, and the extensive coverage provided by these networks ensures that fans never miss a moment of the action. The broadcasts go beyond mere entertainment; they are a vital part of the national culture, uniting people from all walks of life in their shared love for the game.

In Fiji, the partnership between Digicel and Mai TV ensures that rugby league remains accessible to the Fijian audience. The broadcasts are more than just a way to watch games; they are a celebration of Fijian pride, especially when local players take the field. The widespread availability of rugby league on television in Fiji helps to inspire the next generation of players, who dream of one day representing their country on the international stage.

The importance of these broadcasts in the Pacific cannot be overstated. Rugby league serves as a source of national pride, a connection to the wider world, and a symbol of unity in these island nations. By providing live coverage of matches, the broadcasters are not only entertaining their audiences but also preserving the cultural significance of rugby league in the region. The games bring communities together, whether they're cheering for their local team or supporting their favorite players from abroad.

Moreover, the coverage of rugby league in the Pacific has a broader impact on the sport's growth and development. By making the game accessible to a wide audience, broadcasters help to nurture the talent that will shape the future of rugby league in these countries. Young players watching their heroes on TV are inspired to take up the sport, leading to a continuous cycle of growth and development at the grassroots level.

The collaboration between Digicel and local networks like Tonfon TV, TV3, TVWan, and Mai TV ensures that rugby league remains a central part of life in the Pacific. These partnerships are crucial for the sport's sustainability and growth, providing the infrastructure needed to deliver high-quality broadcasts to even the most remote areas. As a result, rugby league continues to flourish in the Pacific, supported by a dedicated fan base and a network of broadcasters committed to keeping the game alive.

The role of television in broadcasting rugby league throughout the Pacific is indispensable. It keeps the sport vibrant and accessible, strengthens cultural ties, and fosters the next generation of players. The extensive coverage provided by Digicel and its partner networks ensures that rugby league will continue to be a beloved and integral part of life in the Pacific for years to come.

Rugby league in the Pacific region is more than just a sport; it's a vital part of the cultural fabric that unites communities across the islands. The role of television broadcasting in ensuring the game's reach and impact cannot be overstated. Through partnerships with networks like Digicel, Tonfon TV, TV3, TVWan, and Mai TV, the sport has managed to transcend the challenges of geography, making it accessible to millions of fans who might otherwise be isolated from the action. This widespread availability has not only maintained but also deepened the connection between the sport and its passionate supporters in the Pacific.

The success of rugby league broadcasts in the Pacific is a testament to the enduring popularity of the game in these regions. The commitment of broadcasters to provide comprehensive coverage, often going beyond just airing the games to include pre- and post-match analysis, player interviews, and behind-the-scenes content, has played a significant role in cultivating a strong and informed fan base. This level of engagement ensures that the sport remains relevant and continues to capture the imagination of new generations of fans.

Moreover, the broadcasts serve as a critical link between the Pacific nations and the broader rugby league world. They allow fans in Tonga, Samoa, Papua New Guinea, Fiji, and other Pacific islands to follow their favorite teams and players, whether they're competing in local leagues or on the international stage. This connection is crucial for maintaining the sport's global presence and ensuring that Pacific nations continue to be recognized as key contributors to the rugby league landscape.

The impact of these broadcasts extends beyond just viewership numbers. They play a crucial role in inspiring young athletes across the Pacific. Watching their heroes on screen, young players are motivated to pursue their own rugby league dreams, knowing that they too could one day play on the world stage. This inspiration is a driving force behind the development of rugby league talent in the region, helping to ensure that Pacific nations continue to produce some of the sport's most exciting and dynamic players.

Furthermore, the collaborative efforts between broadcasters and the rugby league community in the Pacific have helped to raise the profile of the sport globally. As Pacific players make their mark in international competitions, the spotlight on the region intensifies, drawing more attention to the talent and passion that exist within these island nations. This increased visibility benefits not only the players and teams but also the broadcasters, who gain larger audiences and greater influence within the sports broadcasting industry.

The integration of rugby league into the daily lives of Pacific communities through television broadcasts has also reinforced the sport's role as a unifying force. Whether it's gathering with family and friends to watch a match or discussing the latest game at work or school, rugby league fosters a sense of community and shared identity among its fans. This communal experience strengthens social bonds and enhances the sense of pride that Pacific people feel for their nations and their teams.

As we look to the future, the continued success of rugby league in the Pacific will depend heavily on the strength of these broadcasting partnerships. The evolution of technology and media consumption habits presents both challenges and opportunities for broadcasters. Adapting to these changes while maintaining the quality and accessibility of rugby league coverage will be essential for keeping the sport vibrant and engaging for Pacific audiences.

The role of television in the Pacific's rugby league scene is indispensable. The extensive coverage provided by networks like Digicel and their partners ensures that the sport remains a central part of life in these island nations. This coverage not only keeps fans connected to the game but also nurtures the next generation of players, strengthens cultural ties, and reinforces the sport's global presence. As rugby league continues to grow and evolve, the enduring partnership between broadcasters and the Pacific community will remain a cornerstone of its success.

Chapter 64: Global NRL Coverage

Rugby league has grown from a regional sport into a global phenomenon, with fans tuning in from all over the world. Thanks to the wide availability of international broadcasting, the National Rugby League (NRL) can be enjoyed far beyond the shores of Australia, New Zealand, and the Pacific. Through various networks and streaming services, the NRL reaches millions of fans across different continents, bringing the excitement of the game to places where rugby league isn't traditionally played. This chapter explores how the NRL is made accessible to a global audience.

For travelers, the NRL can be viewed even while on the go. Sport24, an in-flight and ship entertainment provider, broadcasts live NRL matches to passengers traveling around the world. Whether on a long-haul flight or a cruise ship, fans don't have to miss any of the action. This service ensures that the NRL remains accessible no matter where fans are located, providing a connection to the sport even in the most remote locations.

One of the most convenient ways to watch the NRL globally is through WatchNRL, a streaming service available worldwide. WatchNRL allows fans to stream live matches, on-demand replays, and other NRL content from anywhere in the world. This service is particularly beneficial for those living in countries where traditional television broadcasts of the NRL are not available. With a subscription, fans can stay up-to-date with their favorite teams and players, making it easier than ever to follow the NRL from abroad.

In Africa, ESPN has taken on the role of broadcasting NRL matches across the Sub-Saharan region, excluding North Africa. This partnership has expanded the reach of the NRL to a whole new audience, exposing rugby league to sports enthusiasts in Africa. ESPN's coverage includes live matches and highlights, helping to build a fan base in a region where rugby league is still growing in popularity.

In Southeast Asia, including Brunei, Malaysia, and Singapore, Premier Sports Asia provides coverage of NRL matches. The network ensures that fans in these countries can watch live games and keep up with the latest NRL news. The availability of NRL broadcasts in this region highlights the global appeal of the sport and its ability to attract viewers from diverse cultural backgrounds.

Premier Sports MENA handles NRL broadcasts in the Middle East and North Africa (MENA) region, including the United Arab Emirates. This coverage brings the excitement of rugby league to a region where other sports, such as soccer, traditionally dominate. By providing access to NRL matches, Premier Sports MENA helps to diversify the sports content available to viewers in these countries, offering an alternative for sports fans who want to explore different games.

In Canada, the NRL can be watched on Sportsnet, one of the country's leading sports networks. This coverage allows Canadian fans to enjoy live NRL matches and stay connected to the sport. The presence of NRL broadcasts in North America is significant, as it demonstrates the sport's growing influence in a region where rugby league is not as widely known. Sportsnet's coverage helps to raise awareness of the NRL and introduces the game to a new audience.

In Europe, the NRL has a solid presence thanks to broadcasters like beIN Sports in France and Sky Sports in the United Kingdom and Ireland. These networks ensure that rugby league fans in Europe can watch live NRL matches, follow their favorite teams, and enjoy in-depth analysis and commentary. The partnership with European broadcasters has been crucial in maintaining and growing the NRL's fan base in a continent where rugby union often overshadows rugby league.

In the United States, Fox Soccer Plus provides NRL coverage, bringing the sport to American audiences. Although rugby league is not as popular in the U.S. as other sports, the availability of NRL broadcasts helps to introduce the game to new fans and expand its reach in a country known for its love of sports. Fox Soccer Plus ensures that American fans have access to high-quality NRL content, contributing to the sport's slow but steady growth in the U.S.

Finally, in German-speaking countries like Germany, Austria, and Switzerland, Sport1+ was the network that broadcasted NRL matches until 2020. While the coverage in these countries has been discontinued, the presence of the NRL in these regions demonstrates the sport's potential to capture the interest of fans in non-traditional rugby league markets. The challenge now lies in finding new ways to reintroduce and grow the sport in these countries.

The global reach of the NRL is a testament to the sport's universal appeal. Through various networks and streaming services, fans around the world can enjoy the thrill of rugby league, regardless of where they are. This widespread availability not only strengthens the NRL's global presence but also fosters a sense of community among fans who share a love for the game. As the NRL continues to grow, the importance of maintaining and expanding its international broadcasting partnerships will be crucial in ensuring that the sport remains accessible to fans everywhere.

The NRL's expansion into global markets underscores the sport's rising popularity and its ability to connect with audiences far beyond its traditional heartlands. The extensive network of broadcasters and streaming services now available to fans across various regions highlights the league's commitment to making rugby league accessible to as many people as possible. This global reach is not just about broadcasting games; it is about building a larger, more inclusive community of rugby league enthusiasts who can share in the excitement, passion, and culture of the sport.

The availability of NRL matches on platforms like Sport24, which offers coverage to travelers on flights and ships, ensures that fans can stay connected to the sport no matter where they are in the world. This is a significant achievement for the league, as it demonstrates a commitment to keeping the fan experience seamless and uninterrupted. Whether on a plane, a ship, or in a different country, fans can now watch live matches and feel part of the action, which is a remarkable advancement in sports broadcasting.

WatchNRL has revolutionized how fans outside of traditional rugby league regions access the sport. By providing a streaming service that can be accessed globally, the NRL has opened up new opportunities for fans to engage with the sport. This service is particularly valuable for those in regions where rugby league is not broadcast on traditional television networks. The ease of access and the ability to watch games live or on-demand has undoubtedly contributed to the sport's growing international following.

In regions like Sub-Saharan Africa, the Middle East, and North Africa, the introduction of NRL broadcasts through networks like ESPN and Premier Sports MENA has introduced rugby league to new audiences. These partnerships are crucial in building the sport's global fan base, as they bring the excitement of NRL matches to areas where the sport is still relatively unknown. The success of these broadcasts could pave the way for more targeted efforts to grow rugby league in these regions, potentially leading to the development of local leagues and increased participation.

In Europe, the presence of NRL broadcasts on networks like beIN Sports and Sky Sports ensures that rugby league continues to thrive in markets where rugby union has traditionally been more popular. By offering comprehensive coverage, including live matches and expert commentary, these networks help maintain interest in the sport and encourage more fans to engage with rugby league. This is particularly important in countries like France and the UK, where the NRL has a strong, albeit niche, following that is critical to the sport's international success.

The NRL's foray into North America, particularly through broadcasts on Sportsnet in Canada and Fox Soccer Plus in the United States, is a bold move that highlights the league's ambition to tap into one of the world's largest sports markets. While rugby league is still in its infancy in North America compared to other sports, the availability of NRL content on major networks represents a significant step towards growing the sport's profile. This effort could lead to increased participation at the grassroots level, more interest in local leagues, and a stronger presence of rugby league in the American sports landscape.

Despite the discontinuation of NRL broadcasts in some regions, such as Germany, Austria, and Switzerland, the league's previous presence in these markets demonstrates the sport's potential to attract fans in non-traditional rugby league countries. The challenge now is to find new and innovative ways to reintroduce the sport to these regions, perhaps through digital platforms or new broadcasting partnerships. The NRL's continued global expansion will depend on its ability to adapt to changing market conditions and explore new opportunities for growth.

Ultimately, the NRL's global broadcasting strategy is about more than just reaching new markets; it is about creating a worldwide community of rugby league fans. By making the sport accessible to people from different cultures and regions, the NRL is fostering a sense of belonging among its international fan base. This global community, united by a shared passion for rugby league, is what will drive the sport's continued growth and success on the world stage. The future of the NRL lies in its ability to maintain and expand these connections, ensuring that rugby league remains a truly global sport.

Chapter 65: NRL Online: Global Streaming and Access

In today's digital age, rugby league fans across the world have more ways to watch NRL matches than ever before. Outside of Australia, New Zealand, and the Pacific Islands, the primary way to watch live NRL games is through the subscription streaming service Watch NRL. This service makes it possible for fans from countries all around the globe to tune in and enjoy the excitement of rugby league, no matter where they are.

Watch NRL is operated by Fox Sports Australia, and it offers all matches in high definition. This means fans can experience the games with top-notch visual quality, bringing the action on the field to life. Whether it's a crucial State of Origin clash or a regular season game, Watch NRL ensures that fans don't miss a moment of the action, even if they are far from the traditional NRL broadcasting regions.

The service is accessible through both a dedicated website and an app, making it convenient for users to watch matches on various devices. Whether you're at home on your smart TV, on the go with your smartphone, or relaxing with a tablet, Watch NRL has you covered. This flexibility is a key part of the service's appeal, as it allows fans to follow their favorite teams and players wherever they are.

One of the great features of Watch NRL is its ability to stream live games as they happen. Fans don't have to wait for replays or highlights; they can watch the game in real-time, sharing the thrill and intensity with millions of other fans around the world. This live-streaming option keeps international fans connected to the NRL, making them feel just as much a part of the game as those watching in Australia or New Zealand.

In addition to live streaming, Watch NRL offers on-demand viewing. This means that if a fan misses a game, they can catch up at a time that suits them. The on-demand feature is particularly useful for fans in different time zones, as they can watch matches at a time that's convenient without worrying about spoilers or missing out on the action.

Beyond live games, Watch NRL also offers a range of additional content to keep fans engaged. This includes full match replays, condensed highlights, and special shows that delve into the latest news and analysis from the NRL. This extra content helps fans stay informed and connected to the league, even when they can't watch games live.

For those who enjoy a bit of nostalgia, the NRL also offers a selection of classic matches available for free on the league's official website. These games allow fans to relive some of the greatest moments in NRL history, from thrilling grand finals to iconic State of Origin clashes. These classic games are a treat for long-time fans and a great way for newer fans to learn more about the sport's rich history.

The global reach of the NRL through Watch NRL and the league's website has significantly expanded the sport's fan base. It has brought the excitement of rugby league to new audiences, helping to grow the game in regions where it was previously less known. This international accessibility is a crucial part of the NRL's strategy to become a truly global sport.

As the NRL continues to evolve and expand, the role of online streaming services like Watch NRL will only become more important. By making rugby league accessible to fans everywhere, the NRL is ensuring that the sport continues to grow and thrive on the world stage. Whether you're a die-hard fan or a newcomer to the sport, the internet is your gateway to the thrilling world of the NRL.

The role of the internet in delivering NRL content to fans around the world cannot be overstated. In an era where digital connectivity is a cornerstone of modern life, the NRL has wisely embraced this shift, ensuring that rugby league remains accessible to its global audience. Through platforms like Watch NRL, the league has extended its reach far beyond the traditional broadcast boundaries of Australia, New Zealand, and the Pacific Islands, effectively bringing the excitement of the game to every corner of the globe.

Watch NRL has become a vital tool for fans who live outside of the primary NRL broadcast regions. By offering live streaming of every match in high definition, the service ensures that fans never miss a moment of the action, no matter where they are. This ability to watch games in real time has created a more connected and engaged global fan base, as fans from different time zones can tune in and share in the excitement as it happens. The convenience of accessing these games through a dedicated website and app further enhances the viewing experience, making it easier than ever for fans to follow their favorite teams and players.

The on-demand feature of Watch NRL is another significant advantage, allowing fans to catch up on matches at their convenience. This flexibility is particularly important for international viewers, who may find it challenging to watch games live due to time zone differences. By providing the option to watch full replays and highlights at any time, the NRL ensures that its content is accessible to fans worldwide, regardless of their schedules. This approach not only caters to the needs of existing fans but also helps attract new viewers who may be discovering rugby league for the first time.

In addition to live and on-demand content, Watch NRL offers a range of supplementary programming that keeps fans informed and engaged with the league. From expert analysis to in-depth discussions, these programs provide valuable insights into the game, enhancing the overall viewing experience. The availability of classic NRL matches on the league's website is another excellent resource for fans, offering a glimpse into the sport's rich history and iconic moments. These features contribute to a more immersive and comprehensive understanding of the NRL, further solidifying the bond between the league and its global audience.

The success of Watch NRL and the league's online presence underscores the importance of digital platforms in the modern sports landscape. By making rugby league accessible to fans around the world, the NRL has positioned itself as a forward-thinking organization that understands the evolving needs of its audience. This global accessibility not only strengthens the league's existing fan base but also paves the way for future growth as more people are introduced to the sport through these digital channels.

As the NRL continues to innovate and expand its digital offerings, the potential for reaching new audiences is vast. The internet has opened up new avenues for fan engagement, allowing the NRL to connect with viewers in ways that were previously unimaginable. Whether through live streaming, on-demand viewing, or exclusive online content, the league is ensuring that its fans remain at the heart of the action, no matter where they are in the world.

Looking ahead, the continued development of the NRL's digital strategy will be crucial in maintaining and growing its global presence. As more fans turn to online platforms for their entertainment, the league's ability to adapt and innovate will determine its success in this increasingly competitive landscape. By staying ahead of the curve and offering a seamless, high-quality viewing experience, the NRL is well-positioned to continue its growth on the international stage.

The internet has transformed the way fans interact with the NRL, making the sport more accessible and enjoyable for a global audience. Through services like Watch NRL, the league has successfully expanded its reach, bringing the excitement of rugby league to fans everywhere. As the NRL continues to evolve and embrace new technologies, its commitment to delivering top-tier content to its fans remains unwavering. This dedication ensures that rugby league will continue to thrive in the digital age, reaching new heights and captivating audiences around the world.

Chapter 66: On the Airwaves – NRL Radio Coverage

Radio has long been a vital medium for NRL fans, allowing them to stay connected to the game no matter where they are. Whether they're driving, working, or simply unable to watch the match on television, fans can rely on radio broadcasts to bring them live play-by-play commentary, analysis, and interviews. In Australia, several key radio stations hold exclusive rights to broadcast NRL matches, ensuring that the excitement of the game is just a dial away.

One of the most prominent radio broadcasters of NRL games is 2GB, which has the commercial rights to cover four matches each week. The coverage is delivered through the popular program, the Continuous Call Team. This show has become a staple for NRL fans, known for its lively commentary, in-depth analysis, and engaging banter. 2GB doesn't just stop at regular-season games; they also broadcast all representative games, including the highly anticipated State of Origin series, as well as every match during the finals series and the Grand Final. The station's coverage is networked across the country, ensuring that fans from all corners of Australia can tune in.

ABC Local Radio is another major player in NRL radio broadcasting. With the rights to seven matches each week, ABC provides extensive coverage across the Australian Capital Territory, Queensland, and New

South Wales. ABC's approach to broadcasting is more traditional, focusing on clear, informative commentary that appeals to a broad audience. Their coverage is particularly valued in regional areas, where television access might be limited, making radio the primary source of NRL action for many fans.

Triple M offers a different flavor of NRL coverage, with exclusive rights to Thursday night, Saturday 4 pm, and Sunday night matches. Known for its energetic and often humorous commentary style, Triple M's broadcasts are popular among fans who enjoy a more relaxed and entertaining take on the game. In addition to regular-season matches, Triple M also covers the State of Origin series, the finals, and the Grand Final, providing fans with comprehensive access to the biggest events on the NRL calendar.

In the past, other stations like 2SM and 2UE also held broadcasting rights, adding to the variety of NRL coverage on the airwaves. 2SM, for instance, used to air Thursday Night and Sunday 4 pm games via NRL Nation, reaching a wide audience through its network of affiliates across New South Wales. Although these stations no longer hold the rights, their contributions to NRL radio broadcasting have helped shape the landscape of sports radio in Australia.

For those who prefer digital access, all radio broadcasts of NRL matches can be streamed live from the NRL website. This feature has become increasingly important as more fans turn to online platforms for their media consumption. Whether through a traditional radio or a streaming service, fans can easily access live NRL commentary, ensuring they never miss a moment of the action.

The presence of multiple broadcasters covering NRL matches ensures that fans have a choice in how they experience the game. Each station brings its own style and perspective to the commentary, catering to different tastes and preferences. Whether a fan prefers the in-depth analysis of 2GB, the straightforward coverage of ABC, or the lively banter on Triple M, there is something for everyone on the NRL radio airwaves.

Radio remains a crucial part of the NRL experience, especially for those who can't always be in front of a screen. The ability to listen to live matches while on the go, combined with the variety of coverage available, makes radio an enduring and valuable medium for NRL fans. As the NRL continues to evolve and adapt to new technologies, radio broadcasting remains a steadfast companion for the game's passionate supporters, keeping them connected to every kick, pass, and try.

As we reflect on the significance of radio in NRL coverage, it becomes clear that this medium plays a vital role in connecting fans with the game. Radio has a unique ability to reach listeners in places where television or streaming services might not be available. Whether it's in the car, at work, or in remote areas, radio brings the excitement of the NRL directly to the ears of fans. This accessibility is crucial in ensuring that the sport remains inclusive, allowing people from all walks of life to stay engaged with their favorite teams and players.

The diversity of radio broadcasters in Australia offers fans a range of perspectives and styles, catering to different tastes and preferences. Stations like 2GB, ABC Local Radio, and Triple M each bring their own flavor to NRL commentary, providing listeners with options that suit their individual preferences. This variety not only enriches the listening experience but also fosters a deeper connection between the fans and the sport. By offering different insights, analyses, and entertainment styles, radio broadcasters help to create a more dynamic and multifaceted understanding of the game.

Radio's role in NRL coverage goes beyond just delivering play-by-play commentary. It also serves as a platform for discussion, analysis, and debate, allowing fans to engage with the sport on a deeper level. Programs like the Continuous Call Team and Triple M's broadcasts are not just about reporting the action on the field; they are about creating a dialogue with the audience. This interaction between broadcasters and listeners helps to build a sense of community among NRL fans, making the sport more than just a game—it becomes a shared experience.

In addition to regular-season coverage, radio plays a crucial role in broadcasting some of the most significant events in the NRL calendar, such as the State of Origin series and the Grand Final. These broadcasts are not just about covering the games; they are about capturing the atmosphere, the excitement, and the drama that make these events so special. Radio has the power to bring these moments to life in a way that is both immediate and intimate, making listeners feel as though they are right there in the stadium, experiencing the highs and lows of the game in real-time.

The evolution of digital technology has expanded the reach of NRL radio broadcasts, making them more accessible than ever before. With the ability to stream live coverage online, fans can now listen to NRL matches from anywhere in the world. This has opened up new possibilities for how fans engage with the sport, allowing them to stay connected even when they are far from home. The combination of traditional radio and digital streaming ensures that NRL coverage remains relevant in an increasingly digital world, adapting to the changing needs and preferences of its audience.

Despite the rise of television and online streaming, radio has retained its place as a beloved medium for NRL fans. Its ability to provide live, real-time coverage, coupled with its accessibility and variety, makes it an indispensable part of the NRL experience. For many fans, listening to the game on the radio is more than just a way to stay informed—it's a tradition, a ritual that brings them closer to the sport they love.

As the NRL continues to grow and evolve, the role of radio in its coverage will remain essential. The medium's ability to reach a wide and diverse audience, its capacity for in-depth analysis and discussion, and its adaptability to new technologies ensure that radio will continue to be a vital part of the NRL's future. For fans, the comforting familiarity of tuning into their favorite station, hearing the voices of trusted commentators, and sharing the experience with fellow listeners is something that will endure, keeping the spirit of the game alive and well for generations to come.

Chapter 67: The Role of Print Media in NRL Coverage

Print media has long been a crucial part of NRL coverage, serving as a key source of information, analysis, and entertainment for rugby league fans. Over the years, several print publications have become synonymous with the sport, offering insights that go beyond what is seen on the field. However, the landscape of print media in the NRL has undergone significant changes, especially in recent years, reflecting broader trends in the media industry.

For many years, *Big League* was the official publication of the NRL, providing fans with comprehensive coverage of the competition. Released every Thursday, *Big League* was a go-to source for team news, player profiles, match previews, and in-depth analysis. Produced by News Magazines, it offered a weekly deep dive into the world of rugby league, helping fans stay informed and engaged with their favorite teams and players. However, in 2020, *Big League* ceased operations, marking the end of an era and leaving the NRL without an official print program.

Another major publication that played a significant role in NRL coverage was *Rugby League Week*. This magazine was a staple for rugby league fans, offering not only match reports and news but also opinion pieces, interviews, and features that delved into the personalities and stories behind the sport. *Rugby*

League Week was known for its passionate coverage and its ability to capture the drama and excitement of the NRL. However, in April 2017, after decades of publication, *Rugby League Week* also ceased production, reflecting the broader challenges faced by print media in the digital age.

With the closure of these two iconic publications, the print media landscape for NRL coverage has changed dramatically. The only print magazine currently in circulation dedicated to rugby league is *Rugby League Review*, a bi-monthly publication that has been running since 2002. *Rugby League Review* continues to provide fans with detailed coverage of the sport, maintaining a focus on both the NRL and the broader rugby league community. Its longevity speaks to the enduring appeal of print media, even in a world increasingly dominated by digital content.

In addition to *Rugby League Review*, there are also digital alternatives that cater to rugby league fans. One such publication is LeagueUnlimited's *Front Row Magazine*, which provides an unofficial match program each week in a digital magazine format. This publication offers a blend of traditional print-style content with the convenience of digital access, making it accessible to a wide audience. The shift to digital formats like *Front Row Magazine* reflects the changing consumption habits of fans, who now expect content to be available anytime and anywhere.

Despite the decline in traditional print media, the role of magazines and printed publications in NRL coverage remains significant. These publications offer a level of depth and analysis that is often missing from other forms of media. They provide a space for long-form journalism, where stories can be explored in detail, and where fans can gain a deeper understanding of the sport they love. In a fast-paced world where news is often consumed in bite-sized pieces, print media offers a chance to slow down and engage with the content on a more meaningful level.

The changes in the print media landscape also reflect the broader challenges faced by the NRL in reaching and engaging with its audience. As fans increasingly turn to digital platforms for their news and entertainment, the NRL and its media partners must continue to adapt to these shifts. The success of digital publications like *Front Row Magazine* suggests that there is still a strong appetite for rugby league content, but it also highlights the need for innovation in how this content is delivered.

While the heyday of print media in NRL coverage may be behind us, its legacy continues through publications like *Rugby League Review* and digital counterparts like *Front Row Magazine*. These platforms ensure that fans still have access to the in-depth coverage and analysis that has long been a hallmark of rugby league journalism. As the media landscape continues to evolve, the NRL will need to navigate these changes carefully, ensuring that it continues to engage its audience in both traditional and new ways.

The role of print media in the coverage of the NRL has seen a significant transformation over the years, shaped by broader shifts in the media industry and the evolving consumption habits of sports fans. As we look back on the history and current state of NRL-related print publications, it becomes clear that while traditional print media has faced challenges, it has also adapted in various ways, ensuring that the passion and depth of rugby league coverage continue to reach its dedicated audience.

Big League and *Rugby League Week*, two of the most iconic publications in NRL history, once stood as pillars of rugby league journalism. They provided fans with a weekly dose of analysis, player interviews, match previews, and post-game breakdowns, becoming indispensable to the rugby league community. However, their closures in 2020 and 2017, respectively, marked a significant shift in how NRL content is delivered to fans. These closures weren't just about the end of print publications but reflected the broader transition in media from traditional print to digital formats.

The decline of traditional print media has been driven by several factors, including the rise of the internet, changing consumer preferences, and the increasing cost of print production. As fans began to seek faster and more accessible content, the immediacy of digital platforms became more appealing. This shift was not unique to rugby league or sports media but part of a global trend where digital content became the dominant mode of information dissemination.

Despite these challenges, the spirit of print media lives on through publications like *Rugby League Review* and the digital magazine *Front Row Magazine*. *Rugby League Review*, a bi-monthly print magazine, continues to offer detailed coverage of the NRL, appealing to those who appreciate the tangible nature of print media. Its continued success demonstrates that there is still a place for print in the modern media landscape, particularly among a niche audience that values in-depth coverage and the tactile experience of a physical magazine.

Similarly, *Front Row Magazine* represents the evolution of print media in the digital age. While it is delivered in a digital format, it maintains the structure and feel of a traditional magazine, offering a blend of long-form journalism, analysis, and commentary. This digital format allows for broader distribution, reaching a global audience while retaining the essence of what made print magazines so popular. It's a testament to how print media can adapt and thrive in a new environment by embracing technology while preserving its core strengths.

The transition from print to digital also highlights the importance of content diversity in NRL coverage. Fans today have access to a wider range of perspectives and analysis than ever before. From podcasts to online articles, social media commentary to video content, the variety of media formats available allows fans to engage with the sport in ways that suit their preferences and lifestyles. This diversity is crucial in keeping the fan base engaged and ensuring that rugby league remains relevant in a crowded media landscape.

However, the challenges facing traditional print media also underscore the need for innovation within the NRL and its media partners. As the media landscape continues to evolve, it will be essential for the NRL to explore new ways of delivering content that meets the changing demands of its audience. Whether through new digital platforms, enhanced fan engagement initiatives, or innovative content formats, the NRL must continue to adapt to stay connected with its fan base.

The evolution of print media in NRL coverage reflects broader changes in how sports content is consumed. While the era of iconic print magazines like *Big League* and *Rugby League Week* has passed, the essence of in-depth, thoughtful coverage continues in both print and digital formats. As the NRL navigates this evolving media landscape, it will be critical to balance tradition with innovation, ensuring that fans continue to receive the high-quality coverage they have come to expect, regardless of the platform. The future of NRL media is one of adaptation, creativity, and, above all, a commitment to delivering the best possible content to rugby league fans around the world.

Part Nine: Chasing Greatness: The Records That Define the NRL

Chapter 68: Official NRL Statistics

Official NRL statistics are a crucial part of the league's history, encompassing all first-grade competitions that have been played over the years. These records include the New South Wales Rugby League (NSWRL), Australian Rugby League (ARL), Super League, and the current National Rugby League (NRL). Each of these competitions contributed to the rich history and evolution of the sport, and the records kept provide a window into the performance, milestones, and achievements that have shaped rugby league in Australia and beyond.

The New South Wales Rugby League (NSWRL), established in 1908, is the oldest competition in this history. The records from this era are a foundation of the sport, highlighting the early days of rugby league and the players who first made their mark. These records reflect the simpler times of the game, where professionalism was just beginning to take hold, and the sport was growing in popularity. They capture the rise of legendary players, pioneering clubs, and the first grand finals that would become iconic events in Australian sport.

When the Australian Rugby League (ARL) was formed in 1995, it built on the NSWRL's foundation. The ARL sought to expand the game nationally, bringing in new teams and creating a broader competition. The records from the ARL era are crucial for understanding how the sport evolved during a time of national expansion and increased professionalism. They document the impact of this growth on player performance, club success, and the overall development of rugby league in Australia.

The Super League, which ran concurrently with the ARL in 1997 during the infamous "Super League War," adds another layer to the official NRL statistics. This competition, though short-lived, was significant in the history of the game. The records from the Super League provide insight into a turbulent time for rugby league, where the sport was split, and players and clubs were divided. Despite this, the statistics from the Super League are part of the official NRL records, showcasing the performances of teams and players who participated in this unique chapter of rugby league history.

The modern NRL, established in 1998 following the reunification of the ARL and Super League, represents the current era of rugby league. The official statistics from the NRL are the most comprehensive, covering everything from individual player achievements to team records and grand final outcomes. These records are meticulously maintained, offering detailed insights into every aspect of the game. From try-scoring feats and goal-kicking accuracy to attendance figures and winning streaks, the NRL statistics capture the ongoing evolution of the sport.

One of the most important aspects of these official records is their role in recognizing the achievements of players and teams. Individual records, such as most tries, most points, and most appearances, are celebrated milestones that highlight the careers of rugby league's greatest talents. Team records, including longest winning streaks, highest scores, and premiership victories, reflect the dominance and success of the most formidable clubs in the competition.

These records also serve as a benchmark for future generations. Aspiring players and teams look to these statistics as goals to be surpassed, driving the competitive spirit of the sport. Whether it's breaking a long-standing record or setting a new one, the pursuit of excellence is a key motivator in rugby league, and the official NRL statistics provide the context for these achievements.

In addition to celebrating success, these statistics also document the challenges and setbacks faced by players and teams. Injuries, losses, and near misses are all part of the official records, offering a complete picture of the sport's history. These moments of adversity are as much a part of rugby league's story as the victories, and they contribute to the rich tapestry of the game's heritage.

The official NRL statistics are more than just numbers on a page; they are the chronicles of rugby league's journey through time. From the early days of the NSWRL to the present-day NRL, these records capture the essence of the sport, the triumphs, the struggles, and the moments that have defined rugby league in Australia and around the world. They are a testament to the enduring legacy of the game and a source of inspiration for all who are part of the rugby league community.

The records kept by the NRL are more than just numbers; they are a living history of the game, a testament to the athletes, teams, and moments that have defined rugby league over the years. These statistics offer a window into the evolution of the sport, reflecting the changes in strategy, skill, and competition that have shaped the league from its earliest days in the NSWRL to the present era of the NRL.

Through these records, we can trace the careers of the greatest players who have graced the field, from the legends of the past to the stars of today. These numbers tell the stories of individual brilliance, such as the most tries scored, the most points tallied, or the most games played. Each record is a milestone that marks the achievements of players who have reached the pinnacle of their craft, setting benchmarks for future generations to aspire to and surpass.

Team records, too, are a crucial part of the NRL's statistics. They highlight the dominance of certain clubs during particular eras, showcasing the strategies, cohesion, and resilience that have led to historic winning streaks, grand final victories, and overall supremacy in the league. These team achievements are a source of pride for clubs and their supporters, solidifying their place in the annals of rugby league history.

The records also document the evolution of the game itself. Over the decades, rugby league has undergone significant changes in rules, format, and structure, each of which is reflected in the statistics. These changes have influenced the way the game is played, the strategies employed by teams, and the skills developed by players. By studying these records, we can see how the game has adapted and grown, becoming faster, more dynamic, and more globally recognized.

The inclusion of records from the NSWRL, ARL, Super League, and NRL eras underscores the continuity and growth of the sport. Each era has contributed its own unique chapter to the history of rugby league, and together, they form a comprehensive narrative of the sport's development. The decision to incorporate these records into a single official NRL archive ensures that the contributions of all players and teams, regardless of the era or competition, are recognized and remembered.

For fans, these records provide a connection to the past, allowing them to relive the greatest moments in rugby league history. Whether it's a legendary try in a grand final, a remarkable comeback in a regular season game, or a player's record-breaking performance, these statistics keep those memories alive. They allow fans to compare eras, debate the greatest players and teams, and celebrate the rich heritage of the sport they love.

For players, the records serve as both a source of motivation and a challenge. The desire to leave a mark on the game, to etch one's name into the record books, drives athletes to push their limits and achieve greatness. Breaking a record is not just a personal triumph; it's a contribution to the legacy of the sport, ensuring that one's achievements will be remembered long after they have left the field.

In a broader sense, these records contribute to the identity and culture of rugby league. They reflect the values of hard work, determination, and excellence that are at the core of the sport. They also highlight the importance of teamwork, resilience, and sportsmanship, as many of the greatest achievements in the game have been the result of collective effort rather than individual glory.

As the NRL continues to evolve and grow, these records will remain a vital part of its history. They will continue to be updated, with new names, new teams, and new milestones added to the list. But no matter how much the game changes, the records will always serve as a reminder of where rugby league has come from, the challenges it has overcome, and the incredible feats that have been accomplished along the way.

In the end, the official NRL statistics are more than just a record of the past; they are a living, breathing part of the game's present and future. They inspire us to celebrate the achievements of those who came before us, challenge us to push the boundaries of what is possible, and remind us of the enduring legacy of rugby league.

Chapter 69: Unforgettable Team Records

In rugby league, team accomplishments hold a special place in history, highlighting the collective power, strategy, and resilience of a group of players working together toward a common goal. The records set by teams in the NRL are not just statistics; they are milestones that represent the highest peaks of success, as well as the challenges that teams have overcome throughout the league's history. From the most premierships won to the longest winning streaks, these records tell the stories of legendary clubs and their remarkable achievements.

The South Sydney Rabbitohs stand tall with the most premierships in the history of rugby league, having secured an impressive 21 titles. This record is a testament to their enduring success and ability to compete at the highest level over many decades. Their journey to these victories has seen countless memorable moments, iconic players, and passionate supporters, all contributing to a legacy that is deeply woven into the fabric of the sport.

On the other hand, the Sydney Roosters boast the most minor premierships, having finished the regular season at the top of the ladder 20 times. This achievement underscores their consistent excellence, with the Roosters often setting the pace for the rest of the competition. Their ability to dominate across multiple seasons highlights their strategic prowess and depth of talent, making them one of the most formidable teams in the league.

St George holds a record that may never be broken—most premierships in a row, with an incredible 11 consecutive titles from 1956 to 1966. This streak is often regarded as one of the greatest dynasties in rugby league history. The Dragons of that era were a powerhouse, blending skill, determination, and teamwork in a way that left an indelible mark on the sport. Their success set the standard for what it means to be a champion team.

However, not all records are about winning. The Western Suburbs Magpies hold the record for the most wooden spoons, having finished last on the ladder 17 times. While this might seem like a negative mark, it also reflects the struggles and challenges faced by the club over the years. These experiences have shaped the Magpies' identity, fostering resilience and a never-give-up attitude that continues to inspire their supporters.

The highest score in a single game is another record that stands out, with St. George scoring a staggering 91 points against Canterbury in 1935. This match showcased the Dragons' offensive firepower, as they relentlessly attacked their opponents, setting a record that remains unchallenged nearly a century later. In the same game, they also set the record for the largest winning margin, defeating Canterbury by 85 points. This dominant performance is a reminder of the unpredictable and thrilling nature of rugby league, where anything can happen on game day.

Eastern Suburbs Roosters and Melbourne Storm share the record for the longest winning streak, with both teams achieving 19 consecutive victories in 1975 and 2021, respectively. These streaks reflect periods of sheer dominance, where everything clicked for these teams, and they were virtually unstoppable. For the Roosters, their 1975 season was one of complete control, while the Storm's 2021 run was marked by their consistent execution and tactical superiority.

Another remarkable feat is the longest undefeated streak, held by Eastern Suburbs from 1935 to 1938. During this period, the Roosters were a force to be reckoned with, avoiding defeat in 35 straight matches. This streak is a testament to their ability to maintain high standards over multiple seasons, a rare and impressive accomplishment in the competitive world of rugby league.

Finally, the University club holds the record for the longest losing streak, with 42 consecutive losses from 1934 to 1936. While this is a difficult record to hold, it also speaks to the perseverance and dedication of the players and supporters who stuck with the team through tough times. It's a reminder that every team, regardless of their success or struggles, contributes to the rich history of the sport.

These team records are more than just numbers on a page; they are the stories of triumph, adversity, and the enduring spirit of rugby league. They capture the highs and lows of the game, celebrating the achievements of teams that have left an indelible mark on the sport. As new seasons unfold, these records inspire current and future teams to strive for greatness, knowing that they, too, can etch their names into the history books of rugby league.

The records held by NRL teams are a reflection of the league's rich history, showcasing the evolution of the sport and the legacy of its most iconic clubs. These records are more than mere statistics; they are the milestones that define the character and resilience of the teams that achieved them. Whether it's the triumphs of the South Sydney Rabbitohs with their record 21 premierships, the dominance of the Sydney Roosters with their 20 minor premierships, or the unmatched streak of 11 consecutive titles by St George, each record tells a story of excellence, dedication, and the pursuit of greatness.

These achievements highlight the dynamic and competitive nature of rugby league, where every match and every season contributes to the broader narrative of the sport. The records are not just about success but also about the challenges faced by teams like the Western Suburbs Magpies, who hold the record for the most wooden spoons. Their perseverance through tough seasons reflects the enduring spirit of the league, where every team, regardless of their position on the ladder, plays a crucial role in the competition's history.

The extraordinary performances, such as St. George's 91-point game against Canterbury and Eastern Suburbs' 35-match undefeated streak, are etched into the annals of rugby league, serving as benchmarks for future generations. These records are reminders of what is possible when a team comes together with a shared vision and executes their game plan to perfection. They inspire not only the players but also the fans, who are an integral part of the league's culture and history.

In addition to the records of success, the league also honors the persistence and resilience of teams like the University club, which endured a 42-match losing streak. Such records, while challenging, are also a testament to the strength of the human spirit and the unwavering commitment of the players and supporters who continue to believe in their team, no matter the odds. It is this mix of triumph and adversity that makes rugby league such a compelling and beloved sport.

As the league continues to grow and evolve, these records serve as a foundation upon which new achievements will be built. They are the touchstones that connect past, present, and future generations of rugby league players and fans. Each record is a chapter in the ongoing story of the NRL, a story that is shaped by the teams that strive to reach new heights and by the moments of brilliance that capture the imagination of millions.

Looking ahead, the records set by these teams will continue to inspire and challenge future players and teams to push the boundaries of what is possible in rugby league. They remind us that the sport is not just about the final score, but about the journey, the effort, and the passion that goes into every match. Whether breaking existing records or setting new ones, the pursuit of excellence will always be at the heart of rugby league.

The team records of the NRL are a testament to the enduring legacy of the league and its clubs. They celebrate the highs and lows, the victories and the challenges, and the never-ending quest for greatness that defines rugby league. As the sport moves forward, these records will remain a vital part of its history, inspiring all who love the game to strive for their own place in the storied tradition of the NRL.

Chapter 70: Remarkable Individual Achievements

Rugby league is a team sport, but individual players have left an indelible mark on the game through their extraordinary achievements. The records set by these players are a testament to their skill, dedication, and impact on the game. In this chapter, we'll explore some of the most significant individual records in the history of the NRL, which highlight the exceptional talents and contributions of some of rugby league's greatest players.

Cameron Smith is arguably one of the most iconic figures in rugby league history. His record for the most games played, with 430 appearances, is a remarkable achievement that showcases his longevity and consistency at the highest level. Smith's ability to perform at an elite level for such an extended period is a testament to his professionalism and dedication to the sport. His leadership on the field and his ability to control the game from the dummy half position have made him a legend in the eyes of fans and players alike.

Not only is Smith the record-holder for the most games played, but he is also the leading point scorer in NRL history. With 2,810 points, including 48 tries, 1,307 goals, and 4 field goals, his contribution to the scoreboard is unparalleled. Smith's accuracy with the boot and his ability to convert opportunities into points have been crucial to his teams' successes over the years. His record as the leading point scorer cements his status as one of the greatest players to have ever graced the rugby league field.

When it comes to crossing the try line, no player has been more prolific than Ken Irvine. With 212 tries, Irvine holds the record for the most tries scored in NRL history. His speed, agility, and ability to read the game made him a constant threat to opposition defenses. Irvine's record has stood the test of time, and his name remains synonymous with try-scoring excellence. His incredible try-scoring ability is a benchmark for future generations of players aspiring to achieve greatness in the sport.

Some individual records are set in a single season, showcasing a player's dominance during that period. Hazem El Masri's record for the most points in a full season, including finals, is one such example. In 2004, El Masri scored an incredible 342 points, consisting of 16 tries and 139 goals. His ability to consistently rack up points throughout the season was instrumental in his team's success, and his record remains one of the most impressive in the sport's history.

Similarly, Reuben Garrick's record for the most points in a regular season, with 300 points in 2021, demonstrates his outstanding goal-kicking and try-scoring abilities. Garrick's consistency throughout the season was remarkable, and his contribution to his team's performance was invaluable. These records highlight the impact that individual players can have on the outcome of a season and underscore the importance of consistency in achieving success.

Dave Brown's achievements in the 1935 season are nothing short of legendary. His record for the most tries in a season, with 38 tries, and the most points in a game, with 45 points, showcase his dominance during that period. Brown's ability to find the try line and his knack for scoring points in large quantities made him one of the most feared players of his era. His records from that season remain unmatched, and they serve as a reminder of the extraordinary talent he possessed.

Frank Burge's record for the most tries in a game, with 8 tries in 1920, is another incredible individual achievement. Scoring that many tries in a single match is a rare feat, and Burge's performance in that game is still talked about today. His record stands as a testament to his prowess on the field and his ability to make a significant impact in a single game.

These individual records are more than just numbers; they are stories of players who pushed the boundaries of what was thought possible in rugby league. They highlight the extraordinary talent, determination, and dedication required to achieve greatness in the sport. As the game continues to evolve, these records will inspire future players to strive for excellence and to leave their mark on the history of rugby league.

The individual achievements outlined in this chapter underscore the profound impact that exceptional players can have on the game of rugby league. These records are not just statistical milestones; they are emblematic of the players' immense skill, determination, and ability to perform under pressure. Each record tells a story of dedication, years of hard work, and a relentless pursuit of excellence. These players have etched their names into the history of the sport, becoming legends whose accomplishments will be celebrated for generations to come.

Cameron Smith's record for the most games played and his title as the leading point scorer highlight his unparalleled consistency and leadership on the field. His career, spanning over two decades, exemplifies what it means to be a professional athlete at the highest level. His influence on the game extends beyond his records, as he has inspired countless players with his work ethic and mastery of the game's nuances.

Ken Irvine's try-scoring record is a testament to his extraordinary athleticism and game sense. His ability to find the try line with such regularity made him a constant threat to opponents and a crucial player for his team. Irvine's record, standing for decades, reflects not just his talent but also the enduring legacy he has left in rugby league. His achievements have set a high bar for future generations of try-scorers.

The remarkable feats of Hazem El Masri, Reuben Garrick, Dave Brown, and Frank Burge showcase the brilliance of individual performances within the context of a team sport. El Masri's and Garrick's point-scoring records in a single season demonstrate the significant impact that a player can have over the course of a year, contributing to their team's success through consistent excellence. Dave Brown's and Frank Burge's records from the early days of the sport remind us of the rich history of rugby league and the incredible talents that have graced the field over the years.

These records are benchmarks in the sport, serving as goals for future players to aspire to. They represent the pinnacle of individual achievement in rugby league and illustrate the heights that can be reached through a combination of talent, hard work, and determination. While some records may eventually be broken, the stories behind them will remain an integral part of rugby league's history.

In celebrating these records, we also acknowledge the evolution of the sport and the increasing levels of competition that make such achievements even more impressive. The fact that many of these records have stood for so long is a testament to the greatness of the players who set them and to the challenges faced by those who seek to surpass them.

As we reflect on these individual accomplishments, it is important to recognize the broader context in which they occurred. Each of these players was part of a team, and their records were achieved within the framework of team success. Their individual brilliance contributed to the achievements of their teams, adding to the rich tapestry of rugby league history.

The records outlined in this chapter are a celebration of the human spirit's capacity for greatness. They remind us of the extraordinary individuals who have shaped the game of rugby league and the enduring legacy they have left behind. As the sport continues to grow and evolve, these records will remain as milestones, inspiring future generations of players to reach for greatness and to make their own mark on the history of rugby league.

Chapter 71: The Future of the National Rugby League

The National Rugby League (NRL) has long been a cornerstone of Australian sport, and as it moves forward, the league faces both challenges and opportunities that will shape its future. The battle for football supremacy in Australia between the NRL and the Australian Football League (AFL) is an ongoing saga, with both codes seeking to expand their influence and secure their place in the hearts of sports fans. As the NRL charts its course into the future, it is poised to make significant decisions that could alter the landscape of rugby league for years to come. The rivalry between the NRL and AFL is more than just about sports; it's a battle for cultural dominance, fan loyalty, and commercial success. How the NRL responds to these challenges will determine whether it can maintain its stronghold or risk losing ground to its southern competitor.

The decisions made in this period could significantly impact the sport's growth, both in terms of audience and participation, potentially redefining the way rugby league is played and perceived across the country. The NRL has an opportunity to solidify its position as Australia's premier rugby league competition, but this will require careful planning and bold moves. From expanding into new territories to enhancing the fan experience, the league's future depends on its ability to innovate while staying true to its roots. The next decade will be crucial in shaping the NRL's legacy, and the choices made now will echo in the sport's history for years to come.

A History of Expansion

The NRL's history is marked by expansion, with the league gradually extending its reach beyond its traditional strongholds. The introduction of new teams, such as the Canberra Raiders in 1982, marked the beginning of this expansion. Over the years, teams from Brisbane, Melbourne, and even Auckland have joined the league, broadening its appeal and bringing rugby league to new audiences. This growth has not only increased the league's popularity but also its competitiveness, as new teams bring fresh talent and rivalries. The NRL's willingness to expand demonstrates its commitment to evolving with the times and meeting the demands of a growing fan base.

The most recent addition, the Redcliffe Dolphins in 2023, demonstrates the NRL's commitment to growth. However, the league is not done yet, with plans to expand to 20 teams by the end of the decade. This growth reflects the NRL's ambition to not only consolidate its presence in Australia but also to explore new markets and fan bases. The league's expansion efforts are driven by a desire to increase viewership, sponsorship, and player development opportunities, ensuring that rugby league remains a vibrant and dynamic sport. As the NRL continues to expand, it must balance the excitement of growth with the challenges of maintaining quality and integrity across the competition.

Resurrecting the Bears

One of the most talked-about possibilities is the resurrection of the North Sydney Bears, a club with a rich history in the sport. However, this would not be a simple return to their original home. The Bears are likely to be reborn in a new location, such as the Central Coast or Perth. The Central Coast option is appealing due to its strong rugby league fan base and existing stadium in Gosford. This region has long been a rugby league heartland, and bringing the Bears to the Central Coast could reinvigorate the local community's passion for the sport. The move would also provide a geographically strategic location, potentially attracting fans from both Sydney and Newcastle.

On the other hand, a move to Perth would allow the NRL to tap into the growing sports market in Western Australia, offering a bold new frontier for the league. Reintroducing the Bears could also serve as a way to honor the legacy of the club while adapting to the evolving demands of the modern game. The Perth Bears would bring rugby league to a largely untapped market, expanding the sport's reach beyond the traditional rugby league strongholds. However, this move would require significant investment and a long-term commitment to building the sport's presence in the region. Despite the challenges, the potential rewards of establishing a team in Perth could be substantial, making it an exciting possibility for the NRL's future.

Exploring New Zealand

Another avenue for expansion is New Zealand, where rugby league continues to grow in popularity. The success of the Auckland-based Warriors has sparked interest in adding a second team in the country, with potential locations including Wellington and Christchurch. A Wellington team, potentially named the Orcas, would strengthen rugby league's presence in the North Island, while a Christchurch team could open up new opportunities in the South Island. Both options would build on the existing popularity of the sport in New Zealand and provide new pathways for local talent. Expanding into New Zealand would not only increase the NRL's footprint but also deepen the trans-Tasman rivalry, adding more excitement to the competition.

The introduction of a second New Zealand team could also enhance the trans-Tasman rivalry, adding more excitement to the competition and fostering deeper cultural connections between the two nations through sport. Rugby league has a passionate following in New Zealand, and a second team could help to cultivate even greater interest in the sport. It could also provide more opportunities for New Zealand players to compete at the highest level without leaving their home country. As the NRL considers this expansion, it must weigh the potential benefits against the logistical challenges of establishing a new team in a different country. However, the success of the Warriors suggests that New Zealand is ready for another NRL team, making this a promising avenue for growth.

A Bold New Horizon Up North

Perhaps the most ambitious proposal is the inclusion of a team from Papua New Guinea (PNG). Rugby league is more than just a sport in PNG; it is a unifying force in a country with incredible cultural diversity. The PNG bid has garnered support from both the Australian and PNG governments, with the aim of using rugby league as a tool for social cohesion and development. The idea of a PNG team in the NRL is exciting, but it also comes with challenges, including concerns about safety and the potential impact on other forms of development assistance in the region. The challenges are significant, but so are the potential rewards. A PNG-based NRL team would not only represent a major step forward for the sport in the Pacific but also serve as a symbol of the deep ties between Australia and PNG.

Despite these challenges, a PNG team would not only elevate the profile of rugby league in the Pacific but also serve as a powerful example of sport's ability to drive positive social change. The potential impact of a PNG team extends beyond the field, offering opportunities for economic development, social unity, and international diplomacy. Rugby league could become a key part of PNG's national identity, bringing people together and providing hope and inspiration to future generations. However, the NRL would need to carefully consider the long-term sustainability of such a venture, ensuring that it benefits both the sport and the communities involved. The decision to include a PNG team in the NRL would be a bold move, but it could also be a transformative one, redefining the league's role in the Pacific region.

A Fourth Option Closer to Home

Closer to home, the Ipswich region in Queensland is another contender for a new NRL team. The Ipswich Jets were strong candidates for the recent expansion spot that went to the Dolphins, and the region remains a rugby league heartland with a growing population. Establishing a team in Ipswich would solidify the NRL's presence in Southeast Queensland, but it would also mean adding yet another team in a region already well-served by the league. The area's rich rugby league history, combined with its rapidly growing population, makes it an attractive option for expansion. A new team in Ipswich could help alleviate some of the pressure on existing clubs in the area, while also tapping into a passionate local fan base.

This expansion could reinforce the NRL's dominance in Queensland, ensuring that the league continues to grow its fan base in one of its strongest markets. Additionally, an Ipswich team could foster local talent development and provide more opportunities for players and coaches in the region. However, it could also face challenges in differentiating itself from the existing Queensland teams, requiring a strong brand and identity to capture the hearts of local fans. The introduction of a new team in Ipswich would likely enhance the competitiveness of the NRL, with the added benefit of intensifying regional rivalries within Queensland. This option represents a safer, more traditional expansion route for the NRL, but one that still holds significant potential for growth and development.

The NRL's Big Decisions

The NRL's goal of reaching 20 teams presents both opportunities and challenges. The league must carefully weigh the benefits of sticking to traditional rugby league territories, such as adding teams in the Central Coast, Ipswich, and New Zealand, against the potential rewards of venturing into new markets like Perth and PNG. Each option has its merits, and the decisions made in the coming years will have a lasting impact on the league. Expanding into familiar territories may offer stability and a guaranteed fan base, but it could also limit the league's growth potential. On the other hand, venturing into new markets presents exciting opportunities but also carries risks that need to be managed carefully.

As the NRL navigates these choices, it must also consider the broader implications for the sport's identity, fan engagement, and commercial viability.

Balancing these factors will be key to ensuring that the league not only expands successfully but also remains true to its roots while embracing innovation. The expansion could lead to a more diverse and competitive league, attracting new fans and sponsors while providing fresh challenges for existing teams. However, the NRL must also be mindful of the potential downsides, such as overextending its resources or diluting the quality of competition. Ultimately, the league's leadership will need to make strategic decisions that align with their long-term vision for rugby league, ensuring that the sport continues to thrive in an increasingly competitive sporting landscape.

Looking Ahead

The future of the NRL is bright, but it is also filled with uncertainty. As the league considers its next steps, it must balance the need for growth with the importance of maintaining its core identity. Whether through expanding into new regions or strengthening its presence in existing markets, the NRL is poised to continue its evolution as a premier sports competition. The decisions made today will determine the shape of the league for generations to come, ensuring that rugby league remains a vital part of Australian and Pacific culture. The league's ability to adapt to changing circumstances while staying true to its roots will be crucial in determining its long-term success.

In doing so, the NRL has the potential to not only secure its place as a dominant force in Australian sports but also to become a global ambassador for rugby league, spreading its values and excitement to new audiences around the world. As the NRL looks to the future, it must also consider the role it plays in the broader sports ecosystem, both in Australia and internationally. By making thoughtful, strategic decisions, the NRL can ensure that it continues to grow and thrive, while also contributing to the global development of rugby league. The next chapter in the NRL's history is set to be an exciting one, full of challenges, opportunities, and the promise of even greater achievements to come.

As the National Rugby League (NRL) looks ahead to its future, it stands at a crossroads filled with possibilities and challenges. The league's expansion, both in Australia and potentially beyond, is not just a strategy for growth but a statement of ambition. The potential inclusion of new teams in regions like Perth, Papua New Guinea, New Zealand, and Ipswich signals a bold move toward cementing rugby league's place as a dominant force in the sporting landscape. These decisions will not only shape the league's structure but also influence the broader dynamics of the sport, from player development to fan engagement. The NRL's leadership must carefully consider the balance between expanding into new territories and maintaining its traditional strongholds. This balance is crucial for ensuring that the league grows sustainably while preserving the rich heritage that has made rugby league a beloved sport in Australia.

The proposed expansion brings with it a unique set of challenges. Establishing new teams requires more than just financial investment; it involves building a community, fostering local talent, and cultivating a new fan base. In regions like Perth and Papua New Guinea, where rugby league is either emerging or has a different cultural context, the NRL must approach expansion with sensitivity and a long-term vision. The potential rewards, however, are immense. A successful expansion could open new markets, attract international attention, and enhance the league's global profile. But these gains must be weighed against the risks, including the potential strain on resources and the possibility of diluting the league's competitive quality. The NRL must also consider the logistical challenges of travel and infrastructure, especially if teams are established in geographically distant locations like Perth or PNG.

Moreover, the expansion of the NRL is not just about adding new teams; it's about reimagining the league's identity in a rapidly changing world. As the league grows, it must stay true to the values that have made rugby league a cornerstone of Australian culture while also embracing innovation and diversity. This includes addressing issues such as player welfare, community engagement, and the broader impact of the sport on society. The NRL has a responsibility to ensure that its growth benefits not just the league itself but also the communities it serves. This involves creating pathways for young talent, supporting grassroots initiatives, and ensuring that the sport remains accessible and inclusive.

The introduction of teams in new regions also presents an opportunity to deepen the cultural connections that rugby league fosters. For instance, a team in Papua New Guinea would not only provide a platform for local talent but also strengthen the bonds between Australia and PNG. Similarly, a second team in New Zealand could enhance the trans-Tasman rivalry and further integrate the league into the fabric of New Zealand society. These expansions could also serve as powerful symbols of rugby league's ability to unite diverse communities and promote social cohesion. However, the NRL must navigate these opportunities with care, ensuring that the league's expansion does not overshadow the importance of maintaining its roots and supporting its existing clubs.

As the NRL charts its course into the future, it faces the task of balancing ambition with tradition. The league's expansion plans are ambitious, and if executed well, they could lead to unprecedented growth and success. However, the NRL must also be mindful of the challenges that come with such expansion, including the need to maintain competitive balance and the risk of overextending its resources. The future of the NRL depends on its ability to make strategic decisions that are guided by a clear vision for the league's long-term success. This vision must be informed by a deep understanding of the sport's history, the needs of its players and fans, and the changing dynamics of the global sports landscape.

Ultimately, the decisions made by the NRL in the coming years will have a lasting impact on the league and the sport of rugby league as a whole. Whether through the resurrection of historic clubs, the establishment of new teams in untapped markets, or the reinforcement of traditional rugby league strongholds, the NRL's future is filled with potential. The league's ability to navigate this period of growth and change will determine its place in the hearts of fans and its legacy in the world of sports. The NRL is not just building the next chapter of its history; it is shaping the future of rugby league, a future that holds the promise of greater inclusivity, diversity, and global reach.

In the end, the NRL's success will be measured not just by the number of teams it adds or the markets it enters but by the strength of the league as a whole. The NRL must remain committed to its core values while also embracing the opportunities that come with expansion. By doing so, the league can ensure that it continues to thrive in an ever-changing world, bringing the excitement and passion of rugby league to new audiences while staying true to the traditions that have made it great. The future of the NRL is bright, but it will require careful stewardship and bold decision-making to realize its full potential. The journey ahead is challenging, but it is also filled with possibilities that could redefine the sport and secure its place in the hearts of fans for generations to come.

Conclusion: Reflections and Future Horizons

The National Rugby League (NRL) has a long and storied history that reflects the evolution of rugby league in Australia and beyond. From its humble beginnings in the early 20th century to its current status as one of the premier sporting competitions in the world, the NRL has grown and changed in ways that few could have imagined. This book has taken you through that journey, exploring the key events, figures, and developments that have shaped the NRL into what it is today. As we conclude, it is important to reflect on how far the league has come and what the future might hold.

Over the decades, the NRL has faced numerous challenges, from the Super League war that threatened to tear the sport apart to the ongoing competition with other football codes in Australia. Yet, through resilience, innovation, and a deep connection with its fan base, the NRL has not only survived but thrived. The league's ability to adapt to changing circumstances, whether through expansion, rule changes, or embracing new technologies, has been a key factor in its success. The NRL has shown that it is not afraid to make bold decisions to secure its future, even if those decisions come with risks.

The history of the NRL is also a story of great players, unforgettable matches, and passionate supporters. The legends of the game, from Dally Messenger to

Cameron Smith, have left an indelible mark on the sport, inspiring future generations of players and fans alike. The iconic moments, whether it be a last-minute try in a grand final or a fierce State of Origin clash, have provided memories that will last a lifetime. The supporters, with their unwavering loyalty and love for the game, have been the backbone of the NRL, driving its growth and success.

As the NRL moves forward, it must continue to honor this rich history while embracing the opportunities of the future. The league's recent expansion plans, its focus on player welfare, and its efforts to grow the game internationally are all signs of a sport that is looking ahead with optimism. However, the NRL must also remain grounded in the traditions that have made it great, ensuring that the values of community, teamwork, and fair play are always at the heart of the game. The balance between innovation and tradition will be crucial as the NRL seeks to build on its legacy.

The role of the NRL in Australian culture cannot be overstated. Rugby league is more than just a sport; it is a part of the national identity, particularly in the heartlands of New South Wales and Queensland. The game brings people together, whether they are cheering for their favorite team at a packed stadium or watching a match with family and friends at home. The NRL has the power to unite communities, create lifelong memories, and inspire young people to pursue their dreams. As the league grows, it must continue to nurture this connection with its fans, ensuring that rugby league remains a sport for everyone.

Looking to the future, the NRL faces both challenges and opportunities. The ongoing battle for supremacy with other football codes, the need to attract and retain young talent, and the pressures of an increasingly globalized sports market are all issues that the league must address. However, with strong leadership, a clear vision, and the continued support of its fans, the NRL is well-positioned to navigate these challenges and seize the opportunities that lie ahead. The future of the NRL is bright, but it will require continued effort and innovation to maintain its place at the top of the sporting world.

As we conclude this book, it is clear that the history of the NRL is far from over. The league will continue to evolve, creating new stories and memories for future generations. The players, coaches, administrators, and fans who have contributed to the NRL's success can take pride in what they have achieved, knowing that they have played a part in shaping one of the greatest sports competitions in the world. The NRL's journey is ongoing, and the next chapter promises to be just as exciting as the last.

In the end, the NRL is more than just a league; it is a celebration of the passion, skill, and spirit of rugby league. The history of the NRL is a testament to the enduring appeal of the game, its ability to adapt and grow, and the deep connection it has with its fans. As the NRL looks to the future, it does so with the confidence that comes from a rich and proud history. The story of the NRL is one of triumph, challenge, and resilience, and it is a story that will continue to unfold for many years to come.

Thank You for Reading This Book

As we reach the end of this journey through the history of the National Rugby League (NRL), it's important to reflect on the incredible stories, achievements, and moments that have shaped the sport into what it is today. Rugby league is more than just a game; it's a reflection of the communities, cultures, and passions that drive millions of people across Australia, New Zealand, and beyond. This book has aimed to capture the essence of that spirit, from the earliest days of the game to its current status as one of the most popular sports in the world.

The NRL's evolution has been a remarkable journey, marked by milestones that have pushed the boundaries of what the sport could be. From the early formation of clubs, the challenges faced during wars and economic hardships, to the modern era of professionalization and commercialization, the league has constantly adapted to the changing landscape of sports and society. Each chapter of this book has delved into different aspects of the NRL, shedding light on the players, teams, and events that have left an indelible mark on the history of the game.

Throughout this book, we've explored the triumphs and tribulations that have defined the NRL's rich history. We've looked at the legendary players who have dazzled fans with their skill, the teams that have dominated seasons, and the unforgettable matches that have become part of rugby league folklore. But just as important are the moments of struggle, the controversies, and the setbacks that have tested the resilience of the sport and its community. These stories remind us that rugby league, like life, is full of highs and lows, and it is this unpredictability that keeps fans coming back for more.

The NRL's influence extends far beyond the field. It has played a significant role in shaping the social fabric of communities, providing a platform for cultural expression, and promoting values such as teamwork, perseverance, and sportsmanship. The league has also been at the forefront of efforts to promote inclusivity and diversity, embracing players and fans from all walks of life. These efforts have not only enriched the game but have also made it more accessible and relatable to a broader audience.

As we look to the future, the NRL faces new challenges and opportunities. The ongoing expansion of the league, the increasing importance of digital media, and the need to maintain the integrity of the sport in the face of commercial pressures are just a few of the issues that will shape the next chapter of rugby league history. The decisions made today will determine the direction of the sport for years to come, and it is up to the players, administrators, and fans to ensure that the values that have made rugby league great are preserved and strengthened.

This book is not just a chronicle of past events; it is also a tribute to everyone who has contributed to the NRL's success. From the players who have given their all on the field to the fans who have passionately supported their teams, from the coaches and administrators who have guided the sport's development to the volunteers who work tirelessly behind the scenes – this book is a celebration of the collective effort that has made rugby league what it is today.

To all the readers who have embarked on this journey with us, thank you. Your interest in the history of the NRL is a testament to the enduring appeal of the sport. Whether you are a lifelong fan or someone new to the game, we hope that this book has provided you with insights, stories, and a deeper appreciation for the rich tapestry that is rugby league. The story of the NRL is far from over, and as we close this chapter, we look forward to the exciting future that lies ahead.

Rugby league will continue to evolve, bringing new challenges and opportunities. But one thing remains certain: the passion, loyalty, and love for the game that have defined the NRL will continue to burn brightly. This is not the end, but merely a pause before the next thrilling chapter begins. Thank you for being part of this journey, and we hope to see you on the sidelines, in the stands, and cheering on your favorite team as the history of the National Rugby League continues to unfold.

If you enjoyed this book, please consider leaving a review by clicking here.

In the spirit of sportsmanship and camaraderie, James Bren.

Other Books by James Bren

The History of MMA

The History of the NFL

The History of the NHL and the Stanley Cup

The History of the UFC – Book 1

111 Weird, Fun, and Random *Facts About the UFC*

The History of the NHL

The History of Bellator

The History of the NBA

The History of Major League Baseball

The History of the UFC – Book 2

The History of Mixed Martial Arts

MMA Manuscripts: 30 Must-Reads in the World of MMA and Combat Sports

The History of NASCAR

The History of FIFA

The History of the PGA TOUR

The History of the Association of Tennis Professionals

The History of Wimbledon

Printed in Great Britain
by Amazon